CUTTING EDGE

EFL
Q

ADVANCED

D0996117

STUDENTS' BOOK

Longman

sarah cunningham   peter moor

with jane comyns carr

Module	Skills and vocabulary	Task
Module 1 Going global **p.6**	**Vocabulary and listening:** what does globalisation mean for us? **Reading and speaking:** the effects of globalisation on one city **Listening and speaking:** changing English in a changing world **Vocabulary:** words and phrases relating to globalisation	**Preparation for task:** complete a Learner questionnaire (reading, writing) **Task:** devise an action plan to improve your English (reading, writing, extended speaking)
Module 2 Mixed emotions **p.16**	**Vocabulary and speaking:** how would *you* feel? **Reading:** what makes you laugh? **Listening:** an actor's first public performance **Vocabulary:** feelings (*overjoyed, flabbergasted*, etc.)	**Preparation for task:** match phrases to pictures (reading, speaking) **Task:** telling a story to make people laugh ... or cry (extended speaking, reading/listening)
Module 3 How you come across **p.26**	**Speaking and vocabulary:** the right way to behave **Reading and vocabulary:** *Perfect behaviour in an imperfect world* **Listening and speaking:** improving your communication skills **Vocabulary:** describing behaviour (*disrespectful, over the top*, etc.)	**Preparation for task:** read about difficult situations and discuss solutions (reading, speaking) **Task:** decide what to say in a difficult situation (extended speaking, writing)
Module 4 Mind, body and spirit **p.36**	**Vocabulary and speaking:** body and spirit **Reading and speaking:** complementary therapies **Listening:** self-help books **Vocabulary:** health and well-being (*allergic, dizzy spells*, etc.)	**Preparation for task:** news items about courageous people (listening, speaking) **Task:** who wins the award? (extended speaking, writing)
Module 5 Learning for life **p.46**	**Vocabulary and speaking:** education **Reading and speaking:** education: fact or myth? **Listening and speaking:** what life skills should you learn at school? **Vocabulary:** education (*qualifications, vocational*, etc.)	**Preparation for task:** match instructions to diagrams (speaking, reading, listening) **Task:** teach a practical skill to others (extended speaking)

Grammar	Writing	Further skills and vocabulary
Grammar extension: continuous verb forms *Patterns to notice*: introducing points in an argument		**Wordspot**: *world, earth, ground, floor* **Real life**: varieties of English
Grammar extension: perfect verb forms *Patterns to notice*: cleft sentences	**Writing**: a music review	**Wordspot**: idioms with *laugh, cry* and *tears*
Grammar extension: modals and related verbs *Patterns to notice*: abstract nouns and relative clauses	**Writing**: emails *Optional writing* (task): a playscript	**Real life**: getting people to do things
Grammar extension: adjectives and adverbs *Patterns to notice*: patterns with comparatives and superlatives	**Writing**: a leaflet *Optional writing* (task): a short news article	**Wordspot**: idioms to do with the body
Grammar extension: use and non-use of passive forms *Patterns to notice:* particles which add meaning to verbs	**Writing**: writing tips from notes	**Wordspot**: *way*

Module	Skills and vocabulary	Task
Module 6 In the money **p.56**	**Vocabulary and speaking:** double your money! **Reading:** TV quiz shows **Listening:** the case of Stella Liebeck **Vocabulary:** words and phrases relating to money (*broke, priceless,* etc.)	**Preparation for task:** four cases where people sued for compensation (reading, listening, speaking) **Task:** decide how much compensation people should get (extended speaking, listening)
Module 7 Living together **p.66**	**Speaking and vocabulary:** who you live with **Listening:** leaving home **Reading and vocabulary:** *The Bluffer's Guide to Men and Women* **Vocabulary:** describing characteristics (*grumpy, laid-back,* etc.)	**Preparation for task:** descriptions of possible participants in a TV programme (listening, reading) **Task:** decide who will go on *Shipwrecked!* (extended speaking)
Module 8 A question of taste **p.76**	**Vocabulary and speaking:** a question of taste **Reading and speaking:** style icons **Listening:** *You're so vain* **Vocabulary:** descriptive adjectives (*contemporary, cluttered,* etc.)	**Preparation for task:** people's pet hates (reading, listening, speaking) **Task:** rant about something you hate (extended speaking)
Module 9 21st century lifestyles **p.86**	**Vocabulary and speaking:** work and play in the 21st century **Reading and speaking:** *What didn't come to pass* **Listening and speaking:** the changing face of tourism **Vocabulary:** work, lifestyle and health (*teleworking, sedentary, epidemic,* etc.)	**Preparation for task:** discuss interesting periods of history (speaking) **Task:** create a time capsule for future generations (extended speaking)
Module 10 Truth and lies **p.96**	**Vocabulary and speaking:** Is it ever OK to lie? **Listening:** *The Unicorn in the Garden* **Reading and speaking:** *How do you know when someone is lying?* **Vocabulary:** truth and lies (*testify, rumour,* etc.)	**Preparation for task:** listen to people playing *The Truth Game* (listening, speaking) **Task:** find out if your partner is lying (extended speaking)

Communication activities pp. 106–114

Grammar	Writing	Further skills and vocabulary
Grammar extension: time and tense *Patterns to notice*: inversion with negative adverbials	**Writing**: summarising statistical information	**Real life**: expressing quantities imprecisely
Grammar extension: infinitives and *-ing* forms *Patterns to notice*: describing typical habits; compound phrases	**Writing**: a report	**Wordspot**: *just*
Grammar extension: adverbs *Patterns to notice*: adding emphasis with auxiliaries	**Writing**: a tactful letter	**Real life**: comment adverbials
Grammar extension: future forms *Patterns to notice:* describing trends		**Wordspot**: *well* **Real life**: computer terms
Grammar extension: noun phrases; ellipsis and substitution *Patterns to notice:* patterns with *as ... as* + verb	**Writing**: a news article	**Real life**: expressing surprise and disbelief

Grammar extension bank pp. 115–155   Tapescripts pp. 156–175

module 1

Going global

- ► **Reading**: extract from a travel book
- ► **Listening**: an interview
- ► **Task**: prepare an action plan to improve your English
- ► **Vocabulary**: globalisation
- ► **Continuous verb forms**
- ► **Introducing points in an argument**
- ► **Wordspot**: *world, earth, ground, floor*
- ► **Real life**: varieties of English

Vocabulary and listening

What does globalisation mean for us?

1 What can you see in the pictures? Which countries do you think they were taken in? All of them relate to the idea of globalisation. What does this term mean to you?

UNITED COLORS OF BENETTON.

2 Check the words and phrases in **bold** if necessary. Which of these things do you do? Compare answers in groups.

- watch foreign films and TV programmes
- listen to music from around the world
- buy international **brands** like Benetton or Nike
- eat food **imported** from across the world
- go shopping in a **neighbouring** country
- watch **domestic** sport from another country, e.g. Italian league football in Spain
- eat in international **fast food chains**
- eat in different **ethnic** restaurants
- use English as a **lingua franca** to communicate with other **non-native** speakers
- work for a **multinational corporation** with people from different countries
- travel abroad to work or study

3 Which of these phrases do you associate with the pictures? Compare your answers in groups.

international investors	small local businesses
locally-produced goods	cultural diversity
multi-ethnic societies	a high standard of living
a traditional way of life	a clash of cultures
emigration and immigration	Americanisation
worldwide communication networks	mass tourism

4 **a)** Which ideas reflect globalisation? Why?

b) Make a list of five advantages of globalisation, and five disadvantages. Compare answers.

5 **a)** 🔊 [1.1] You will hear five extracts in which people talk about what globalisation means to them. Listen and make notes about headings 1 and 2 below.

Example: Richard

1) Topics mentioned	American TV and films, other foreign films
2) Attitude (positive/negative/mixed)	positive
3) Main points they make	great to have a wide choice

b) Listen again and make notes about heading 3. Did anyone say anything you disagree with?

6 What are the differences between these pairs of words and phrases?

emigration	immigration
imports	exports
multinational	multi-ethnic
cultural diversity	a clash of cultures
a brand	goods
a business	a corporation
your standard of living	your way of life

▶ Phrase builder

Reading and speaking

1 **a)** One by one, read the extracts below from a travel guide to a famous city. Can you guess which city it is?

- smartly dressed people clutching mobile phones
- road signs and advertising billboards are now in English
- a majestic political and architectural marvel
- a forest of construction cranes and bulldozers
- shopping malls and five-star hotels rise from the rubble
- The city is changing so rapidly it makes you dizzy.
- most youngsters disdain socialist sacrifice and are more interested in money, motorbikes, fashion, video games and rock music
- bicycles and ox carts were the main form of transport a decade ago but both are now prohibited on the new freeways and toll roads
- It may be something of a showcase, but what capital city isn't?

b) Look at p.8 to check the identity of the city. Were you surprised? What impressions did you previously have of this city?

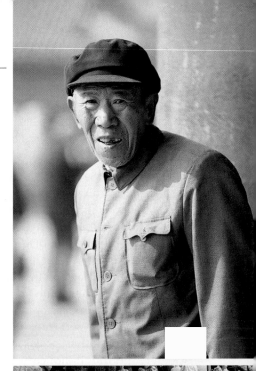

2 Read the text taken from the Lonely Planet guide to Beijing.
  Which of the following statements do/do not reflect the author's
  views? In pairs, discuss why.

a) Beijing has the same attraction today that it has always had for the
   people of China.
b) These days, people in Beijing have the same aspirations as people
   anywhere else.
c) It's hard to keep up with the pace of change in modern Beijing.
d) Beijing has been completely ruined by modernization.
e) Life in Beijing is more comfortable materially than it was in the 1980s.
f) Beijing is an amazing place that all visitors will love.

3 Underline words and phrases in the text which show that the
  following sentences are true.

a) Lots of people come to Beijing from the countryside to pursue
   their dreams.
b) The capital is extremely attractive to these people.
c) The differences between old and young people's attitudes are very
   obvious in Beijing.
d) Old people are very enthusiastic about the Communist past.
e) Many young people have no respect for Communist ideals.
f) The builders are in a great hurry.
g) Many new buildings are luxurious.
h) Traditional homes have been replaced by big blocks of apartments.
i) In the 1980s no-one expected to have such things as a TV set or a
   washing machine.
j) A lot of people now have these things.
k) People usually wear western clothes now.
l) Near Beijing there are some extremely impressive things to see.

4 What are the main changes that have taken place in Beijing since
  the 1980s? Comment on the following:

- buildings
- material goods
- clothes
- transport
- attitudes

5 Discuss these questions in pairs.

- Do you think the changes described are mainly positive or mainly
  negative?
- Do they make you more or less interested in visiting Beijing?
- Are any of these changes happening in your city/country?
- Are there any other ways that globalisation has affected your
  city/country?
- What influences lie behind these changes?
- Have they had a good or bad effect on your city/country?

▶ Phrase builder

A changing city

1 For centuries, Beijing has been the promised land of China. Originally a walled bastion for emperors and officials, it remains a majestic political and architectural marvel. Today, people from the countryside still flock to the city in search of the elusive pot of gold at the end of the rainbow. The government encourages them to go home, but the lure of the capital proves too enticing. Meanwhile, down the road by the Friendship Store, smartly dressed customers clutching mobile phones head for the nearest banquet or disco.

2 Perhaps nowhere else in China more than in Beijing is the generation gap more visible. Appalled by the current drive to 'modernise', many older people still wax euphoric about Chairman Mao and the years of sacrifice for the socialist revolution. But most youngsters disdain socialist sacrifice and are more interested - like youngsters everywhere – in money, motorbikes, fashion, video games and rock music (though not necessarily in that order).

3 Foreigners seem to enjoy Beijing since the city offers so much to see and do. Things have changed drastically in the last ten years or so. The Beijing of today is a forest of construction cranes, bulldozers and 24-hour work crews scrambling to build the new China. Plush shopping malls and five-star hotels rise from the rubble. A good number of the road signs and advertising billboards are now in English. Whatever one says about Beijing today, it probably won't be true tomorrow. The city is changing so rapidly it makes you dizzy. Travellers of the 1980s remember Beijing as a city of narrow lanes with single-story homes built around courtyards. These have given way to the high-rise housing estates of the 1990s. TV sets and washing machines – unimaginable luxuries in the 1980s – are now commonplace. Whereas bicycles and ox carts were the main form of transport a decade ago, both are prohibited on the new freeways and toll roads that now encompass the city. Whereas not so long ago every one wore the Chairman Mao suit, now jeans and T-shirts, leather jackets and suits are the norm.

4 Whatever impression you come away with, Beijing is one of the most fascinating places in China. It may be something of a showcase, but what capital city isn't? Within its environs you will find some of China's most stunning sights – the Forbidden City, the Summer Palace and the Great Wall, to name just a few. The city itself offers so much of interest that the main complaint of most visitors is that they simply run out of time before seeing it all.

Grammar extension
Continuous verb forms

1 Look at the verbs in **bold**. Find examples of:

> a simple form a continuous form
> the Future Continuous a continuous passive
> a continuous infinitive the Present Perfect Continuous

a) Everywhere you go nowadays people seem **to be speaking** English.
b) Many experts are worried because so many languages in the world **are disappearing**.
c) Every city centre **seems** the same these days.
d) Old buildings **are being pulled down** and replaced by ugly new ones.
e) Another new shopping mall **is coming** soon.
f) Beijing may well **be changing** faster than any other city on earth.
g) When I **was growing** up there were no fast food chains in my town.
h) Advertisers **are** always **trying** to sell us some new brand of clothes or trainers.
i) In thirty years' time I don't suppose anyone **will be wearing** traditional dress any more.
j) Recently the government **have been taking** measures to preserve the local way of life.

2 Find a continuous form that describes an action in progress: a) at a point in the past, b) at a point in the future and c) at the present moment.

3 **a)** How does the meaning of sentences a), b), d) and f) in Exercise 1 change if you put the verb into the simple form?

b) Why can't you put sentence c) into the continuous form? Do you know any other verbs like this?

4 **a)** Which sentence in Exercise 1 describes:

- a situation which is gradually changing?
- a repeated habit which is strange or annoying?
- a definite plan for the future?

b) Think of three examples of:
- changes that are taking place in the world today.
- annoying things that advertisers or the government do in your country.
- plans for new buildings/developments in your town.

▶ Grammar extension bank pp.115 – 119

Listening and speaking
Changing English in a changing world

1 Discuss in groups. In what circumstances will you use English in the future? Think about work, travel, social situations, the Internet, etc.

2 Read the facts about the English language. Just one piece of information is false. Can you guess which? (see p.109). Do any of the facts surprise you? Why?

Did you know ...?

1 There are far more non-native speakers of English in the world today than native speakers. About 350 million speak it as their mother tongue, whereas it is thought that around 1.5 billion speak it as a second or foreign language!

2 It is believed that around 80% of the data on the world's computers is stored in English.

3 It has been estimated that about 20,000 English words spread into other languages every year.

4 Special simplified forms of English exist to help various professions to communicate internationally, for example 'air-speak' for pilots and air-traffic controllers; 'police-speak' to help deal with international crime, and 'doctor-speak' to simplify communication between doctors.

5 The grammar and vocabulary used by native speakers varies a lot, even in the UK.
In some local accents people say 'we was' or 'they was'; a few kilometres away, they say 'he were' and 'she were'.

6 Modern British people probably wouldn't have been able to understand the English spoken in Shakespeare's time. Many words had different meanings, for example, 'nice' meant 'foolish' in the sixteenth century!

3 Read these statements and mark them (✓) if you agree, (✗) if you disagree, and (?) if you are not sure. Compare answers in pairs.

a) I am more likely to use English to speak to native speakers (e.g. British and American people) than I am to speak to other non-native speakers.

b) All learners of English should try to pronounce the language as closely as possible to the way native speakers do.

c) It is important for learners of English to have a good command of British and American idioms.

d) People can't understand you when you speak a foreign language unless you use the grammar correctly.

e) English doesn't just 'belong to' British or American people. It belongs to everyone in the world who uses it.

f) When I speak English I don't want to imitate a British or American person. I want to keep my own identity.

4 🖭 [1.2] Listen to Dr Jennifer Jenkins talking about 'English as an International Language'. Which statements above does she agree/disagree with? Why?

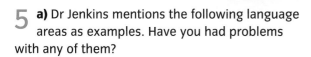

5 **a)** Dr Jenkins mentions the following language areas as examples. Have you had problems with any of them?

> the pronunciation of *th*
> British and American idioms
> uncountable nouns like *information*
> the third person 's' in the Present Simple

b) What does Jennifer Jenkins think may happen to these things as English as an International Language develops? How does she think dictionaries in the future will be different? Listen again if necessary.

6 **a)** Do you agree with Dr Jenkins? Has she made you change your mind about any of your answers to Exercise 3 above?

b) Interview your teacher and find out what he/she thinks. Think of at least three questions to ask him/her.

▶ Phrase builder

Patterns to notice

Introducing points in an argument

1 Notice how the points are introduced:
Well, there are two things. **One thing** is that … they're intelligible to each other.
The second thing would be that … nobody owns English any more.
One advantage would be that … learners have less to do.

How do these introductory phrases help the listener?

2 Here are some similar ways of introducing points:

One important	point to consider	
	reason	
Another (important)	disadvantage	is that …
The most important	drawback	would be that …
The second	problem	might be that …
A further	concern/issue	
The main	consideration	
	explanation	

One important issue is that many people use English over the Internet.
Another problem is that there are so many different varieties of English.

Which ways do you think are the most/least formal?

7 Introduce each of these arguments **for** and **against** globalisation in a different way.

For

a) … people are much more aware of other cultures and ways of life.

b) … there are more and more opportunities to travel.

c) … there is a lot more choice available than there used to be.

Against

a) … a lot of small local businesses cannot compete with big multinationals.

b) … big multinational corporations have so much power.

c) … a lot of local skills and customs are being lost.

8 Give your opinions on one of the questions below. Aim to speak for 30 seconds to one minute, but first decide what you will say. Try to use some of the phrases from the box above to make your points.

• Is it a good thing to have English as a global language?

• Will the Internet increase the spread of globalisation?

• Should each country/region try to preserve their traditions and way of life? How?

Personal vocabulary

Preparation for task

1 Look at the Learner questionnaire on p.13. Have you done a questionnaire like this before? Why do you think this is useful?

2 Answer the questions about yourself.

Task

1 Compare answers in pairs. Read the Learning tips on pp.106 – 107. Underline like this (_____) useful advice for yourself, and like this (∼∼∼∼) useful advice for your partner.

▶ Useful language a

2 Help your partner to devise an 'action plan' to improve his/her English during this course. Write your own action plan on a piece of paper to give to your teacher. Make notes under the headings below.

▶ Personal vocabulary

Useful language

a Giving personal views

I'm (not) the kind of person who …

One thing I'm good at is …

One of my worst faults is that I (never) …

I feel pretty happy about my …

For me, I (don't) feel … is very important/useful

Personally, I'd like to concentrate on…

b Explaining your targets

My main aim is to …

… is one of my main priorities because of …

Another important area for me is …

So for that reason, I'm aiming to …

Another thing I thought might be a good idea is to …

I'd find it really useful to look at …

▶ Phrase builder

ACTION PLAN   *Name:* ....

1) *Areas where I feel confident*
   Areas where I need to improve

2) *Areas in this course syllabus I particularly want to study*
   Other useful features of the book

3) *Questions to ask my teacher*

4) *SIX targets for this year (Be realistic!)*
   In class
   1) *Speak more in group work; answer more questions in class*
   2) ....
   3) ....
   Outside class
   1) *Do my homework — esp. writing exercises!*
   2) *Buy monolingual dictionary and use it for homework*
   3) ....

---

3 Present your targets to the class, or in groups, explaining why you have chosen these areas to work on. Write out your targets and stick them on the inside cover of your coursebook.

▶ Useful language b

Learner questionnaire

2) What kind of learner are you?

a) I *never/sometimes/often* practise my English outside class.

b) I am usually *very active/quiet/rather lazy* in class, and I *never/sometimes/often* ask questions.

c) I'm *very/reasonably/not at all* confident about speaking English in front of a group of people.

d) I *worry a lot/worry a bit/don't worry at all* about making mistakes.

e) I *always/sometimes/never* make notes during the lesson.

f) I *have/don't have* a monolingual dictionary. I *sometimes/never/often* use it *in class/for my homework*.

g) Expanding my vocabulary *is/isn't* one of my main priorities.

h) I am *very/fairly/not very* interested in work on English phrases and idioms.

i) Studying and remembering grammar rules *is/isn't* very important to me. I *feel/don't feel* I need to do a lot of work on grammar.

j) I *feel/don't feel* I need to revise a lot of the grammar and vocabulary I have learnt in the past. (Especially ....)

k) I think it's *extremely important/quite important/not very important* to have good pronunciation in English. Improving my pronunciation *is/isn't* a priority for me.

l) For me, writing essays, letters, etc. in English is *reasonably easy/a real problem/not that important*.

1) Why are you learning English?

a) I'm learning English *for pleasure/because I have to* for ....
....
....
....

b) I'm attending this course because *I need/will need* English *in my job/for my studies/at some point in the future*.

c) I *intend/do not intend* to take (name of exam(s)) ....
....
....

d) *Reading/writing/speaking/listening/all four* are particularly important for me because ....
....
....
....
....
....
....

Wordspot

world, earth, ground, floor

1 Do you have exact equivalents for these four words in your language?

2 Choose words or phrases from the box to complete the explanations.

> floor   floorboards   earth   in the world   on the ground
> think the world   worldwide   on earth   top of the world
> this world   the earth   floor   grounded   off the ground

a) You have plenty of time, and so you don't have to hurry: you have all the time ....
b) Added for emphasis to a question, or to show you are very surprised or annoyed: e.g. What .... is she wearing?
c) An idiom to say that something is very expensive: it costs ....
d) The land at the bottom of the sea is known as the ocean ....
e) If you have great affection and respect for someone, you .... of them.
f) At a club/disco, the place where people dance: the dance ....
g) If parents punish their child by not letting him/her go out, (s)he is ....
h) An informal way of saying that something is so good it's unbelievable: out of ....
i) If a plan or business starts to succeed, it gets ....
j) If you feel absolutely fantastic, you feel like this: on ....
k) To keep your feet .... means to be realistic and practical, not over-ambitious.
l) If something happens or exists in most or all countries, it happens ....
m) The planks of wood in a wooden floor are called ....
n) An event or news which is .... -shattering is extremely shocking and important.

3 Complete the diagrams below with words and phrases from Exercise 2.

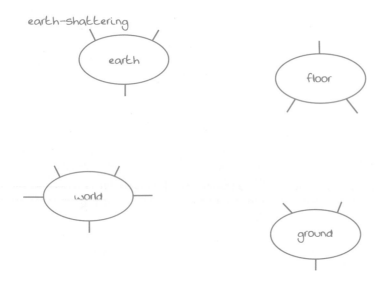

4 The sentences below contain mistakes with one of the words or phrases from Exercise 2. Find the mistakes and correct them.

a) Although no plants grow there, the ocean ground is home to many varieties of deep-sea fish.
b) Everybody thought worlds of Mayor Conlon, and people in the city were absolutely devastated when he died. Putting up a memorial statue has been suggested several times, but the idea has never really come off the ground.
c) What on the earth do you think you're doing coming home at this time in the morning? You were supposed to be home at 12! You're floored for the next week, young man!
d) The police became suspicious when they noticed that there were several loose flooring-boards.
e) A holiday in the Seychelles would suit you perfectly: there's constant sunshine and, if you go at the right time, it needn't cost the world to get there.
f) After the earth-smashing events of last month, there has been wideworld condemnation of the terrorist attacks.
g) It needed something very special to win the game, and United's winning goal was truly out of this planet.
h) Understandably, new pop sensation Jake Salinas is feeling at the top of the world at the moment. His song *Bring Me Back Home* was an enormous hit on the dancing floors of Europe this summer. 'All this fantastic success could easily have changed me, but luckily I have my wife and child to help me keep my foot on the ground,' he told *Pop Star* magazine.
i) Take it easy, relax … we've got all the hours in the world to get to know each other.

▶ Phrase builder

Real life

Varieties of English

1 **a)** 🖭 [1.3] The radio programme *From Our Reporter in....* features news reports from around the world. Listen to the three items from the US, India and Australia, and make brief notes in the table.

	American story	Indian story	Australian story
Where the event is happening			
Main event described			
Key numbers/statistics			

b) The three reporters spoke American English, Indian English and Australian English. Can you hear any differences between the way they speak and standard British English?

2 🖭 [1.4] **a)** Compare the pronunciation of the phrases below. Tick if you can hear the difference. Can you imitate American/Indian/Australian/ pronunciation?

British English and American English
a) globalisation policies
b) police were on duty
c) four European finance ministers

British English and Indian English
a) more than 70 million Hindus
b) the religious festival
c) a thirty-square-mile tent city

British English and Australian English
a) the past fortnight
b) eight hours
c) no lives have been lost

b) Which accent do you like best? Why?

module 2
Mixed emotions

▶ **Reading**: humorous texts
▶ **Listening (1)**: extract from an autobiography
▶ **Listening (2)**: song
▶ **Task**: tell a story to make people laugh … or cry
▶ **Writing**: an album or concert review
▶ **Vocabulary**: feelings
▶ **Perfect verb forms**
▶ **Cleft sentences**
▶ **Wordspot**: idioms with *laugh*, *cry* and *tears*

Vocabulary and speaking
How would *you* feel?

1 How do the different people in the pictures feel? Write down three adjectives for each picture, using words/phrases from the box and others you know.

relieved	apprehensive	proud
delighted	cross	overjoyed
stressed out	furious	insecure
determined	flabbergasted	
sorry for yourself/someone else		
desperate	scared stiff	
depressed	shattered	horrified
disillusioned	let down	
disappointed	pleased	

2 Which adjectives in Exercise 1 can you group together according to meaning? Which ones have a 'strong' meaning (S)? Which have a 'weaker' meaning (W)?

Example: desperate (S)
sorry for yourself (W)

Add other words you know to these groups.

16

3 In groups, choose five of the situations below to discuss. What emotions would you go through at different stages (e.g. beforehand, during, afterwards)? Here are some useful phrases.

> It wouldn't bother me much
> I'd be looking forward to it
> I'd feel a sense of … (satisfaction/dread, etc.)
> It would make me feel (as if) …

How would you feel?

★ You've been learning to drive for months and finally the big day arrives – your driving test. Unfortunately, a few minutes beforehand you lock yourself out of your car and can't take the test in the end.

★ Your company/college offers you the opportunity to do a special course in the USA for nine months away from all your family and friends.

★ Your brother and sister-in-law ask you to look after their three pre-school children for the weekend while they go to a wedding. It turns out to be a wet, freezing weekend.

★ You fail an important exam because you haven't done any studying. To make matters worse, all your friends seem to have passed with flying colours.

★ A colleague you dislike is giving an important presentation. Her delivery is completely incoherent, and she keeps going red and apologising. Members of the audience are sniggering openly.

★ Things have been going fantastically well with your new boyfriend/girlfriend. Then suddenly he/she starts being late for dates, or doesn't turn up at all. There's no good reason that you can see.

★ You have finally got to play for the football team of your dreams. In the first half hour of the biggest match of your career you score a vital goal, only to have it disallowed by the referee a few seconds later.

★ You are in your mid-forties with three teenage children. Out of the blue, you/your wife discover that you are having another baby.

4 In pairs, choose three words or phrases from Exercise 1 that you did not use. Describe three situations like those above to other students. Can they guess which feeling you had in mind?

▶ Phrase builder

Reading
What makes you laugh?

1 Which of the following tend to make you laugh? Which would you never choose to read/watch? Compare answers, giving examples of your favourites.

- a **comic** book or your favourite **cartoon**
- a **witty** column in your favourite newspaper or magazine
- old-fashioned **slapstick comedians** (like Laurel and Hardy)
- modern **stand-up comedians**
- comedy films
- a classic comedy play (e.g. by Shakespeare or Oscar Wilde)
- articles or **sketches** sending up some serious contemporary issue or politician

2 a) The texts on the right are intended to make people laugh, but the punchlines are missing. Can you guess any of them?

b) Match the punchlines in the box to the texts.

> ## Punchlines
>
> 1 'You lose,' replied the great man grimly and relapsed into his customary silence for the rest of the meal.
> 2 'You're not eating properly.'
> 3 ... marry himself.'
> 4 ... between the land and the sky.
> 5 No-eye deer.
> 6 And found that his dream had come true.
> 7 ... off the edge of a cliff.
> 8 you wouldn't have in your home.

3 Check your answers on p.114. Which did you like best? Which didn't you like? Were there any that you didn't 'get'? Can other students explain?

4 The following words and phrases describe the different text types. Match the descriptions to the texts.

an anecdote	a put-down	an epigram
a corny joke	a limerick	a pun
a non-p.c.* joke	a scene from a sitcom	

* 'politically correct'

▶ Phrase builder

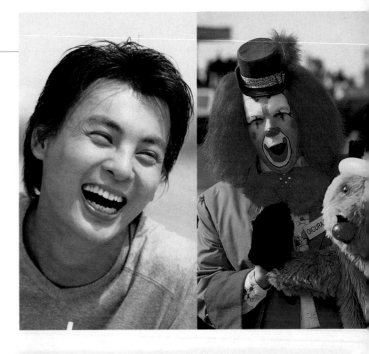

(a) **(said by Frank Sinatra about actor Robert Redford)**
'Well, at least he has found his true love, what a pity he can't ....

(b)
Television is an invention that permits you to be entertained in your living room by people

....

(c) US President Calvin Coolidge was known as a man of few words. One day, he found himself sitting next to a young lady at a public dinner. Bringing all her charm to bear, the young lady said:

'Mr President, I have made a bet with my friends that I can make you say at least three words to me during dinner.'

....

(d)
– What's the definition of mixed emotions?
– **Seeing your mother-in-law driving your new car** ....

(e) A man went to the doctor's with a cucumber in his left ear, a carrot in his right ear, and a banana up his nose.
'What's wrong with me?' he asked the doctor.
'It's simple,' said the doctor.

....

f
There once was a man from Peru
Who dreamed he was eating his shoe
He awoke with a fright
In the middle of the night
....

g
'What do you call a deer with no eyes?'
'
....'

h

Mrs Richards:	And another thing – I asked for a room with a view.
Basil:	(to himself) Deaf, mad and blind. (goes to the window) This is the view as far as I can remember, madam. Yes, this is it.
Mrs Richards:	When I pay for a view I expect something more interesting than that.
Basil:	That is Torquay, madam.
Mrs Richards:	Well, it's not good enough.
Basil:	Well ... may I ask what you were hoping to see out of a Torquay hotel bedroom window? Sydney Opera House, perhaps?
Mrs Richards:	Don't be silly. I expect to be able to see the sea.
Basil:	You can see the sea. It's over there ....

Grammar extension
Perfect verb forms

1 Read the quotes about laughter and happiness. Which do you like best?

a 'One must laugh before one is happy, or one may die without ever having laughed at all.'
Jean de la Bruyère
(French writer 1645–1696)

b 'The most wasted of all days is that on which one has not laughed.'
Nicholas Chamfort
(French writer 1694–1778)

c 'To be happy, you must have taken the measure of your powers, tasted the fruits of your passion, and learned your place in the world.'
George Santayana
(Spanish-born philosopher 1863–1952)

d 'If the caveman had known how to laugh, History would have been different.'
Oscar Wilde
(Anglo-Irish playwright 1854–1900)

e 'To have been happy is the most unhappy form of fortune.'
Boethius
(Roman statesman c.489–524)

f 'Telling bad jokes is not habit-forming. I should know. I've been doing it for years.'
(American comedian)

2 a) Underline the perfect form(s) in each quote. Find examples of:

the Present Perfect Simple   the Past Perfect
the Present Perfect Continuous   a perfect infinitive
a perfect -ing form

b) What do all perfect forms have in common in the way that they are **formed**?

3 With all perfect forms, the speaker is **looking back** from one point in time, to a time before that. In which quote is the speaker:

a) looking back over a day?
b) looking back over the whole of his/her life?
c) looking back over history?

▶ Grammar extension bank pp.120 – 123

Listening
My first public performance

1 Discuss these questions.

- Have you ever performed in public (e.g. given a speech or appeared in a play)? How did it go?
- Here are some things that could go wrong. Can you add any more ideas?
  - you forget your lines
  - you make a joke and no one laughs
  - –
- Has anything like this ever happened to you or anyone you know? Which of these things would you find most embarrassing?

2 You are going to listen to a British actor, Michael Crawford, describing his first stage appearance in a school play at Brixton Town Hall in the 1950s. In the extract he describes two stories:

1 the plot of the play he appeared in
2 an anecdote about what happened when the play was performed.

Which story (1 or 2) do you think the following relate to?

a) Michael Crawford's shorts 2
b) Victorian England 1
c) the Mayor of Lambeth
d) coverage in the local press
e) Sam, a child chimney sweep
f) the headmaster, Mr Livingston
g) ripping off raggedy old clothes
h) two villainous adult chimney sweeps

3 🔲 [2.1] Read the questions below then listen. If necessary listen again.

1 What was the name of the play and what was it about?
2 What part did Michael Crawford play in the production?
3 What part did Mr Livingston play?
4 What was supposed to happen to Sam's clothes during the play?
5 Why was it an important occasion and who was in the audience?
6 How did Michael Crawford feel before the performance began?
7 Why did young Michael cling on to his ragged trousers and was he successful?
8 How did the audience react?
9 What about his headmaster?

4 Michael Crawford often uses language for dramatic effect. Underline phrases in the tapescript on p.158 that mean the same as a)–h).

a) exactly then
b) Sammy **asks** 'Please don't send me up again.'
c) they **remove** Sammy's shirt
d) the hall was **full**
e) I was **very nervous**
f) I stood there **with no clothes on**
g) Mr Livingston was **very angry**
h) He **used his hands** to close the curtains

5 a) Who do you think felt the following emotions?

> proud   terrified   furious   sorry for Michael
> embarrassed   amused   nervous   horrified/disgusted

b) Imagine you are one of these people. Retell the story to other students from this person's point of view without saying who you are. Can they guess?

▶ Phrase builder

Patterns to notice

Cleft sentences

1a) Compare these two ways of giving the same information:

> Mr Passey saw I could also act.
> It was Mr Passey who saw I could also act.

b) What is the difference in emphasis? What changes are there in the construction of the sentence?

2 Here are some other ways of making cleft sentences with *it* and with *what*:

I didn't invite them.	▶ **It wasn't me who** invited them.
I began to suspect something then.	▶ **It was then that** I began to suspect something.
You should tell her the truth.	▶ **What you should do is** tell her the truth.
I like the way she smiles.	▶ **What I like (about her) is** the way she smiles.

6 Rewrite these sentences as cleft sentences. Use the word in brackets to begin the sentence.

a) You need a few days' rest and recreation. (*What*)
b) Money is the thing people care about nowadays. (*It*)
c) We need someone to help us, not someone to criticise. (*What*)
d) I like the way he always listens sympathetically. (*What*)
e) His attitude towards other people really annoys me. (*It*)
f) I don't understand why you had to lie to me. (*What*)
g) I didn't decide to take a short cut across country! (*It*)
h) The world needs love, peace and understanding. (*What*)

7 Complete the sentences below using your own ideas, as in the example. Compare your ideas.

a) What I really dislike about my city ̲i̲s̲ ̲t̲h̲e̲ ̲t̲e̲r̲r̲i̲b̲l̲e̲ ̲t̲r̲a̲f̲f̲i̲c̲ ̲a̲n̲d̲ ̲t̲h̲e̲ ̲p̲o̲l̲l̲u̲t̲i̲o̲n̲.̲
b) What I like about my city is ....
c) It's the .... (in my country) that really .... me.
d) What I'd really like to do in my English class is ....
e) It's .... that I find really difficult in English.
f) What my country needs is ....
g) It was .... who taught me to ....
h) What I don't understand about .... (a famous person) is why (s)he ....

Wordspot

Idioms with *laugh*, *cry* and *tears*

1 In pairs, complete the gaps with *laugh*, *cry* or *tears*. Which phrases do you already know? Which can you guess?

a) a shoulder to .... on
b) to be in floods of ....
c) to have the last ....
d) to .... your eyes out
e) to be bored to ....
f) it's no ....ing matter
g) to burst out ....ing
h) to burst into ....
i) to .... your head off
j) to be close to ....

2 a) Replace the phrase in **bold** with one of the idioms with *laugh*, *cry* and *tears*. (There may be more than one possibility.)

1 I'm not sure you realise just how serious the parking situation is around here. It's **a very serious problem**.
2 I don't know what the matter was, but when I went past her room, she was **crying a lot**. Poor Linda!
3 Despite the bad reviews from the critics, the show was a great success, so Pinter **was proved right in the end**.
4 When I asked Bill where Tara was, he **began crying suddenly**.
5 Jenny was very upset when her father died, and Tom was very sympathetic. I think he gave her **support when she was depressed**.
6 I really enjoyed taking my nephew to the cinema. He **laughed and laughed and laughed** at all the jokes.
7 We tried to stay serious, but when we saw Ella wearing that ridiculous hat, we couldn't help it: we looked at each other and **suddenly started laughing**.
8 The way John read the elegy was very moving – many people listening were **nearly crying**.
9 It's such a sad story – I **cried and cried** at the end.
10 I wish our teachers had made more effort at school to make maths lessons more interesting. I was always **completely bored**.

b) Check your answers with another student.

▶ Phrase builder

Personal vocabulary

Task: tell a story to make people laugh ... or cry

Useful language

Describing feelings

Feeling completely (mystified/desperate/ashamed), he/she/they ...

To his/her horror/surprise/amusement/relief ...

In desperation/despair, he/she ...

He/she/they were in for a surprise/shock.

Time phrases

Before long ...

By this time ...

At that point ...

From that day on ...

From that moment onwards ...

Ten weeks/months/years went by ...

Ending the story

In the end ...

But the story doesn't end there, because ...

▶ Phrase builder

20 years later

d

e

f

Preparation for task

1 a) Which of the following phrases definitely relate to the story on the left?

> starving and penniless   a half-empty bottle of perfume
> ashamed of herself   play a trick   had to retire
> the pupils' past records   begged for money
> a messy child who needed a bath   in floods of tears
> the smartest child in the class   laid out on the bed
> a great comic actor   a note   a terminal illness

b) Do you think it is a funny or a sad story?

2 The class divides into two halves, A and B. A look at the story on these pages. B look at the story on p.108.

a) In small groups, put your pictures in order to make a story. Start with picture b in each story.

b) Use phrases from Exercise 1, and ask your teacher for other words you need.

▶ Personal vocabulary

c) Practise telling your story in your groups.

▶ Useful language

Task

1 Work with someone from the other half of the class. Tell your story using the pictures to illustrate it.

2 📟 [2.2 a + b] **a)** *Either* read the tapescript on p.160 *or* listen to the recording of **your partner's** story (i.e. group A listens to story B, group B listens to story A).

b) How close was your partner to the original story? What were the differences?

3 Tell your partner where he/she was right/wrong. Which of you was closest to the original story?

Optional writing

Write a funny/sad/touching story that you know (either a true story or a story from a novel or film that you like). Use phrases from the Useful language box to help you tell the story.

The Tears of a Clown

Oh, yeah yeah yeah
Now if there's a smile on my face
It's only there trying to fool the public
But when it comes down to fooling you
Now, honey, that's quite a different subject

Don't let my glad expression
Give you the wrong (1) ....
Really I'm sad
Oh, sadder than sad
You're gone and I'm hurting so (2) ....
Like a clown I pretend to be (3) ....

Now there're some sad things known to man
But there ain't too much sadder (4) ....
The tears of a clown
When there's no one around

Oh, yeah baby ... now if I appear to be carefree
It's only to camouflage my sadness
In order to shield my pride I try
To cover this hurt with a show of (5) ....
But don't let my show convince you
That I've been happy (6) .... (2 words)
Decided to go
Oh, I need you (7) ....

I'm hurt and I want you to (8) ....
But for others I put on a (9) ....
There're some sad things known to man
But there ain't too much sadder (10) ....
The tears of a clown
When there's no one around
Oh, yeah baby ...

Just like Pagliacci did
I try to keep my sadness (11) ....
Smiling in the public eye
But in my lonely room I (12) ....
The tears of a clown
When there's no one around

Oh, yeah, now if there's a smile on my face
Don't let my glad expression
Give you the wrong (13) ....
Don't let this smile I wear
Make you think that I don't (14) ....
Really I'm sad
Hurting so (15) ....

Smokey Robinson was one of the leading American songwriters of the 1960s, known for the clever wordplay of his lyrics. One of his most famous songs is *The Tears of a Clown*, originally a hit in 1967.

Song

🎵 *The Tears of a Clown*

1 Read about Smokey Robinson. Are you as good at rhyming as he was? How many rhyming words can you add to the groups below in **three** minutes?

a) sad/mad   Dad, had, bad
b) man/ran
c) expression/depression
d) sadness/madness
e) go/blow
f) wear/dare
g) did/lid

2 📼 [2.3] Guess which words go in the gaps. (They rhyme with the previous word in red.) Listen and check.

3 Explain the title of the song. Do you behave like this when you are sad, or do you show your feelings? What about other people you know?

Writing

A music review

1 What different kinds of music do you enjoy listening to, and in what situations? Who are your favourite singers/groups/composers?

2 Would you find the phrases below in a review of a concert, an album or both? Use the phrases to complete the reviews on p.25.

> a masterful performance   the opening act
> deafening applause   giving the audience 100%
> highly acclaimed   a powerful rendition
> refreshingly new and different   its appeal lies in
> the atmosphere changed   the encore
> poignant final track   voice is unmistakable
> the legendary   stands out

Macy Gray at the Roseland Ballroom

Macy Gray's show last Friday did not get off to an auspicious start. Technical difficulties, extra-strict security and an hour-long wait between 1) .... and Macy Gray's set made the audience impatient and rather listless. However, the moment the singer and her band appeared, 2) .... from lethargic to electric. Macy Gray came on in a shimmering red outfit and her 13-piece band were all dressed in white. The show opened with 3) .... of *Do Something*, one of the most danceable tunes on the debut album *On How Life Is*, and suddenly everyone was on their feet dancing, as if pulled by a mysterious force.

Ms Gray went on to give 4) ...., belting out her personal views on life, relationships and romance with a fiery passion. As well as the originals, she performed an array of cover versions which demonstrated her wide variety of musical influences. The best of these were the Beatles' *With a Little Help from my Friends* and Doris Day's *Que Sera Sera*. But whatever she sang, it was clear that Gray was 5) .... and was getting back the same. When the band finally launched into *I Try*, which they had saved until the end of 6) .... , the crowd went wild and sang along enthusiastically and very loudly with all the choruses.

The show ended with 7) .... and chanting from fans demanding another encore, but Ms Gray has enough experience to know: always leave them wanting more. I know that I certainly did.

Artist: **Macy Gray**
Album: ***On How Life Is***
Label: **Sony**

The voice of Macy Gray is a wonderful thing. It can be sugar sweet on one song, harsh and scratchy on another. The obvious comparison is to 8) .... Billie Holiday, but there are traces of other influences too, such as Nina Simone and Tina Turner. Yet in the end, Macy Gray sounds like no one but herself: within ten seconds of any song on her debut album 9) ...., *On How Life Is*, the 10) ....

Featuring confessional lyrics sung in a distinctive 'earthy' style, and a unique blend of hip hop, soul and rock, the album appeals across age and musical boundaries. It takes everything from breezy ballads to aggressive dance tunes and makes them sound 11) .... Of the ballads, the hit *I Try* definitely 12) .... : a hymn to the joy and pain of romantic dependence, part of 13) .... the catchy chorus, which showcases Gray's vocal talent. Other tracks which deserve a mention are the smoky ballad, *Still*, reminiscent of early Aretha Franklin, the comical *I've Committed Murder*, one of the album's up-tempo songs, and the 14) ...., *The Letter.*

On How Life Is sounds like a drive through the neighbourhoods of contemporary Los Angeles: roll down your window, and you can hear Macy Gray's roots and her inspirations. And if you haven't got this inspiring album, drive on down to the record shop and buy it now.

Rating: ★★★★

---

3 **a)** What information is contained in each paragraph of the two reviews?

b) Read again and find six more phrases which describe albums and concerts. Use these categories.

1 Songs/Tracks - cover versions
2 Voice
3 Audience
4 Concert - technical difficulties

4 **a)** Think of an album or concert that you have enjoyed recently and make notes on the following:

- the name(s) of the artist(s), the type of music
- reasons why you like the album or enjoyed the concert (e.g. the singer's voice, the atmosphere ...)
- descriptions of particularly good songs/tracks.

b) Write your review. Collect the reviews into a music guide for other students to read.

module 3

How you come across

Speaking and vocabulary

The right way to behave

1 Read a journalist's view on manners. Do you agree?

'I believe schools would be far better employed spending an hour a week on manners and charm, instead of banging on about Maths. Looking people in the eye, saying thank you, offering compliments at appropriate moments, giving up your seat to an elderly lady with shopping, the correct mode of address to a Belgian policeman while inebriated after a victory at football – these topics would be much more useful than most of the stuff on the curriculum.'

Matthew Engel *The Guardian*, Tuesday June 20, 2000

2 Write down six things you were taught about good and bad manners by your parents/at school. Compare lists with other students.

3 **a)** Look at the words in **bold**. Which describe polite behaviour (+) and which describe rude behaviour (–)?

it's very **good manners** **+**	it's **revolting**
it's **disrespectful** **–**	it's too **familiar**
it's not considered **acceptable**	it's considered **gentlemanly**
it **creates a** good **impression**	it's **sexist**
it's **over the top**	it's **unhygienic**
it's a way of **showing respect** to older people	it's **unprofessional**
it might make other people feel **awkward/embarrassed**	it might be **offensive to** some people
	it could be **misinterpreted**

b) Look back at the ideas on your list in Exercise 2. Could you use any of the phrases in the box above to describe them?

Is it the right thing to do?

- standing up when a teacher, boss, etc. enters or leaves the room
- men opening doors for women and helping them to take off and put on their coats
- calling people you don't know very well by their first name
- dropping in at someone's house without being invited
- smoking in someone else's house without asking permission
- asking people how much they earn or how old they are
- a man paying for a woman's meal and drinks if he takes her out on a date
- coughing, sneezing or yawning without putting your hand over your mouth
- touching people when you talk to them, e.g. patting them on the back or putting your arm round them
- shouting or holding loud conversations in public places
- swearing or blaspheming
- men whistling or shouting comments at girls they find attractive
- couples kissing and cuddling in public
- arriving half an hour late to a social engagement (without a good reason)
- phoning people after ten o'clock in the evening

4 **a)** Social behaviour varies in different situations. Read the list on the left and decide which of these:

- is always/never acceptable
- depends on people's ages or the social context (e.g. at work, with your friends, etc.).

b) Compare answers in groups. Explain your opinions, using phrases from the box in Exercise 3. What is the right way to behave in these situations?

> You could easily give the impression that …

> I think you might come across as being very …

> A lot of people might feel …

> I think it's much better to …

c) If you come from different countries, what are the differences?

5 Give a short talk about **one** of these topics:

- the kind of rude behaviour that infuriates you
- the six most important things a child should be taught about manners
- good manners between men and women
- the social taboos in your country that a foreigner should know about.

▶ Phrase builder

27

Reading and vocabulary

1 Discuss these questions.

- How has people's concept of good manners changed since your parents' and grandparents' generation?
- Is there any particular 'etiquette' attached to using modern technology, such as cash dispensers, mobile phones, computers, email, etc.?

2 Read seven questions sent in by readers to a newspaper advice column. Answer the questions below in groups.

a) What is the query in each case?
b) Have you ever wondered about any of these things?
c) What do you think the experts will advise?

3 Read quickly. Match the answers to the questions.

4 Answer these questions.

a) How does John Morgan say you should greet people you are meeting for the first time?
b) Why should you only kiss people on the cheek?
c) Explain what a 'double diary device' is.
d) Underline three words/phrases that show John Morgan disapproves of the way the woman with the mobile phone behaved.
e) What does Drusilla Beyfus suggest about the photos of the ex-girlfriend?
f) If you cannot understand another person's accent, what should you do?
g) In what ways can the person help his friend who has been sacked? Is it OK to discuss the subject with him, or not?

Perfect behaviour in an imperfect world

Q 1 My wife and I recently had a guest who took two calls on her mobile phone while she was with us. Both brought the conversation to a halt while we listened in uneasy silence. Can you advise on the etiquette of using mobile phones? I deplore my aural space being invaded on public transport and in restaurants, and dislike my home being turned into someone else's telephone box.

Q 2 There seems to be confusion about the etiquette of social kissing. When – and whom – should we kiss on the cheek? Are we supposed to kiss once, twice or even three times like in some countries? Standardisation of a practice which can cause awkwardness and embarrassment is surely long overdue.

Q 3 Do you have any recommendations for responding to a situation in which my close friend and colleague has been sacked?

Q 4 Whenever I am telephoned out of the blue by a friend with a ghastly invitation, I find it hard to think of an excuse fast enough, and always end up either accepting or sounding like a complete liar. Can you help me with a nifty formula?

Q 5 Is it offensive to ask your interlocutor, whose accent or dialect you are unable to understand well, to repeat what they are saying?

Q 6 May I suggest that my boyfriend removes the photos of his former girlfriend from his flat when I go round?

Q 7 When is it acceptable to tell someone there is something about their appearance that they would find embarrassing, such as having spinach on their teeth, their flies open, or, as I witnessed at a party, a woman with her skirt tucked in her knickers?

John Morgan from The Times replies:

1 *A Social kissing, as the name suggests is usually reserved for social life. It is cross and presumptuous to kiss people you are meeting for the first time: a traditional handshake or small nod of the head is all that is called for. The only site for a social kiss is on the cheek; attempts at mouths, foreheads or any other part of the anatomy display distinctly sexual rather than social intentions. One kiss is usual for the older generation, two permissible for young people, but three is quite excessive for any age. (JM)*

2 *A You need a 'double diary device'. It allows you to play for time while you make up your mind. All you have to say is: 'I'd love to, but first I have to look in my office/husband's/other diary. Can I ring you back?' (JM)*

3 *A Space does not permit my going into the ins and outs of mobile phone use here. However, I can quite unequivocally say that your guest displayed very bad mobile manners. It is very poor form to take calls when in any sort of social situation with others. Instead she should have left her phone either resolutely switched off, or on voice mail, thus giving you her undivided attention. (JM)*

4 *A Always. (JM)*

Drusilla Beyfus from The Mail on Sunday replies:

5 *A To me this seems a very dodgy notion. Why not have some good shots taken of yourself, leave them lying around, and hope that the penny drops? (DB)*

6 *A Much depends on the way in which you ask. Don't put the person down. This situation can be embarrassing, as it is very likely that the other person will be sensitive on the point. It would probably be crass to give as an explanation your inability to understand their accent, even with an apology. Make light of your apparent dumbness and ask for a replay. Or you might rephrase your understanding of the other person's remarks in a way that would allow them the advantage of correcting you, had you got it wrong. (DB)*

7 *A I believe that the stigma attached to your friend's ill luck has lost much of its power, now that redundancy has become one of the facts of working life. Few of us have no knowledge of the experience. The topic is liberated for discussion without a sense that the person concerned would be embarrassed. This doesn't mean that commiseration isn't in order. Very much so – getting the sack is usually confidence-shaking. What the person will need, most likely, are any promising tips on job offers. Former colleagues may be able to help by passing on any interesting enquiries. And offers of sociable treats are likely to be more than ever desirable when spirits are at a low ebb, and perhaps, finances are stretched. (DB)*

5 Match the words and phrases 1–10 to the definitions a)–j), using the context to help you.

1 crass
2 presumptuous
3 excessive
4 go into the ins and outs
5 dodgy
6 the penny drops
7 put someone down
8 make light of it
9 stigma
10 at a low ebb

a) the person gets the message
b) sense of shame
c) rude and insensitive
d) make someone feel stupid or inferior
e) at a low point
f) discuss all the details
g) make a joke of it
h) not to be relied on
i) too much
j) assuming more than you should

6 Discuss these questions in groups.

- Is the advice as you predicted? Do you find any of the answers strange?
- From their answers, which of these words would you use to describe John Morgan and Drusilla Beyfus? Which phrases give you this impression?

> formal   tactful   blunt
> opinionated   old-fashioned

7 Have you been in any social situations where you haven't known what to do? Ask other students their opinion about what you should have done.

▶ Phrase builder

Grammar extension
Modals and related verbs

1 <u>Underline</u> the modal verbs in the sentences below. Match them to the meanings in the box.

> possibility ability request for permission ~~request~~
> obligation advice (un)willingness logical necessity

a) <u>Can</u> you give me some advice about what to wear at the wedding? (request)

b) Children, you must sit quietly and listen to me – it's very rude to interrupt.

c) Many young people these days just won't accept the importance of good manners.

d) I'm terribly sorry to ask, but may I use your phone? It's rather urgent.

e) My uncle was the most charming man I've ever met – he could persuade anyone to do anything!

f) You must be John's niece – it's a pleasure to meet you.

g) Inappropriate social kissing may cause embarrassment in certain cultures.

h) When you're a guest at someone else's house, you should always switch your mobile onto voice mail.

2 **a)** The following sentences contain different modals, and other related verbs. Match them to the same meanings in Exercise 1.

1 You might offend some of the older people if you go to the funeral dressed like that.

2 My son will carry that for you, don't worry. Jeremy, help this lady.

3 <u>Would</u> you thank Alison for the kind invitation and send her my apologies? (request)

4 Sorry to leave early, but we really have to get to the airport or we'll miss our flight!

5 Excuse me, but could I ask you a personal question – where did you buy those shoes?

6 I think you ought to make an effort to be a bit more punctual in future – the boss is getting a bit fed up about it.

7 You can't be Karina's mother, surely? You're far too young!

8 Nicola was extremely annoyed about the way David behaved at her party the other night, but I think I managed to calm her down in the end.

b) Look at the pairs of sentences with the same general meaning. Is there any difference in the way we use the two modals?

Example: a and 3. Both are requests – 'would' is politer and more formal than 'can'.

▶ Grammar extension bank pp.124 – 127

Listening and speaking
Improving your communication skills

1 Read the information below. Are you surprised at this survey? Have you ever been shy?

> When asked in a survey, 25 per cent of the people interviewed said that they were chronically shy, and 80 per cent said that they had been shy at some time in their life. 60 per cent said that they would like to improve their communication skills.

2 Look at the situations below and discuss these questions in groups. How confident/nervous would you feel in these situations? Explain why.

- socialising at a party where you only know one or two people
- suggesting a social arrangement (e.g. a drink) to a new acquaintance or colleague
- meeting your boyfriend or girlfriend's parents for the first time
- asking a friend or colleague to do you a big favour
- talking to someone you fancy for the first time
- socialising for the evening with a group of people you feel are senior to you (senior colleagues, your parents' friends, etc.)
- giving a ten-minute presentation to a group of fifteen or twenty people
- making a light-hearted speech at a wedding or a party
- making a complaint (e.g. in a restaurant or shop)
- phoning someone you know you should have phoned ages ago

3 Do you think you would do these things in any of the situations above?

> blush shake giggle slump and look bored
> talk far too much stumble over your words
> get emotional or aggressive avoid eye contact
> look stiff and uncomfortable
> dry up and not be able to think of anything to say

6 Listen again if necessary, and check. What else did Rosemary say about these things? Did she say anything you disagree with?

▶ Phrase builder

Patterns to notice

Patterns with abstract nouns and relative clauses

In complex sentences, there is often an abstract noun followed by a relative clause:

> People often have problems communicating in **situations where** they're unsure of who they're speaking to.
> A lot depends on **the way in which/that** you say it.

Different nouns collocate with different relative pronouns. Notice these:

> There are many **reasons why** communications skills are important.
> There's **no reason why** you should feel uncomfortable.
> We have seen several **cases where** people have started arguing.
> It is easy to reach **the point where** you become over-emotional.
> We seem to be going through **a period in which** communications are very difficult.
> No one is sure of **the extent to which** this will affect business.
> One of the key elements of clear communication is **the part where** you summarise what the other person says.

Complex sentences like these are found in both writing and speech.

4 🖭 [3.1] You are going to listen to a radio interview with Rosemary Bailey, an expert on communication skills.

a) Which two situations in Exercise 2 does she refer to?

b) Which of the things in Exercise 3 does she feel is important to avoid in these situations?

c) What tips does she give for the best way to behave in these situations?

5 Work in pairs. Which of these statements do you think are true? Can you remember what Rosemary said?

a) People communicate less effectively with people they perceive as being very different from themselves.

b) In social situations, the more questions you ask, the better.

c) You should never pause during conversations with people you don't know very well.

d) You shouldn't look people in the eye for too long or you may give the wrong message.

e) When complaining, don't be distracted by listening too closely to what the other person is saying.

f) It's very useful if you summarise the other person's point of view at the end of your complaint.

g) Many people naturally have good communication skills.

7 Join the pairs of sentences using some of the phrases above. You will need to shorten/change some of the sentences slightly. Start with the word underlined.

Example: Make other people feel important. <u>Many</u> experts say that charm depends on how much you do this.

Many experts say that charm depends on the extent to which you make other people feel important.

a) People talk too much and don't listen properly because they are nervous. <u>I</u> have seen many situations like this.

b) How you stand or sit while you are talking is important. <u>People</u> often judge you unconsciously by this.

c) The two people involved remember different things from the same conversation. <u>It</u> is quite common to come across cases like this.

d) Nervous people forget to smile or make sympathetic noises. <u>There</u> are various reasons.

e) After an emotional argument, calm down and think clearly about what you really want to get across. <u>It</u> is essential to have a time like this.

f) How people express themselves when they complain is important. <u>Many</u> people respond negatively to this.

g) People dread long conversations with senior colleagues at parties. <u>There</u> are a large number of reasons for this.

Personal vocabulary

Useful language

Making suggestions
You/she could always try ...
(-ing)

or else ... might be worth
a try

One way to tackle it might
be to ...

Talking about the wrong things to do
It's best not to ...

There's no point in ... (-ing)

It's important to avoid ...
(-ing)

You don't want to give the
impression that ...

... wouldn't go down too
well

Talking about the right thing to do
The main thing to get across
is ...

He/she needs to feel that ...

The best thing to do would
be to ...

▶ Phrase builder

Task: decide what to say in a difficult situation

Preparation for task

1 Imagine you have a difficult personal problem. Are the responses below likely to help (+), unlikely to help (–), or does it depend (?). Explain why.

You:
talk the problem **over** with friends
get emotional
close up and refuse to discuss it
start **resenting** people who try
  to help
get defensive
tell friends to **mind their own business**
pull yourself together

Your friends/family:
try to be **supportive** +
start criticising you –
make you **face facts**
drop hints about what you
  should do
try to be **encouraging**
lose their patience
make positive suggestions

2 Read about three difficult situations and summarise the problem in each case.

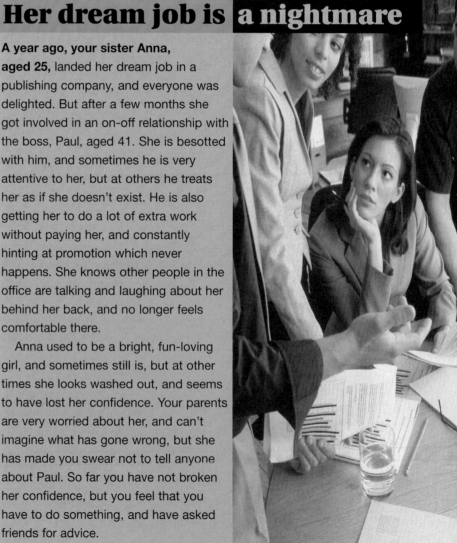

Her dream job is a nightmare

A year ago, your sister Anna, aged 25, landed her dream job in a publishing company, and everyone was delighted. But after a few months she got involved in an on-off relationship with the boss, Paul, aged 41. She is besotted with him, and sometimes he is very attentive to her, but at others he treats her as if she doesn't exist. He is also getting her to do a lot of extra work without paying her, and constantly hinting at promotion which never happens. She knows other people in the office are talking and laughing about her behind her back, and no longer feels comfortable there.

Anna used to be a bright, fun-loving girl, and sometimes still is, but at other times she looks washed out, and seems to have lost her confidence. Your parents are very worried about her, and can't imagine what has gone wrong, but she has made you swear not to tell anyone about Paul. So far you have not broken her confidence, but you feel that you have to do something, and have asked friends for advice.

The flatmate from hell

Monica's parents are very protective, and had always refused to allow her to attend university in a city 100km away. However, when her aunt and uncle bought a flat there for her cousin, Julia, they agreed to let her go, if she lived with Julia. Monica knew Julia was a bit spoilt, but they had always got on fine, and Monica was happy to share with her.

However, she has seen another side of Julia since they started living together. Her cousin never invites Monica to join in when she has friends round, and is selfish in all sorts of small ways. She switches the TV over when Monica is watching something, plays music late at night when she knows Monica has early lectures next day, and uses Monica's clothes, make-up and food without asking. She acts as if Monica owes her something, even though Monica's father is paying rent. Monica likes college, but living with Julia is spoiling everything, and she feels she needs to speak to someone. But who? Her aunt and uncle can see no wrong in their daughter, and she's afraid that her parents might make her go home. She's dropped hints to Julia, but Julia hasn't responded. She's been asking friends' advice.

Task

1 **a)** In groups, choose one of the problems to discuss.

b) Work individually. Make a list of all the different options for handling the problem. Ask your teacher for any vocabulary you need.

▶ Personal vocabulary

2 Discuss in your groups.

- Compare your individual lists.
- What are all the options for tackling the problem?
- What would be the worst thing you could do, in your opinion?
- What else should you avoid?
- What is the best thing to do? (It could be a combination of ideas).

▶ Useful language

3 Present your conclusions to the class. If you cannot agree, explain why and find out what the class think.

Optional writing

1 Write a playscript for a scene in which you discuss the problem with the person involved. Does it go as you planned, or does it all go wrong? How does it end up?

2 Act your scene out for the rest of the class.

Eight months ago, Richard, aged 22, failed his exams and dropped out of university. He got a job for three months but was sacked for being unreliable. Since then he seems to have fallen into a deep depression – he refuses to look for a job or go back to college, and hardly goes out. He's a very intelligent but highly sensitive young man, and tends to fly off the handle if he feels he's being criticised. His father is losing patience rapidly, and his mother is at her wits' end. You've known the family for years, and are close to Richard. A few days ago, his mother phoned you in tears, begging you to talk to him before his father does something terrible, like throw him out of the house. You feel you must help and have asked friends for suggestions.

He's dropped out and depressed

Writing
emails

1 **a)** How often do you use email? Think of three differences between emails and ordinary letters.

b) Read the introduction to the article below. What do you think the problems are?

2 Work in pairs. Think of advice for writing emails to colleagues and to friends. Read the article. <u>Underline</u> any good advice you didn't think of.

The explosive growth of email has created new problems, mainly because there has never been a definitive guide to common standards and expectations.
Shirley Taylor offers advice.

Today's way of conducting business is informal so that's what we should aim for in our business writing too – a friendly, conversational style. We should use short words and simple expressions, short sentences and paragraphs which are clear and concise but still courteous. The only place for standard overused clichés like 'Please find attached herewith' and 'Please be advised' is the recycle bin.

Messages which are sent without much thought or planning, with important details missing, or with spelling and punctuation errors, create a very bad impression. Similarly, the common courtesies of a greeting and sign-off should not be neglected for the sake of speed. Finally, a moment taken to fill in the 'Subject' line will be appreciated by a busy recipient, who will be able to see what your email is about before they decide to open it.

High on the list of annoyances when I did some research recently was the overuse of abbreviations and excessive punctuation. Using abbreviations is fine with a friend who you know will understand them, but should otherwise be limited to those that are already common to the English language, such as FYI (for your information) and BTW (by the way). As far as punctuation is concerned, a row of exclamation or question marks after an important point may be acceptable for chatting with friends, but could look out of place in other contexts. The main point is: don't overdo it.

Last but not least, remember that it's not a computer you're talking to, it's a real live human being – some people seem oblivious to the fact that writing in capitals is the equivalent of SHOUTING, and should be avoided unless you intend to convey excitement: 'WE WON!'

3 Find examples in the emails below where the writer does **not** follow the advice in the article.

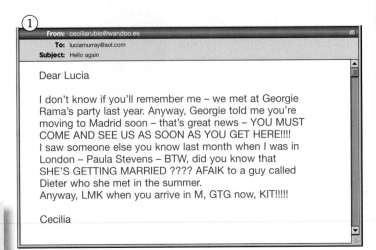

From: ceciliarubio@wandoo.es
To: luciamurray@aol.com
Subject: Hello again

Dear Lucia

I don't know if you'll remember me – we met at Georgie Rama's party last year. Anyway, Georgie told me you're moving to Madrid soon – that's great news – YOU MUST COME AND SEE US AS SOON AS YOU GET HERE!!!!
I saw someone else you know last month when I was in London – Paula Stevens – BTW, did you know that SHE'S GETTING MARRIED ???? AFAIK to a guy called Dieter who she met in the summer.
Anyway, LMK when you arrive in M, GTG now, KIT!!!!!

Cecilia

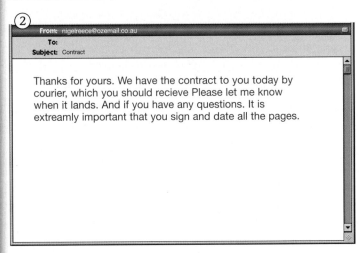

From: nigelreece@ozemail.co.au
To:
Subject: Contract

Thanks for yours. We have the contract to you today by courier, which you should recieve Please let me know when it lands. And if you have any questions. It is extreamly important that you sign and date all the pages.

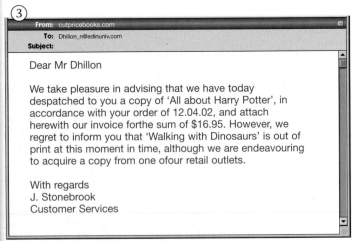

From: cutpricebooks.com
To: Dhillon_n@edinuniv.com
Subject:

Dear Mr Dhillon

We take pleasure in advising that we have today despatched to you a copy of 'All about Harry Potter', in accordance with your order of 12.04.02, and attach herewith our invoice forthe sum of $16.95. However, we regret to inform you that 'Walking with Dinosaurs' is out of print at this moment in time, although we are endeavouring to acquire a copy from one ofour retail outlets.

With regards
J. Stonebrook
Customer Services

4 Rewrite the emails, following the advice in the article. Compare ideas in pairs.

5 Write an email for one of the following situations:

- You have seen a job advertised on the Internet. Decide on the name of the company and what the advertised position is. Write an email showing interest in the position and asking for more information about it.
- An old school friend who you have not seen for several years has invited you to a school reunion. Write an email asking for more information about the reunion (e.g. Will there be other guests? How formal is it? Are partners allowed?) and offering to help with the preparations in some way.
- You have an important meeting (decide the day and the time), but you have realised that you won't be able to make it. Write an email to your colleague, asking if the meeting can be rescheduled and suggesting another time/day.

6 Exchange your email with another student (send it if you can!). Check your partner's work, bearing in mind the advice in the article.

Real life
Getting people to do things

1 📼 [3.2] The pictures show four situations in which one person wants another person to do something. Can you guess what the situations are? Listen and check.

2 a) Which phrases in the box below are used for:

1 interrupting someone?
2 asking for help/persuading?
3 refusing to do something?
4 asking someone to wait?
5 agreeing to do something?

Are you in the middle of something?	If you say so
I'll be right with you	I don't see why I should
Can I ask a really really big favour?	Oh, all right then
Oh, go on	I wonder if you might be able to help
If you'll just bear with me for a minute	
I'd be really grateful	Shall I come back later?
Sorry to disturb you	We would very much appreciate it
I must ask you not to	use your mobile phone

b) Listen again and copy the intonation on the recording.

3 a) Choose the best adjective to describe each speaker's attitude.

cooperative	annoyed/reluctant	fairly polite
extremely polite	uncooperative	casual

b) Read the tapescripts on p.162. Underline other phrases that show the speakers' attitudes – as 5 below.

4 Work in pairs to prepare a short dialogue (15–20 lines). Use the questions on p.114 to help you. Act out your dialogue for the class.

5 Listen to other students' dialogues. Decide what the request is, where the people are, and what the attitudes of the two speakers are.

module 4

Mind, body and spirit

Vocabulary and speaking

Body and spirit

1 **a)** Match the two halves of the sayings. What do they mean?

1	Healthy body ...	a)	by bread alone.
2	The eyes ...	b)	no gain.
3	You are ...	c)	healthy mind.
4	Man does not live ...	d)	what you eat.
5	No pain ...	e)	are the window to the soul.

b) Which sayings do you think are true? Are there similar sayings in your language?

Questionnaire

1 Do you do **weight-training** or **body-building**?

2 Do you ever **meditate**?

3 Have you ever **had your palm read**?

4 Do you **pray** regularly?

5 Do you have a **lucky mascot** or **lucky number**?

6 How important is music in your life?

7 Have you ever practised yoga?

8 Are you prone to headaches or **dizzy spells**?

9 Do you believe in **horoscopes**?

10 Have you ever **had a massage**?

11 Do you take any notice of **superstitions**?

12 Have you ever done a **high risk sport** like hang-gliding or parachuting?

13 Have you ever **sought spiritual advice** before making a big decision?

14 Do you believe that dreams have a meaning?

15 Have you ever climbed a really high mountain?

16 Have you ever **suffered from insomnia**?

17 Do you **believe in** ghosts?

18 If you walked up six flights of stairs, would you be **out of breath**?

19 Have you ever **followed a special diet**?

20 Do you ever do **relaxation exercises**?

21 Do you ever read or write poetry?

22 Have you ever tried any **complementary therapies**, like **aromatherapy** or **osteopathy**?

23 Would you go to a **séance** if you were invited?

24 Could you run for a kilometre without stopping?

25 Which things most **stress** you **out**?

26 Is there any food that you can't eat for health reasons?

27 Are you **allergic to** anything?

28 Do you believe colours can **affect your mood**?

29 Do you ever **lose your appetite**?

30 Do you believe in **life after death**?

2 Read the questions above, checking the phrases in **bold** if necessary. Mark them B if they relate to body, S if they relate to spirit or B/S if they relate to both.

3 Tick (✓) at least ten questions that you would be happy to discuss.

4 **a)** Change books with a partner and look at the questions he/she ticked. Think of suitable follow-up questions.

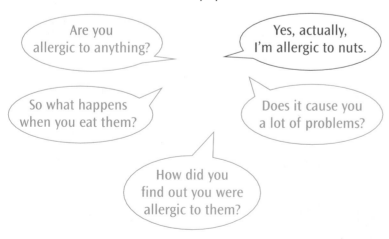

Are you allergic to anything?

Yes, actually, I'm allergic to nuts.

So what happens when you eat them?

Does it cause you a lot of problems?

How did you find out you were allergic to them?

b) Ask and answer your questions. Tell the class anything interesting you discovered about your partner.

▶ Phrase builder

Reading and speaking

1 Many people nowadays say that they are stressed. Make a list of reasons for this, and a list of ways of dealing with stress. Compare in groups.

2 Put the phrases below in the best category. Mark them S if they are related to stress, R if they relate to relaxation.

- feeling tense
- getting things into perspective
- feeling worked up
- things getting on top of you
- taking things in your stride
- chilling out
- being in a trance
- taking a step back
- finding it difficult to unwind
- getting pains in your chest
- feeling bad-tempered
- doing breathing exercises

3 Look below at the introduction of an article from *The Observer* magazine. What is it about?

4 Match the four therapies in the introduction to the photos. What do you think these treatments involve? Can you add any more complementary therapies to this list?

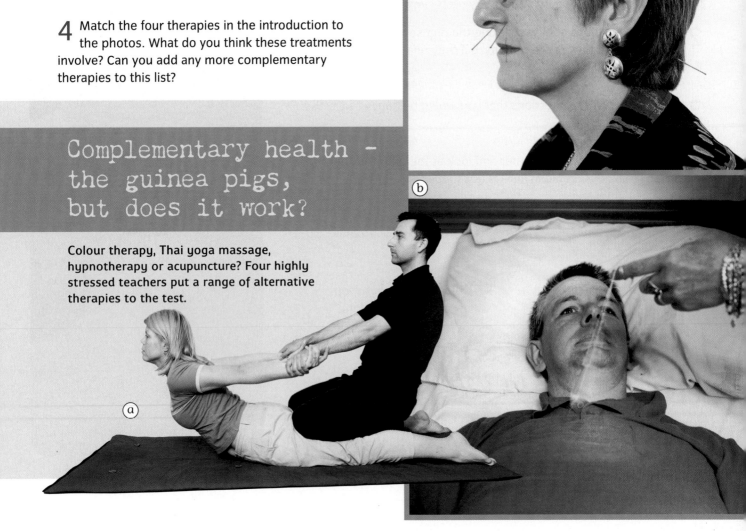

```
Complementary health -
the guinea pigs,
but does it work?
```

Colour therapy, Thai yoga massage, hypnotherapy or acupuncture? Four highly stressed teachers put a range of alternative therapies to the test.

Hypnotherapy

Alison Hatch teaches a class of seven- and eight-year-olds.

'I often get stressed at work, and it makes me feel bad-tempered and really worked up. I get pains in my chest, and an infection flares up in my hair and eyebrows. I'm very open-minded about alternative medicine.'

Prescribed

Hypnotherapy, which involves being induced into a light trance state usually by closing your eyes and listening to the therapist's voice. Though it directs itself to your unconscious mind, you remain aware of your surroundings.

Alison says, 'We spent a large part of the first session looking back at my medical history and my life from when I was very small. She asked me what I was stressed about, to which the answer was "Everything". The discussion was almost like therapy. I'd describe a stressful scenario, and she would look at it in a different way, explaining how things that happened in my childhood affect my reactions now.

'Afterwards, she taught me breathing exercises for relaxation. Then she got me to lie down and imagine a special place where I could go to relax. I thought of a rock pool in a green lagoon. She said that after she counted to ten very slowly she wanted me to be in my relaxed place in my mind, which was where I ended up.

'She would then talk through whatever problems had come up at the beginning of the session, then she counted back to ten and took me out. The idea was that, when stressed, I would be able to close my eyes and remember that state of total relaxation and it's true, I can take myself back there if I want to. The infection hasn't been a problem since I started the treatment. When I find a classroom stressful, I take a step back, breathe and tell myself to chill out. A boy came up to me in the classroom the other day and said, "Miss, what are you doing?" and I said, "I'm counting to ten, Alex." '

Continuing treatment? Yes

5 Read about the teacher who tried hypnotherapy and complete the first column of the grid at the bottom of the page.

6 a) Work in groups of three, Students A, B and C. Each read about one of the other therapies. Complete the correct column of the grid.

Text 2 Colour Therapy p.109
Text 3 Thai Yoga Massage p.111
Text 4 Acupuncture p.114

b) Tell your partners about the text you've read. Listen and complete the rest of the grid.

7 a) Rank the therapies from 1 (= most successful), to 4 (= least successful). Explain why.

b) Discuss these questions.

- Which factors seem to affect how successful the therapy was?
- Would you like to try any of these therapies? Why/Why not?
- The four people in the articles are primary school teachers. Do you think that is a stressful job? Which other jobs do you think are stressful and why?

▶ Phrase builder

	Alison Hypnotherapy	Ray Colour therapy	Dayle Thai yoga massage	Jackie Acupuncture
His/her symptoms of stress				
Initial attitude to therapy				
Brief description of therapy				
Relationship with practitioner				
His/her assessment of the treatment				

39

Grammar extension
Adjectives and adverbs

1 How many of the quiz questions below can you do **without** looking back at the reading texts? Count up your score (maximum points 30).

Adjectives quiz

I Where do the adjectives in brackets go in the following sentences from the texts?

a) I never got that feeling of energy back again. (*instant*)   I point
b) I feel if I do things for myself. (*selfish*)   I point
c) Though it directs itself to your mind, you remain of your surroundings. (*aware, unconscious*)   2 points
d) The practitioner did a consultation. (*initial, thorough*)   I point

For two bonus points: find an example above of an attributive adjective, and an example of a predicative adjective.

2 Some of the adjectives in the text have two parts. What is the missing part of the adjective in these sentences?

a) It makes me feel .... -tempered and really worked ....   2 points
b) I'm very open-........................... about alternative medicine.   I point
c) My husband has even noticed a difference in me. He thinks I'm much more .... back about things.   I point

For two bonus points: think of two more adjectives formed from phrasal verbs (like the second example in 2a).

3 Form the adjective from the noun in brackets.

a) I'd describe a (*stress*) scenario, and she would look at it in a different way.   I point
b) I felt quite (*energy*) after the first session.   I point
c) We spent a large part of the first session looking back at my (*medicine*) history.   I point

For two bonus points: think of two more adjectives which end in each of these ways (no points if you can't come up with all six!).

4 What prefixes were used with these adjectives?

a) When I get stressed at work, I get very ....active.   I point
b) She gave me a lot of advice on .... personal relationships. I point

For five bonus points: think of five more prefixes which modify the meaning of adjectives, and explain what they mean.

5 We use adverbs of degree (e.g. *very*, *really*, etc.) to change the meaning of adjectives. Which adverbs were used with the adjectives below?

a) Four .... stressed teachers put a range of alternative therapies to the test.   I point
b) I felt .... energetic after the first session.   I point
c) I was .... sceptical beforehand   I point

For two bonus points: think of four more adverbs of degree which modify the meaning of adjectives.

2 Use the texts to check answers you are unsure of.

▶ Grammar extension bank pp.128 – 131

Listening
Self-help books

1 Discuss these questions.

* What kind of things do self-help books give advice about?
* Do you ever buy self-help books?
* Have you found them useful?

2 The headings below come from self-help books about relaxation. Choose two or three and guess what the advice will be.

a) Water while-you-wait
b) Musical relief
c) Empty your brain
d) Your mind
e) Unblocking your emotional flow
f) Skip-to-it
g) Stressed out?
h) Getting rid of the clutter in your life
i) Stress in the workplace
j) Instant air-conditioning
k) Colour your thoughts
l) New beginnings

3 [4.1] The advice you will hear comes from two books, one gives serious advice, the other is a joke. Listen and mark the headings for a)–m) in Exercise 2 as follows:

(✓) = from the serious self-help book

(!) = from the joke self-help book

(?) = not sure yet, need to understand it better

4 a) Work in pairs. How much of the advice can you remember? Listen again and check.

b) Which serious pieces of advice were useful/not very useful? Which joke/advice did you like best?

▶ Phrase builder

Patterns to notice

Patterns with comparatives and superlatives

a) Complete these sentences from the recording scripts with a comparative or superlative. Notice the patterns in **bold**.

1 Skipping is **one of the** *quicker/quickest* **ways of** getting up your heart rate.
2 **The** *better/best* **thing about** skipping is, you don't need lots of time, space or expensive clothes.
3 **There is nothing** *more soothing/most soothing* **than** a cup of herbal tea.

b) Here are three other common patterns.

1 **The older** you get, **the less** energetic/**the more** unfit you become.
   The more you practise meditating, **the easier**/**the less** difficult it becomes.
2 **What could be more** refreshing **than** a cool drink on a hot summer's day?
3 A brisk walk is **among the most** effective forms of exercise.

5 [4.2] Use the box to complete the gaps. Notice there are **four extra** words. Listen and check your answers.

than	among	less	one	the	some	better	that	more
about	likely	nothing	most	What	either	of		

The ancient art of reading someone's palm has always been (1) .... the most popular ways of foretelling the future ... after all, you don't have to believe it, and the best thing (2) .... it is that it doesn't require a lot of time or expensive equipment (3) .... But many are sceptical that palm reading has any scientific basis at all. (4) .... could be more ridiculous (5) .... the idea that our future can be predicted from the random lines and creases on our hands? Cynics claim that palmists use other clues to gain their 'amazing' insights ... in other words, the (6) .... experienced and observant the reader is, the (7) .... she becomes at noticing things which help her to 'predict' the future ... while the more cynical the 'victim' is, the (8) .... likely they are to believe a word of it!

However, scientists at the University of Barcelona have discovered that palmistry may have some basis in scientific truth. Having compared the palms of 140 children, they discovered that (9) .... more arches and loops children have on their palms, the more (10) .... they are to be intellectually impaired. And the existence of a Simian line – a rare crease across the palm – appears to be (11) .... of the most reliable indicators of mental deficiency. This may be connected with events between the thirteenth and eighteenth weeks of pregnancy, a crucial time for brain development and the period when fingerprints are formed. So maybe there is some truth in what the palm reader says ... and there's (12) .... more guaranteed to cheer you up than the news that you're about to meet a tall dark stranger who will change your life for the better!

Personal vocabulary

Task: who wins the award?

Preparation for task

1 Read about the 'Mind, body and spirit' award on the right.
From the pictures, can you guess what any of the finalists achieved?

2 📼 [4.3] Listen to news items describing what these people did.
Make brief notes about:
- where/in what context it happened
- what they did
- why they did it/how they feel about it

3 **a)** Work in pairs A and B. Listen again for more detail. Student A
should listen most closely to stories 1, and 3 and Student B should
listen most closely to stories 2 and 4.

b) Compare answers, explaining to your partner the details of the stories
you listened to most closely.

Useful language

a Explaining your choice

He showed great courage/
determination in the way
he ...

He/she could easily have
(done) ...

She must have felt terrified
about ...

They took a big risk when
they ...

What particularly strikes/
impresses/me about ...
is (the fact that) ...

They set a great example
to ...

She is a positive role model

He risked his life to ...

b Expressing reservations

Personally, I don't think she
should have ...

You could argue that it was a
bit stupid/naive to ...

c In your speech

We found it difficult to come
to an agreement ...

After a great deal of
discussion ...

In the end, we decided ...

I am very proud to present
the award to ...

The first prize goes to ...

▶ Phrase builder

Fiona and Mike Thornwill

Camila Batmanghelidjh

PICK OF THE DAY

Mind, body and spirit is a popular TV programme featuring human interest stories about people who have shown exceptional physical, mental or moral courage, in a wide range of situations. At the end of the series, the 'Mind, body and spirit' award is presented to one of the people who have featured in the programme, with a prize of £10,000 (£5,000 for the runner-up). An Internet poll of viewers has produced the short-list of finalists in the pictures.

The 'Have-a-Go Golden Girls':
Joan Windsor, Jean Douglas and Anne Aylward

Police Constable Glynn Griffith

Task

1 a) Work individually. Spend five to ten minutes thinking about the candidates' experiences, and the ways in which they showed courage. Ask your teacher for any vocabulary you need.

▶ Personal vocabulary

b) Write down the nominees in order from 1 to 4 (1= the people/person, who most deserve(s) the award). Note down two or three reasons next to the person/people.

2 a) Work in groups of about four. You are the panel who decides who gets the award. Compare your list of arguments with the rest of the group.

▶ Useful language a and b

b) Decide on the winner and the runner-up for the award.

3 Spend a few minutes preparing a short speech explaining your choice to the class.

▶ Useful language c

4 Listen to the other groups' decisions. Are their arguments the same as yours? Have any of the arguments convinced you to change your mind?

Optional writing

Write a short news article describing the awards ceremony. Use these guidelines.

- Make the winner (and to a lesser extent the runner-up) the main focus of the article: describe what he/she has achieved, why the panel chose him/her, and include some imaginary quotes from the delighted winner.
- Refer briefly to the other finalists, their achievements and possibly why they were not chosen.
- Remember to refer briefly to the TV programme, and describe the atmosphere at the award ceremony, etc.

Wordspot
Idioms to do with the body

1 Use the definitions in blue to guess the appropriate part of the body in the idioms.

1 a ..*shoulder*.. to cry on
   (= a sympathetic listener)
2 keep a straight ....
   (= stop yourself from laughing)
3 ....-raising
   (= very scary!)
4 turn a blind .... to something
   (= pretend not to notice)
5 turn your .... up at something
   (= treat something with contempt)
6 ....-watering
   (= delicious, tasty)
7 up to your .... in it
   (= totally busy and overwhelmed by work)
8 get your .... round something
   (= understand something difficult)
9 ....-rending
   (= extremely sad and moving)
10 to have butterflies in your ....
   (= feel very nervous before you do something)
11 win .... down
   (= win easily)
12 all fingers and ....
   (= very, very clumsy)
13 pull someone's ....
   (= make fun of somebody)
14 put your .... in it
   (= say something that upsets somebody)

2 Spend a few minutes studying the idioms. Which of them could relate to:

a) food and drink?
b) worry, sadness or nerves?
c) embarrassing situations?
d) humour?
e) stressful situations?
f) sport?

3 Work in pairs. Student A looks at the card on p.106 and reads out the questions. Student B answers using one of the body idioms. Student B looks at the card on p.109 and reads out the questions. Student A answers using one of the body idioms.

▶ Phrase builder

Writing
A leaflet

1 Look at the leaflet on p.45. What is it for? What other places have leaflets like this?

2 Match the headings below to the correct section of the leaflet. Why are the headings questions? Think of questions for the other four sections.

Who are the trainers?
What if I don't have much free time?
How long do I have to join for?
What other facilities are there?

3 Complete this advice for writing leaflets using the words and phrases below.

1 The .... should be visually attractive.
2 It is a good idea to use .... , illustrations, colours, etc.
3 The language should not be ....
4 .... should be avoided.
5 Headings should ....
6 .... should be quite short.
7 The information given should move from the ....

> too complex   layout   bullet points   stand out
> sentences   long blocks of prose   general to the specific

4 You have been asked to write a leaflet for a new arts centre in your area. Use the notes below and the advice in Exercise 3.

Arts centre
• types of exhibition the centre puts on
• courses (day/evening/weekend?) – dance, ...?
• theatre(s) for plays, concerts, etc.
• free events, e.g. workshops for children
• cinema (e.g. of films?)
• talks by visiting speakers, e.g. ...?
• café/bar/restaurant, opening times
• crèche, opening times
• shop (which sells ...?)
• directions (by car, public transport, etc.)

5 Put your leaflet on the classroom wall for other students to read. Which leaflet is the most effective and why?

Fit as a Fiddle Health Centre

A DIFFERENT WAY TO GET FIT FOR LIFE

a) ....

Unlike other centres, Fit as a Fiddle allocates a personal trainer to every member. Your trainer will help you to set goals and build up an individualised exercise programme. You don't even have to go to the gym – your trainer can provide you with an exercise video to use at home, if that suits you better.

b) ....

All our trainers are qualified instructors who have a minimum of five years' experience in personal training. Their aim is to motivate and give help and advice, in a friendly 'family' atmosphere.

c) ....

No problem! You are exactly the kind of person our centres are designed for. We can give you a short programme to ease you gently back into exercise and help you to make it a regular part of your life.

d) ....

Even if you can only spare half an hour twice a week, we will find the most beneficial way for you to use it. Most of our centres have 'early bird' openings three or four times a week when they open at 7 a.m., so you could easily fit in half an hour in the gym before work.

e) ....

Yes, we can. Every centre has a nutrition expert who can design a diet for you, based on your needs and lifestyle, or simply give you advice about healthy eating and help you to change bad dietary habits for ever.

f) ....

Other facilities include: a daily timetable of fitness classes such as aerobics, kick boxing and yoga, treatments such as massage and physiotherapy, a sauna and steam room, a range of healthy refreshments.

g) ....

You can join for as little as four weeks to start with. We have a range of membership deals from one month to a year.

h) ....

To find out where your nearest centre is, give us a call on 0800 2312000, or visit our website at fitasafiddle.com.

module 5
Learning for life

- ▶ **Reading:** short articles about education
- ▶ **Listening:** interview with a head teacher
- ▶ **Task:** teach a practical skill
- ▶ **Writing:** tips from notes
- ▶ **Vocabulary:** education
- ▶ **Passive forms**
- ▶ **Particles which add meaning to verbs**
- ▶ **Wordspot:** *way*

Vocabulary and speaking
Education

1 Work in groups. Write the alphabet on a piece of paper. Next to each letter write one word connected to **education**. How many words can you write in two minutes?

2 Complete the A–Z quiz on p.47. Check your answers on p.109.

THE A–Z OF LEARNING

A   The .... year is the time when there are school or university classes.

B   .... **time**, when students can 'have a breather'. In the US it's called **recess**. Many people's favourite part of the school day!

C   is for a series of lessons in a particular subject. It could be a **crash** .... , a **refresher** .... or a **foundation** ....

D   is for degree, diploma, to drop out of university.

E   is for .... school (as it's known in the US) – in the UK it's **primary** school. You go there from age 6 to age 11.

F   is for faculty, final exams, further education.

G   is for .... day. It's traditional in many countries to wear a cap and gown as you receive your degree.

H   is for high school, higher education, history.

I   The Internet, infant school, instructor.

J   is for .... school – in the UK this is a school for 7–11-year-olds; in the US it's a high school for children aged 12–14.

K   is for kindergarten, kids, knowledge.

L   is for .... : university students should attend them and take notes, but sometimes they **skip** them!

M   Numbers which show how well you did in a test – full .... is 100 per cent (unlike **grade**, which is a letter).

N   is for nursery school, numeracy, note-taking.

O   is for .... -learning – in other words, studying via the Internet.

P   is for .... – a teacher at university: in the UK, higher-ranking than a **lecturer**.

Q   is for qualifications, questions, quizzes.

R   is for the three Rs – ...., ... and .... … the three basics of a good primary education … but shouldn't that be the one R, one W and one A?!

S   is for secondary school, school subjects, scholarship.

T   is for .... education – education at a college, university, etc.

U   is for .... – a student studying for a first degree, as opposed to a postgraduate, studying for a Master's or PhD.

V   is for .... courses, which help you to do a specific job.

W   is for work experience, workload, workaholic.

X

Y   is for Yale, one of the USA's most prestigious universities.

Z   is for zoology, which you can take a degree in.

3 **a)** Mark the sentences below (✓) if they are true in your country, (✗) if they are not true, and (?) if you're not sure.

- Children start learning the Three Rs from the age of about six.
- The academic year begins in September.
- Most undergraduates take five or six years to finish their degrees, and many drop out of university.
- University lecturers and professors are badly paid.
- Children at elementary school are usually required to wear a uniform.
- More than two-thirds of students in tertiary education are women.
- Schoolchildren are allowed to smoke during breaks.
- Many postgraduates go abroad to study.
- Secondary school students can do vocational courses as well as courses in academic subjects.
- People celebrate graduation day by jumping into fountains.
- There are skills shortages in many areas, so older people are being encouraged to go back to college and do refresher courses.
- Lectures are often attended by more than 500 students.
- More and more people are doing online language courses.

b) Correct the sentences that are not true, then, in pairs, compare and discuss your answers.

4 **a)** Which of the things in Exercise 3 would you like to see changed in your country?

b) Think of **three** other things about the education system in your country that you would like to change. Compare answers with other students.

▶ Phrase builder

Reading and speaking
Education: fact or myth?

1 Look at the headlines of the five articles. Without reading the articles, decide whether you think they are facts (F) or myths (M).

2 Read the articles and find out what the latest research suggests. Were you right? Are the headlines correct summaries of each article?

3 Tick (✓) the best summary of each article according to the information in the texts.

1 Watching TV programmes
a) seems to benefit all children up to the age of 16.
b) is particularly beneficial for 2- and 3-year-olds.
c) is good for toddlers whatever the programme.

2 According to Richard Roberts, 'evening types' do better in intelligence tests because
a) they sleep more.
b) of their genetic inheritance.
c) they did the tests in the evening.

3 According to Matthew Melmed, the best way for parents to help their children would be
a) to enrol them in extra classes.
b) to spend more time with them.
c) to put less pressure on them.

4 According to Dutch scientists, the children's stress disorders are probably mainly caused by
a) the inability to sleep.
b) problems at school.
c) being separated from their parents.

5 It appears that the 'brain zapper'
a) has only been successful in some cases.
b) had a negative effect generally.
c) is useful for teaching young children.

4 Find the nine words and phrases in **bold** in the texts. Suggest an alternative word with the same meaning. Use the context to help you.

better

Example: a ~~head~~ start in life

5 Discuss these questions.

a) Which research did you find most surprising?
b) Do you think any of the findings might be dubious?
c) Are the trends described in articles 3 and 4 happening in your country too?

▶ Phrase builder

① Watching TV is bad for toddlers

To give your children a **head** start in life, sit them in front of the television. A study of 200 American pre-schoolers has revealed that toddlers who watch TV for two hours a day develop more quickly than those who do without. On average, the two- and three-year-olds who watched TV scored 10 per cent higher in reading, maths and vocabulary. However, the programmes have to be aimed at their age group – children **derive** no benefits from watching TV designed for adults. 'Television opens up the world to many young children and gives them a head start, which is sustained in improved academic achievement throughout their school lives,' said Aletha Huston of the University of Texas. But the positive impact of TV declines with age, reports _The Sunday Times_. Older children who watch more than 16 hours of TV a week perform worse than their peers.

④ The happiest days of your life

One in five modern children suffers from anxieties so severe that they should be classified as psychiatric disorders, say scientists from the University of Maastricht. The researchers interviewed 290 Dutch primary school children aged between eight and thirteen; 20 per cent of them were **beset with** worries so serious that they limited their ability to lead normal lives, reports _The Daily Mail_. Many had trouble sleeping; some were afraid to leave their homes; others had problems interacting with their peers. 'Nobody is really sure exactly why this is, but these disorders are caused by children internalising their anxiety,' said child psychiatrist Peter Muris. 'This could be caused by parents being away from their children for long periods or by children being stressed at school. A parent who does not spend time with their child could miss out on the fact that the child has the problem, meaning it can go untreated and get worse.'

② The early bird catches the worm …

The early bird may catch the worm – but people who lie around in bed in the morning and work into the evening are more intelligent, according to Richard Roberts of the University of Sydney. The scientists asked 400 volunteers to **fill in** questionnaires to work out if they considered themselves early-rising 'morning types' or late-working 'evening types'. Each was then **subjected to** mental agility and memory tests. The researchers discovered that the 'evening types' had significantly better mental speed and memory. 'The results indicate that, contrary to conventional folk wisdom, evening types are more likely to have higher intelligence scores,' Roberts told *The Sunday Telegraph*. He also suggested that the link between intelligence and working late may be a hang-over from prehistoric times, when those who were still alert after dark would be more likely to survive attacks by nocturnal predators.

③ Pushy parents help children succeed

Pushy parents may be doing their children more harm than good, says Washington-based childcare expert Matthew Melmed. Professional parents frequently overstimulate babies and toddlers and buy them educational toys that are too old for them in the belief that they are improving their prospects. In fact, faced with such demands, the children may become frustrated and give up completely. Worse still, the children recognise that they are disappointing their parents and this sense of failure eats away at their self-esteem. The warning comes as an ever-increasing range of educational material is being produced for the very young. In the US, 'hyper-parenting' is rife, says Joanna Coles in *The Times*. **Expectant** mothers are pressured into buying CDs such as *Mozart for Mothers to Be* ('Build your baby's brain!') while no self-respecting newborn would be without educational videos including *Baby Einstein* and *Baby Shakespeare*. By the age of one, enrolment in **a plethora** of classes, from languages to arithmetic, is *de rigueur*.

⑤ We all have genius within us

For years, scientists have speculated that the talents possessed by so-called 'idiots savants' – as depicted by Dustin Hoffman in the film *Rain Man* – may be accessible to us all. According to Professor Allan Snyder of the University of Sydney, it is just a question of switching off the conscious part of the brain. 'I believe that each of us has non-conscious machinery to do extraordinary art, extraordinary memory, extraordinary mathematical calculations,' he told *The Daily Mail*. Now, Dr Robyn Young of Flinders University in Adelaide has tried to prove the theory by using an electronic brain zapper to release the artistic and mathematical skills of 17 volunteers. Using a technique known as transcranial magnetic stimulation, Dr Young switched off the conscious part of the volunteers' brains, then tested their skills in calculation

or drawing. The process did not turn them into geniuses, but five showed improved performance. Dr Young believes that the technique could eventually be used to help children learn to read, or adults to pick up a new language. **In the meantime**, however, the 'brain zapper' seems to do as much damage to the brain as it does good. 'We had **a hard time** recruiting volunteers to get their brain zapped,' admitted Young. 'One guy got lost on his way to work the day after the experiment.'

Patterns to notice

Particles which add meaning to verbs

Many verbs in English are followed by a preposition/particle. Here are three basic types:

A   Verbs with dependent prepositions. The preposition does not add to the meaning of the verb but is grammatically necessary.

1   The programmes have to be **aimed at** their age group.
2   One in five modern children **suffers from** anxiety.

B   Phrasal verbs (a) The verb and particle together have a new meaning which cannot be guessed from their two separate meanings.

1   Children may become frustrated and **give up** (= stop) completely.
2   Scientists asked volunteers to complete questionnaires to **work out** (= calculate/discover) if they were morning or evening types.

Notice there are few consistent patterns with types **A** and **B**. They have to be remembered individually and checked in a dictionary.

C   Phrasal verbs (b) In other phrasal verbs, the verb keeps its normal basic meaning, but the particle adds to or modifies it.

1   People who **lie around** in bed in the morning are more intelligent.
    around adds the idea of pointless activity/inactivity.
    See also:
    messing around, lazing around, lounging around
2   This sense of failure **eats away** at their self-esteem.
    away adds the idea of something happening constantly/for a long time.
    See also:
    chatting away, working away, typing away

There are patterns in the way these particles are used. Here are some more examples:

up = completely	lock up, drink/eat up, tidy up
on = continuation	work on, carry on
out (1) = to different people	hand out, share out, send out
out (2) = loudly/ publicly	speak out, shout out, call out
down (1) = becoming less	slow down, calm down
down (2) = onto paper	write down, take down, note down
off = to another place	drive off, run off

▶ Phrase builder

6 Look at the pairs of sentences below. How does the particle in b) change the meaning of the verb in a)?

1   a)   There was already someone **sitting** outside the door when I got to the classroom.
    b)   We spent the whole day **sitting around** at home, watching videos.
2   a)   Do you know if it's legal for schools to **copy** video tapes?
    b)   The teacher wrote the answers on the blackboard, and we all **copied** them **down**.
3   a)   We **turned** the corner and saw the village a few hundred metres away.
    b)   Can you **turn down** the radio a bit, please?
4   a)   My brother came to **see** me at the airport.
    b)   My brother came to **see** me **off** at the airport.
5   a)   Because of suspension, Lopez can't **play** in Sunday's match.
    b)   After receiving treatment from the physiotherapist, Lopez was able to **play on**.
6   a)   Have you **read** any books by J.K. Rowling?
    b)   The teacher chose Jane to **read out** her composition.
7   a)   Did the teacher **give** you any homework for the weekend?
    b)   The teacher **gave out** the exam papers.
8   a)   We **used** green paint for the bathroom ceiling.
    b)   We've already **used up** the paint you bought the other day.

7 Add a particle to the appropriate verb in the sentences below, to improve the meaning.

a)   For the first few chapters, you might find the book a bit slow, but if you read there's a lot more action.
b)   It wasn't a serious accident, but we took each other's name and address.
c)   We're planning to send over a thousand invitations to the opening party.
d)   I don't know why he was so upset: he just walked without saying a word.
e)   It was so frustrating to be left hanging, waiting for news.
f)   I don't see why we shouldn't complain. I really think it's time someone spoke.
g)   He waited for the boos and whistles to die before he spoke.
h)   Didn't your mother ever tell you to eat all your vegetables?

Listening and speaking

What life skills should you learn at school?

1 Discuss these questions in groups.

a) Were you taught many practical skills at school, or was the focus mainly on academic subjects?

b) How many of the things below did you learn? Which do you think would have been most useful?

- Citizenship
- Cookery
- DIY and woodwork
- Drama
- Drug and alcohol awareness
- Economics
- First aid
- Foreign languages
- How to work in a team
- Managing your finances
- Note-taking and study skills
- Personal organisation
- Racism awareness
- Sex education
- Typing

2 [5.1] Nine people were asked 'Are there any practical skills that you wish you'd been taught at school?' Listen to their answers, and answer the questions.

a) Which topics from Exercise 1b) are mentioned? Number them in the order you hear them.

b) Which person had no complaints about his/her education? Why?

c) What reasons did the other people give? Whose comments do you most identify with?

3 [5.2] Now listen to a radio interview with William Atkinson, the head teacher of Phoenix High School in London, in which he discusses the life skills that they try to teach in his school.

a) Underline the skills from Exercise 1 that he mentions.

b) Why does he think they are important?

4 Listen again. Correct the statements that are not true about William Atkinson's school. Follow the interview with the tapescript on p.165.

a) In their daily assemblies, pupils are encouraged to give their opinions about the organisation and management of the school.

b) The school council is made up of parents who are elected to represent each class.

c) The best lessons for learning how to work in a team are drama and religious education.

d) At the school, they believe that the ability to work in a team is one of the key life skills of the future.

e) The teachers always warn pupils against social evils like drugs, alcohol, racism, etc.

f) The school sometimes brings in ex-criminals and ex-drug addicts to tell pupils about their experiences.

5 Discuss in groups.

- Are policies like those described by William Atkinson common in schools in your country? What do you think of his ideas?

6 Which words from the box collocate with the words and phrases in **bold** in the sentences below?

part (x2)	develop	deal	play	say
involved	pursue	make	share	provide

a) They want their pupils to .... **a** full **part in** society, so they try to **give** them a .... in the organisation of the school, and allow them to .... **observations about** the management of the school.

b) The school tries to .... **the opportunity** for young people to .... team **skills**. They should tolerate others viewpoints and perspectives, rather than just .... **their own interests**. This is important because in real life, everyone is .... **of** some kind of group.

c) The school tries to .... **with** some of the big issues that society is facing, and so, for example, they sometimes ask people who have been .... **in** crime to .... **their experiences with** pupils.

▶ Phrase builder

Grammar extension
Use and non-use of passive forms

1 Which sentences below do not contain a passive form? Are there any sentences where you are not sure?

a) In some countries, pupils are allowed to smoke during breaks.
b) In my day, girls were not expected to go to university and have a career.
c) I wish I'd been taught more about how to use computers.
d) An ever-increasing range of educational materials is being produced for the very young.
e) Expectant mothers are pressured into buying CDs like *Mozart for mothers-to-be*.
f) We encourage youngsters to be able to take different roles within a group.
g) Many schoolchildren's anxieties should be classified as psychiatric disorders.
h) One day, the talents possessed by so-called idiots-savants may be accessible to us all.
i) To be educationally beneficial, TV programmes have to be aimed at their age group.
j) In the future, people will be expected to work in teams even more.
k) Before you take a photo, you should always check the position of the sun.
l) If parents are worried that their children are not learning to read fast enough, they should get them assessed by an expert.

2 In the sentences in Exercise 1, find examples of:

- past, present and future passive forms
- a continuous passive form
- a modal passive
- a passive infinitive
- a 'reduced' passive where only the past participle is used
- a passive where the auxiliary is not *be*.

3 Here are some reasons the passive is often used. Find examples in Exercise 1 to illustrate them. (For each example more than one of these may be true.)

1 The subject of the verb is unimportant, obvious or unknown.
2 The subject of the verb is 'people generally'.
3 The passive is part of the formal/journalistic style.
4 The passive verb is part of a 'set phrase'.

4 The first verbs in f) and k) in Exercise 1 could be expressed in the passive, but they are not. Why not?

5 Is the *get* passive in sentence l) formal in style or not? Which other auxiliary is used in a similar way? Think of some more examples of this kind of passive.

▶ Grammar extension bank pp.132 – 135

Personal vocabulary

Useful language

Ordering your instructions
Before you start …

First of all …

What you need to do first is …

There's something important that I should have mentioned before …

What to do
It's extremely important/it's vital that you … (or … will happen)

The main thing is to …

Make sure you always …

The best way to … is to …

Another way of doing it is to …

What not to do
One common mistake is to …

Avoid …ing

Be careful not to …

What you shouldn't do is …

Don't … whatever you do!

▶ Phrase builder

Task: teach a practical skill to others

Preparation for task

1 Read the list of everyday skills below. Tick (✓) the ones you can do.

- taking a good photograph
- sending a text message
- mending a puncture on a bicycle
- ironing a shirt perfectly
- giving the kiss of life
- making bread
- serving in tennis
- bathing a small baby

2 **a)** You are going to hear someone explaining how to give mouth-to-mouth resuscitation. Which diagrams below do you think these instructions relate to?

- [ ] Tilt back the patient's head.
- [ ] Watch to see if their chest is expanding.
- [ ] You may feel their breath tickling your ear.
- [ ] Cover their mouth with your mouth.
- [ ] You may hear a deep intake of breath.
- [ ] Pinch their nostrils hard.
- [ ] Completely seal their mouth.
- [ ] Turn the person on their side.
- [ ] Place two fingers beneath their chin.
- [ ] Put the patient into the unconscious position.
- [1] Shake them gently by the shoulders.
- [ ] Breathe into their mouth.
- [ ] Try to open up their airway in case it's blocked.
- [ ] Repeat this four to six times.

b) 🖾 [5.3] Listen and check. Were you surprised by any of the instructions?

Task

1 **a)** *Either* choose one of the skills you ticked in Exercise 1 *or* think of a similar skill that you could explain in detail.

b) Spend about ten minutes thinking about how to explain it step-by-step to someone who has never done it before. Use gestures, props or rough diagrams to help you. Make brief notes if necessary.

▶ Useful language

c) Ask your teacher or use a dictionary to find any other phrases you need. Write them in your Personal vocabulary box.

▶ Personal vocabulary

2 Choose two more skills from the list in Exercise 1 that you would like to learn. Find another student in the class who can explain them to you.

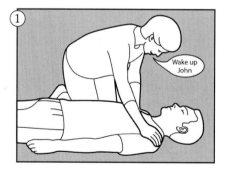
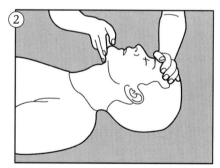
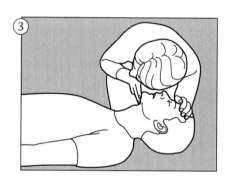
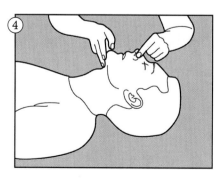
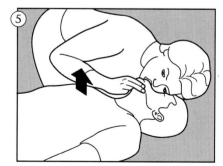
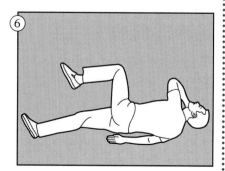

Writing

Writing tips from notes

1 Look at the following words and phrases for talking about computers and the Internet. How many of them are the same in your language?

websites	folder	search	search engine
menu	address	type	save

2 **a)** Complete the notes on Internet searches using a word or phrase from the box above.

<u>INTERNET SEARCHES</u>

Typing a website 1) ....
- No spaces between words.
- Write as one word.
- Be careful with spelling.

Good 2) ....
- Alta Vista
- Google
- Lycos

How to make a 3) .... quicker and more efficient
- 4) .... interesting websites in your Favourites
  5) ....
- 6) .... a plus sign between words.
- Use drop-down 7) .... to visit
  8) .... visited earlier.

b) Compare answers with a partner.

3 **a)** Look at four different ways of writing the same tip.

1 To make your search more specific, a plus sign can be typed between the words.
2 Your search can be made more specific by typing a plus sign between the words.
3 Make your search more specific. One way of doing this is to type a plus sign between the words.
4 Try typing a plus sign between the words. This will make your search more specific.

b) <u>Underline</u> the *-ing* forms and the infinitives with *to*. Which tips have passive forms? What is the effect of this?

4 **a)** You're going to write a set of tips. Read the following advice.

- Start with a short introductory paragraph. This could start with a question like this:

  Are you having trouble finding what you want on the Internet? Well, here are some tips to ...

  Or an explanation like this:

  The Worldwide Web is like a giant magazine with millions of pages. To get the best out of it, you should ...

- Write out your tips, grouped under sub-headings. Include examples where necessary.

- Break up the information under a sub-heading if it is too 'dense', by using numbers or bullet points.

b) *Either* write up the tips on how to use the Internet for research *or* write a set of tips on one of the following topics:
- finding the best English course/university course to suit your needs
- revising for exams
- success in a job interview
- the best ways to learn a foreign language quickly
- improving your speaking skills in English
- using a monolingual dictionary effectively
- another topic of your choice.

5 Read each other's tips. Did you learn anything useful?

Wordspot

way

1 Which phrase with *way* best completes each sentence?

a) Do you find that, when they get lost, men are much more reluctant to *ask the way/find their way/know the way* than women?

b) Many parents say that you shouldn't let children *go out of their way/ have their own way/get in the way* all the time, or they will grow up spoiled and selfish.

c) I just called the taxi firm, and they say that the cab is *in the way/ on its way/under way*.

d) The label's sticking out of the front of your pullover … it's *in a bad way/ the wrong way up/the wrong way round/way too big for you* and you look ridiculous.

e) They started work on the bridge in April and they still haven't done much. *By the way/No way* will it be finished by the end of the year.

2 Put phrases with *way* in the correct place on the diagram.

manner/method

- *This is **the best way to** cook beef.*
- *There is **another way of doing it**.*
- *I hate **the way** he laughs.*
- *I **did it my way**!*

route, direction

- *ask the way* = ask for directions
1 .... = discover the route somewhere
2 .... = be familiar with the route somewhere
3 .... = take extra trouble to do sth
4 .... = arriving soon
5 .... = travel in front

WAY

blocking or avoiding

- *to be/get in the way* = to be blocking the path
6 .... = stop blocking the path

what you want

- *have your own way* = have things as you want them

position/situation

- *in a bad way* = very ill, e.g. after an accident
- *the wrong way round* = reversed
7 .... = reversed

other phrases

- *No way!* = absolutely not!
- *By the way* (= used to change the topic)
8 .... = much too big
9 .... = strange, weird
10 .... = in progress

3 **a)** Complete the dialogues using a phrase with *way*.

1 'Can I get past, please?'
'Oh, I'm sorry … are my bags ....? I'll put them up in the locker.'

2 'Oh, dear! I think we're lost. What do you think we should do?'
'Why don't you stop and ....?'

3 'What do you think we should buy Sophie for her birthday? How about a Barbie doll?'
'...................!!! She's 14 years old. She's .... for Barbie dolls!!'

4 'Were the staff nice at the hotel?'
'Oh yes … they really .... to make us feel at home.'

5 'OK, we'll drive to the restaurant … Do you ....?'
'I'm not sure I remember it … you'd better .... and we'll follow behind.'

6 'When will the new cinema complex open?'
'They expect the work to be .... by the beginning of next month.'

7 'What did you think of the modern art exhibition?'
'Strange. Some of it was a bit .... for my taste … '

8 'How many children does Geraldine have now?'
'Three … and there's another one ....!!'

9 'Poor Frank! Have you seen him since his accident?'
'No, but I've heard he's still ...., unfortunately.'

10 'Is this how I put the ink cartridge in?'
'No, you've got it .... Here, let me do it.'

b) [5.4] Listen and check your answers.

▶ Phrase builder

module 6

In the money

- ▶ **Reading:** a series of articles about TV quiz shows
- ▶ **Listening:** discussion of a court case
- ▶ **Task:** people's court
- ▶ **Writing:** analyse graphic data
- ▶ **Vocabulary:** money
- ▶ **Time and tense**
- ▶ **Inversion with negative adverbials**
- ▶ **Real life:** expressing quantities imprecisely

Vocabulary and speaking

Double your money!

1 Work in pairs. How many questions in the quiz can you answer **without** using a dictionary?

2 ▭ [6.1] Listen and check. For each question you answered correctly, you win the figure stated. Who won the most?

Quiz

£10
What were first minted in ancient Lydia (part of what is now Turkey) about 2,600 years ago?

- A automatic cash machines
- B coins
- C one-armed bandits
- D credit cards

£25
Someone who has no money at all is often described as ...

- A broke
- B broken
- C bust
- D shattered

£50
Which of these might a child receive from his/her parents?

- A a fee
- B a pension
- C pocket money
- D a subsidy

£100
Something so valuable it cannot be bought can be described as ...

- A valueless
- B priceless
- C worthless
- D pricey

£250
If a company goes out of business because it cannot pay its debts, it ...

- A is in the black
- B breaks even
- C is in the red
- D goes bankrupt

£500
Which of these is money given to someone in authority to get them to do something dishonest?

- A a tip
- B a bribe
- C a deposit
- D a ransom

£1,000!
Which of these is **not** a way of describing someone who hates spending money?

- A flashy
- B stingy
- C tight-fisted
- D miserly

3 How much can you remember from the recording? Answer as many questions as you can individually, then compare answers in groups.

a) In what circumstances might someone
  ... receive a **subsidy**?
  ... expect a **tip**?
  ... charge a **fee**?
  ... pay a **deposit**?
  ... demand a **ransom**?
  ... go **bankrupt**?

b) Have you ever
  ... been completely **broke**?
  ... bought something '**valuable**' that turned out to be **worthless**?
  ... won money from a **one-armed bandit**?
  ... paid or been offered a **bribe**?

c) Do you know anyone who is
  ... really **stingy**?
  ... always **in the red**?
  ... really **flashy** with their money?

4 <u>Underline</u> the phrases relating to money in the quiz on p.56 and the tapescript on p.167. Write the words under the headings below.

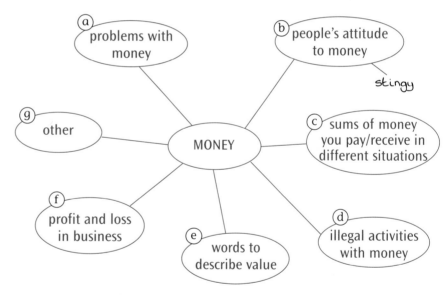

5 **a)** Work in groups. Read the well-known sayings about money. What do they mean? Think of as many arguments as you can for and against each idea.

'Money makes the world go round.'
'Neither a borrower nor a lender be.'
'Money is the root of all evil.'
'Take care of the pennies and the pounds will take care of themselves.'
'In life, the rich get richer and the poor get poorer.'
'Money can't buy happiness.'

b) Your teacher will choose one student to talk for a minute about one of the sayings above. Other students can challenge them if they deviate from the topic or repeat themselves.

▶ Phrase builder

Reading

1 Are there any 'big money' TV quizzes in your country? What do you have to do, and what kind of prizes do you win?

2 Read the text on the right about TV quiz shows. Note:

a) the name of two 1950s quiz shows.

b) when *Who Wants To Be a Millionaire?* began.

c) the names of the three lifelines on *Who Wants To Be a Millionaire?*

d) the name of the first $million winner.

e) why Lertlak Panchanawapron was both lucky and unlucky.

3 Discuss these questions in groups.

- Has there been a version of *Who Wants To Be a Millionaire?* in your country?
- Would you like to appear on a show like this? Why/Why not?
- How many times would you be prepared to phone the contestants' hotline in order to get on?
- What kinds of questions would you most dread in a general knowledge quiz? What would be your strongest areas?
- Can you think of any ingenious ways of winning any TV quiz show that you watch? Tell the class and decide whose idea is the cleverest.

Getting Rich Quick:
The Rise of the TV Quiz Show

Quiz shows first became popular in the USA in the late 1950s, with radio and TV shows such as *The $64,000 Question* and *Twenty-One* pulling in huge ratings. But scandals about feeding correct answers to contestants (later the subject of the Robert Redford movie, *Quiz Show*) undermined the public's faith in the shows, and the TV quiz went into temporary decline – in the US at least. With the growth of television in the '60s and '70s, the prizes gradually got bigger – and the formats for the shows more lavish and imaginative.

A key breakthrough came with the British quiz, *Who Wants To Be a Millionaire?* which first appeared in 1998. The formula was simple –15 multiple-choice questions of increasing difficulty, with the contestant in the hot seat having three lifelines if they're stuck – 'Phone a Friend', 'Ask the Audience' and '50:50', where the computer takes away two wrong answers, and leaves the correct answer and one remaining wrong answer. The big prize money that attracted viewers to the show was funded by an equally simple idea: would-be contestants paid a small charge to call telephone hotlines to enter their names for the show. These proved so popular that viewers had to phone dozens of times to stand any chance of appearing. This ingenious formula proved so successful that the show has been sold to more than forty countries worldwide. In fact, it's probably being shown somewhere in the world as you read this!

John Carpenter became the first $million winner on the American show in 1999 – but things haven't always gone according to plan. On the Thai version of the show, Lertlak Panchanawapron had exhausted her three lifelines by the fifth question when she was amazed to see the answer she thought was correct highlighted on her monitor screen. She picked it and continued choosing the highlighted answers until she had answered all fifteen questions, winning 1 million baht in the process. 'I didn't notice anything,' said the presenter. 'Just that she was very smart despite not having much education.' Unfortunately, the show's producers were more suspicious and Lertlak later confessed to noticing the highlights around the correct answers – the computer was mistakenly showing her the host's screen! After her winner's cheque had been returned, she was given another chance … and failed on the fourth question.

However, contestants have come up with other ingenious ways of reaching that elusive million …

£500,000

4 You are going to read about one quiz show contestant, Patrick Spooner. Read article 1, from an Australian newspaper. Why was the article written about him?

5 a) Can you guess the next stage of Spooner's plan? Read article 2 from the British press and check your ideas.

b) What were the similarities between his TV appearances in Britain and in Australia?

6 a) Predict what Spooner did next. Scan article 3 and check. What happened?

b) Tick the statements that reflect your opinion of Patrick Spooner. Explain why.

- ☐ I feel sorry for him.
- ☐ He got what he deserved.
- ☐ People like him should be banned from games shows.
- ☐ I admire his ingenuity.

7 Can you remember the colloquial phrases used instead of the phrases in **bold**?

a) An English backpacker, who **had so little money** that he slept on a friend's floor …

b) Mr Spooner, 32, **made a lot of money** by answering …

c) But he was **not a complete beginner**.

d) Last year, he **became famous** on the other side of the world.

e) … there's a good chance he will soon **appear unexpectedly** on the American version …

f) With a toss of an old £1 coin **things went badly** for a shocked contestant.

g) He moved to Dublin to **see if he could succeed** on the Irish show.

▶ Phrase builder

---

① Broke backpacker wins $250,000

An English backpacker, who was so broke that he slept on a friend's floor, won $250,000 cash in a television quiz last night. Paddy Spooner, who has only a week left in Australia before his visa expires, scooped the biggest prize so far on Channel Nine's *Who Wants To Be a Millionaire?*

A self-described 'professional backpacker', Mr Spooner, 32, struck it rich by answering 10 multiple-choice questions. The final question which he answered correctly was to name the year in which the last convicts were transported to Freemantle: 1868. He decided to take the money when he didn't know the answer to the next question – worth $500,000 – which asked him to name the science field in which Australian Sir T.W. Edgeworth specialised: geology.

Mr Spooner borrowed a friend's phone to make 215 $1 phone calls before successfully registering for the show.

From Illawara Mercury 29/04/99

② What do you mean 'it's only a game'?

The top prize remains elusive, but *Who Wants To Be a Millionaire?* contestant Paddy Spooner may have found a novel way to win the golden sum. Mr Spooner walked off with £250,000 following his appearance on the top British TV quiz show on Thursday night.

But he was no rookie. The 33-year-old backpacker from Hampshire had already pocketed a fortune on the Australian version of the show. In April last year, he made headlines on the other side of the world when he scooped what was then the record prize of 250,000 Australian dollars. And given that Mr Spooner sees himself as a 'hemispheric commuter' who travels the world escaping from winter, there's a good chance he will soon pop up on the American version of the programme.

Clearly his grasp of general knowledge and doggedness – he called the *Who Wants To Be a Millionaire?* hotline 400 times before being selected – outline him as a budding quiz show professional.

BBC News 31/3/2000

③ A toss of a coin costs contestant dear

With a toss of an old £1 coin, it all went horribly wrong for a shocked contestant on Gay Byrne's *Who Wants To Be a Millionaire?* show last night who left with only €1,000 after winning well over half a million on the British and Australian versions of the show. Patrick Spooner (35) was left in total disbelief after he got a €4,000 question wrong when asked the name of top Irish actor Pierce Brosnan's youngest son.

He first asked the audience, 51 per cent of whom gave him the correct answer of 'Paris', but decided that this margin was too close and on opting for his '50:50' lifeline was left with 'Paris' and 'Tyrone'. A stunned Gay Byrne looked on as Patrick, who was born in Britain, produced an old £1 coin from his pocket and said he was going to flip it to decide the answer.

At this stage Gay reminded Patrick that he could still use his 'phone a friend' lifeline but the tossed coin was already in midair and he opted for the wrong answer of 'Tyrone'. Gay then helped the speechless contestant out of the chair just as the klaxon sounded to end the show.

Patrick has previously scooped $250,000 on the Australian version of the show and another £250,000 on the British version. He moved to Dublin last year to try his hand at the Irish show, making up to 200 phone calls per week to get on. It is understood that his phone bills have reached €900. He now plans to resume his extensive travels which have taken him to 45 countries in four years. He was described as a 'professional backpacker' on the show.

Isabel Hurley
© Irish Independent 4/3/02

Grammar extension
Time and tense

1 Read the text about unsuccessful criminals.

a) Can you name the verb forms <u>underlined</u> in the first paragraph of the text?
Example: 1 Present Simple
b) How many of these forms can you also find in the second paragraph? <u>Underline</u> the examples.
c) Which time do the verbs underlined refer to?
  • the past   • the present   • the future   • no specific time

No criminal ever (1) <u>believes</u> that he (2) <u>will be caught</u> ... but it seems that some (3) <u>are trying</u> to make crime detection as easy as possible for the police. In Japan, a country which (4) <u>has</u> long <u>been</u> famous for its peaceful, law-abiding citizens, one robber (5) <u>burst</u> into a shop and demanded money. But as he (6) <u>was admiring</u> himself in the CCTV camera, he changed his mind and asked the shop workers to call the police. Everything (7) <u>had been going</u> fine, he said later, until he realised he (8) <u>had forgotten</u> to put on his mask.

And have you heard about the two British men who tried to rob a shop? Unfortunately, they had forgotten to cut eyeholes in the woollen masks they were wearing. While they were trying to find the counter, they bumped into each other and knocked each other unconscious. 'Don't worry,' said the owner when the men came round, 'I've phoned the police and they'll be here in a few moments. Do you fancy a cup of tea while you're waiting?'

2 a) How many of the same verb forms can you find in the sentences below? Do they refer to the same **time** as the examples in Exercise 1?

1 (newspaper headline) Broke backpacker **wins** $250,000
2 Have you ever thought about what you'd do if you **won** a big money prize?
3 Mum, I **was wondering** if you could lend me a bit of money until I get paid on Friday.
4 Your father told me this morning that he**'d** already **lent** you £50.
5 If the two robbers **had had** more sense, they might have got away with it.
6 He'll have to leave the country as soon as his visa **has expired**.
7 So, this funny old bloke **walks** up to me and **asks** me to give him twenty quid!
8 I **advise** you not to leave any valuables in your room, Mr Timothy.

b) Are these verb forms used in the same way as in the story?

▶ Grammar extension bank pp.136 – 139

Listening
The Case of Stella Liebeck

1 You are going to hear the story of Stella Liebeck, from New Mexico, USA, and what happened when she ordered a coffee with her takeaway meal.

a) Which pictures do these words go with?

to drop someone off	a lid	
to tug	damages	scalding
to sue	jury	horrified

b) 🔲 [6.2a] Listen and put the pictures below in order.

2 [image: cassette] [6.2b] Listen to two people arguing about the case. What new information do you learn:

a) in favour of Stella?
b) in favour of the company?

Who do you agree with?

3 Discuss these questions.

- What was Stella entitled to, if anything, in your opinion?
- Is it common in your country to sue for compensation?
- If so, what kind of institutions tend to be sued?
- What are the disadvantages of a 'compensation culture'?

Patterns to notice

4 [image: cassette] [6.3] Here are three sentences from the recordings. Put the phrases in order to make a correct sentence. Listen and check. Is this the usual word order in English?

a) consult/did/a lawyer/only/Stella/then
b) did/not once/her fault/it was/admit that/she
c) all that money/have been given/no way/she/should

Inversion with negative adverbials

1 The following adverbials come at the beginning of a sentence and are followed by an inversion.

Only then **did I understand** what was happening.
Only now **can I appreciate** the difficulties of the situation.
Not once **did he offer** to pay.
Rarely/Seldom/Never before **have I experienced** such kindness and hospitality.
No longer **will we accept** these low standards.
Under no circumstances **should you wander** around alone after dark.
On no account **must you overexert** yourself.
Not only **did he take** all our money, *but he also* **betrayed** our trust.

They are often used to give greater emphasis in formal language.

2 The phrase *No way* means 'It's completely impossible' and is common in informal, spoken language. It is also followed by an inversion.

No way **will we be finished** by 10.

---

5 Make the sentences below more formal using the phrase in brackets in the 'front' position. Make any other changes necessary with negatives, inversion, etc.

a) Our country does **not** need to rely on foreign investment **any more**. (*No longer*)
b) You **certainly** should **not** borrow money without checking the interest rates. (*Under no circumstances*)
c) **Now** we are **finally** seeing the benefits of the government's careful policies. (*Only now*)
d) A change of government has **not often** had such a dramatic effect on the economic outlook. (*Rarely*)
e) Frederick looked for his wallet to pay. **At that moment** he realised he had left all his money at home. (*Only then*)
f) **You definitely shouldn't** reveal the details of your bank account over the telephone. (*On no account*)
g) This country has **not** witnessed such a serious financial crisis **before**. (*Never before*)
h) **It's rare that** a politician admits publicly that he has made a mistake. (*Seldom*)
i) George had to pay a large fine, **and** he had to spend some time in prison **as well**. (*Not only … also*)

▶ Phrase builder

Personal vocabulary

Useful language

a Comparing ideas

I think he should be entitled to ...

I think she deserves a bit more/less.

That's far/a bit too much.

That's not nearly enough.

b Trying to reach a conclusion

Do we all agree about ... ?

The key issue is whether or not ...

Shall we move on to ... ?

Shall we come back to ... later?

c Presenting your conclusions

In the circumstances, we feel that ...

We agreed unanimously that ...

We found it very difficult to agree ...

Some people felt that ... while others felt that ...

▶ Phrase builder

Task: decide how much compensation people should get

Preparation for task

1 🖭 [6.4] The stories opposite describe four cases where people sued successfully. Listen and complete the gaps in each of the stories.

2 Work in pairs and look at the words and phrases in **bold**. Use the context to guess the meaning.

Task

1 **a)** Work individually or in pairs. For each of the cases, decide how much each person should receive. You can choose any amount between $100 and $3 billion.

b) Make a brief list of reasons why you think this should be the case. Ask your teacher for any vocabulary you need.

▶ Personal vocabulary

2 Work in larger groups of four. Compare ideas and try to reach an agreement about the amount of compensation.

▶ Useful language a and b

3 Present your conclusions to the class. How far did the different groups agree?

▶ Useful language c

4 🖭 [6.5] Listen and find out how much money the people in question really received. Are there any you find particularly surprising or unfair? Which group's awards were most similar to the real ones?

A, an American actor, once the star of a major (1) ...., moved to London and started a career in the theatre as a writer and director when his TV career began to fade. When one of his plays appeared at a theatre, a **reviewer** in a newspaper claimed that it was 'without doubt the worst thing he had ever seen on the London stage'. The show (2) .... soon afterwards, and A decided to sue the newspaper. It emerged in court that the reviewer had not actually been present at the performance, but had relied on information supplied by (3) .... He had also claimed that the performance had been poorly attended, when in fact it had been (4) .... The reviewer's lawyer said his client apologised for the (5) .... in the article. The judge awarded A **damages**.

B, a man from California, was diagnosed with **terminal** lung cancer in his (1) .... He had started smoking when he was 13, and had smoked (2) .... of the same brand of cigarettes a day for most of his adult life. He said that he had tried to stop (3) ...., but resumed after those attempts failed. He claimed that he had been 'tricked into smoking' by the tobacco industry, which he said had made him think that cigarettes were (4) .... without making him (5) .... of the danger to his health. He sued the tobacco company in question, and was eventually awarded a sum of money by the court.

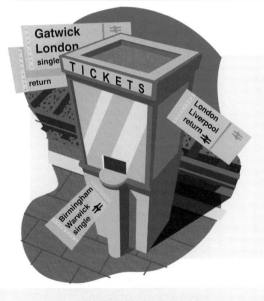

C, a rail worker employed as (1) ...., had to sit in a **ticket booth** checking passengers' tickets as they left the platform. However, C, who weighed (2) .... kgs and was 1 metre 82 cm tall, claimed that the ticket booth was (3) .... for him to work in comfortably. When he went off sick suffering from severe (4) ...., he was sacked. C said the rail company had treated him unfairly because his working conditions were to blame for his poor health, and he sued his employers for (5) .... C eventually won his case and was awarded a sum of money in compensation.

D, a 26-year-old woman, was working as (1) .... when she met an elderly Texas **oil tycoon**. The man showered the young dancer with gifts and money, and three years later the couple got married. They were married for only (2) .... before he died, aged 89, leaving an estate worth an estimated (3) .... D did not have a **prenuptial agreement** with her late husband and there was no mention of her in his **will**. However, she claimed that he had always said he would take care of her, and had promised to leave her (4) .... This claim was contested by the man's son, who said he was the sole **beneficiary** of his father's will. He said that D had 'exploited' his late father and should receive (5) ....

Writing
Writing about statistics

1 Roughly how much do you spend per month on these things? Who spends the most/least in the group?

- cinema, theatre and concert tickets
- football pools
- lottery tickets
- tickets for spectator sports

2 **a)** Look at the bar charts showing family spending on these items in the UK. Where did the amount of money spent:

- increase slightly?
- more than double?
- fall steadily?
- drop sharply?
- rise significantly?
- change very little?

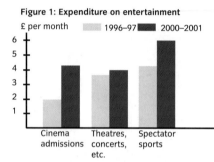

Figure 1: Expenditure on entertainment

£ per month   ▨ 1996–97 ■ 2000–2001

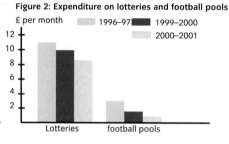

Figure 2: Expenditure on lotteries and football pools

£ per month   ▨ 1996–97 ■ 1999–2000 ▨ 2000–2001

b) Correct the factual mistakes in the summary below.

> Figures 1 and 2 show how much was spent on entertainment, lotteries and football pools in a four-year period between 1996 and 2001. **Overall**, there has been a decrease in expenditure on entertainment, whereas spending on lotteries and football pools has increased.
>
> The biggest increase was on cinema admissions, which more than trebled from £2 to £4.25. Expenditure on spectator sports also rose significantly by almost three-quarters to £6 per month. **In contrast**, the amount spent on theatre and concert tickets only increased slightly.
>
> **By far** the largest expenditure in the period was on lotteries, as illustrated in figure 2. However, spending on this item fell dramatically, from £11 in 1996–97 to £10 in 1999–2000 and £9 in 2000–2001. **Much less** was spent on football pools, and the amount dropped sharply, by about two-thirds, between 1999–2000 and 2000–2001. Spending on this item changed very little from 1996–1997 to 1999–2000, falling from 80p to 60p per month **respectively**.

3 Use one of the words or phrases in **bold** from the summary to complete each of the sentences below.

a) Contrary to ministers' claims, the report says that .... money will be available for public transport next year.

b) The number of people taking their cars to work has soared in recent years. .... , numbers using the railways have plummeted.

c) The average price of a house or a flat has increased by 20 per cent and 15 per cent ....

d) .... , people are spending more on videos and DVDs, and less on going to the cinema.

e) .... the most popular toy last Christmas was the 'Robodoll'.

4 **a)** Look at Table 1 on p.65 which compares the spending patterns of boys and girls aged 7–15. Which of the figures do you find surprising? How would you account for the differences between the boys' and girls' spending patterns?

b) Read this summary, and look at the underlined phrases describing amounts. Which are not grammatically correct?

Different age groups in society spend their money in different ways. As young people gain access to money, they are able to make choices about the way that they spend it. In 2000–2001, more than <u>third of</u> the expenditure of children aged 7 to 15 was on food and soft drinks, and <u>similar proportion</u> was spent on leisure goods and leisure services. Only <u>7 per cent of</u> their expenditure was <u>household goods</u> and services, reflecting the fact that <u>the majority</u> young people under the age of 16 live in the family home. Transport and fare costs counted for only <u>6 per cent</u> children's expenditure, as their fares tend to be paid for by their parents, and public transport fares for young people are subsidised by the government.

There are differences in the spending patterns of boys and girls. Girls spent <u>twice as much than</u> boys on clothing and footwear, and <u>almost half the amount</u> that boys spent on fares. Conversely, boys spent <u>one and half times</u> more than girls on leisure goods and services.

Table 1: Children's* expenditure: by gender and type of purchase, 2000–2001

United Kingdom		Percentages	
	Males	Females	All aged 7–15
Food and soft drinks	37	36	36
Leisure goods	29	17	23
Clothing and footwear	8	16	12
Leisure services	11	8	10
Household goods and sevices	5	8	7
Transport and fares	7	4	6
Other goods and services	4	10	7
All expenditure (= 100%) (£ per week)	10.60	10.80	10.70

* Children aged 7 to 15
Source: Family Expenditure Survey Office for National Statistics

5 **a)** Look at Table 2 below comparing student expenditure in 1996–1997 and 2000–2001.

- How is student expenditure different to that of other young people?
- How could you account for the changes in their spending patterns over the period?

Table 2: Student* expenditure, 1996–1997 and 2000–2001

United Kingdom	Percentages	
	1996–97	2000–1
Essential expenditure		
Accommodation	23	20
Food, bills, household goods	20	18
Course expenditure	10	7
Essential travel	3	6
Children	1	–
All essential expenditure	57	51
Other expenditure		
Entertainment	26	31
Non-essential travel	4	3
Other**	12	16
All other expenditure	10.60	10.80
All expenditure (= 100%)	£5,031	£5,403

* Students under the age of 26 in higher education
** Includes non-essential consumer items and credit repayments
Source: Student Income and Expenditure Survey, Department for Education and Employment

b) Write a summary of the information in about 150 words. Look back at the examples in Exercises 2 and 3 to help you.

Real life
Expressing quantities imprecisely

1 Which of the phrases from the box can replace the phrases in **bold** in the sentences below?

> the overwhelming majority of   a while
> a huge sum of money   a handful of   a dash
> an enormous portion   dozens of   a pinch
> a vast number of people   a great deal of time
> a small quantity   a small percentage

a) The company is spending only **2 per cent** of its annual budget on research and development.
b) Galvin was arrested when police dogs discovered **10 grams** of an illegal drug hidden in his luggage.
c) **14 million people** in this country still do not have access to the Internet.
d) I'd like a black coffee with just **0.2 ml** of milk.
e) I can't believe anyone can be so greedy!! He ate **2 kilograms** of potatoes, and still had dessert!
f) **95 per cent** of people in this country are in favour of reforming the tax system to make it fairer.
g) The only reason they could afford such an enormous house was because they won **$5 million** in the state lottery.
h) Just add **0.001 grams** of salt to help bring out the flavours of the dish.
i) The council has spent **two years** looking into ways of saving money.
j) We have received **72** enquiries about our latest offer.
k) It was disappointing that only **five or six** people actually took the trouble to attend the meeting.
l) You must be tired after such a long run. You should sit down and rest for **ten minutes**.

2 Use your own ideas, and the phrases in Exercise 1 to make true sentences. Compare in pairs.

a) .... people in my country speak English.
b) Learning to speak a foreign language fluently requires ....
c) It's possible to win .... money by ....
d) There are .... women politicians in my country.
e) To become President you need ....
f) The government wastes .... money on ....
g) .... road accidents are caused by ....
h) Some people like to add .... of .... to their coffee.
i) .... people of my age have no interest in pop music.

module 7
Living together

Speaking and vocabulary

Who you live with

1 Read the news extract. Is there a similar trend in your country?

... statistics show that for the first time in the UK, households consisting of two parents and their children are in the minority. The majority of households are now made up of single people living alone, single people sharing, and single parents and their children. The government believes that this trend is set to continue ...

2 Discuss in groups.

• Do you live, or have you ever lived away from your family?
• If not, would you like to? Under what circumstances?
• What are/were the advantages and disadvantages of living alone or with friends, rather than with family?

3 Read the descriptions of people you might live with and check any unknown vocabulary. Mark them + (easy to live with); – (difficult to live with) and ? (mixed/depends).

• someone with a very **negative attitude**, who **moans** a lot
• someone very **chatty** and **lively**, who **likes company**
• someone very quiet, who **keeps him/herself to him/herself**, and **respects your privacy**
• someone who is often **grumpy** and **irritable**
• someone very **laid-back**, who never worries about anything
• someone who likes background noise, and has the TV or music on all the time
• someone **unpredictable**, whose moods change **for no apparent reason**
• someone very **neat** and **fussy**
• someone who **leaves their stuff all over the place**, and doesn't **do their share** of the housework
• someone who **likes things their way**, and **won't listen to other people's points of view**
• someone very **dynamic** and **active**, who never sits down
• someone who **lounges around** doing nothing for hours on end
• someone who **sulks** rather than **saying what is on their mind**

Patterns to notice

Describing typical habits

1 Notice the use of *will/would* and the Present/Past Continuous (+ *always*) to describe typical behaviour (good or bad).

Present habits:

> She**'ll** tell you everything she's done that day.
> She**'s always** laugh**ing**.
> She**'s always** moan**ing**.

Past habits:

> One day he**'d** be really friendly, and the next he**'d** be really down.
> He **was always** pick**ing** things up and **sighing**.

2 Past habits (but not present habits) can also be described with *used to*.

> He **used to go** mad at me if I left things lying around.

3 The verbs *tend to* and *keep (on)* + *-ing* are also common here. *Keep on* emphasises that the action is repeated frequently.

> Sorry, I **keep on forgetting** your name!
> He just **kept asking** her to marry him, until in the end she said *yes*!

Tend to is used with repeated actions and typical states.

> She **tends to speak** very loudly.
> My parents **tended to be** very easy-going.

4 **a)** Compare and explain answers in groups. Which characteristics on the list would you personally find most difficult? Is there any behaviour not mentioned that also drives you mad?

b) Does anyone you live or have lived with have the faults described in Exercise 3? Are **you** guilty of any of these bad habits?

5 **a)** 🔲 [7.1] Listen to seven people describing a person they find or found difficult to live with. Who are they talking about? Which of the characteristics above do they mention?

b) Listen again. Give more details about why they find or found these people difficult to live with.

6 Choose three of the following people:

- someone you live with now
- someone you used to live with
- a colleague or acquaintance who irritates you
- a neighbour you don't/didn't like
- someone who looked after you a lot when you were a child
- a teacher from primary or secondary school.

Think of three or four typical habits (good and bad) that that person has or had. Tell your partner about them using the verb forms above.

> My grandmother was always telling us stories that she had made up.

> He'll stand at his window for hours watching what we're doing.

> She kept shouting at us all the time.

▶ Phrase builder

Grammar extension

Infinitives and *-ing* forms

1 Read what six people say about 'behaviour that drives me mad'. What is it in each case? Who do you agree with?

2 Underline as many examples as you can of:

a) *-ing* forms.
b) infinitives with *to*.
c) infinitives without *to*.

3 Find at least one example of:

a) a verb followed by an *-ing* form.
b) a verb followed by an infinitive.
c) an *-ing* form that is an adjective.
d) a negative *-ing* form and a negative infinitive.
e) a passive *-ing* form and a passive infinitive.
f) a perfect *-ing* form and a perfect infinitive.
g) two infinitives together.

4 What's the difference between a gerund and a present participle? Find examples of each.

5 Complete five of the sentences below about behaviour you can't stand, using the forms above. Compare answers with other students.

a) I hate seeing people …
b) I don't like hearing people …
c) I hate people …
d) …ing … is incredibly annoying
e) I can't stand being …
f) I hate not …ing …
g) I try hard not to …
h) Everyone should try not to …

▶ Grammar extension bank pp.140 – 143

Behaviour that drives me **mad**

We asked people to tell us about behaviour they can't stand.

' I hate people interrupting all the time, and not listening properly to what other people are saying, it's really infuriating! '
(Paul, 32, graphic designer)

' I can't stand seeing parents shouting at their children in the shop, and threatening them with what they'll do when they get home – it really upsets me. '
(Zara, 19, shop assistant)

' I hate people beating about the bush and not saying what they really mean – it drives me crazy, especially in meetings at work. '
(Belinda, 33, sales manager)

' Watching my colleagues creep round the boss is pretty disgusting, especially when I know what they say about him behind his back! I really despise that kind of thing – I try hard not to do it myself. '
(Sula, 26, receptionist)

' Not having had the benefit of a good education myself, although I would very much like to have gone to university, I get really irritated when I see well-educated people acting and speaking as if they are half-illiterate – I can't understand it myself. '
(John, 66, retired)

' This is probably my problem, but I really hate being told what to do! I'd hate to be forced to go into the army, with all that discipline, it would be my personal nightmare. '
(Ben, 23, student)

At the age of 18, Peter left home for the first time to do military or 'national' service. In the 1950s, soldiers doing national service were often stationed abroad. National service was abolished in the UK in 1961.

At the age of 11, Liz from Australia was sent to a boarding school where she lived throughout the term, only going home in the holidays.

After taking French 'A' level at the age of 18, Catherine went to be an au pair in Brittany, northern France, where she stayed with a family and looked after their two young children.

Listening

1 Discuss in groups.

a) What's the longest you've ever been away from home? What were the circumstances? How did you feel about it?

b) Make a list of six reasons why people might leave home. What are the most common reasons?

2 a) You will hear three people discussing their experiences of leaving home. Look at the photos and read the information. Why did each person leave home?

b) Look at the list of topics mentioned during the conversation. Who do you think talked about each one?

	Who mentioned it?	What did they say?
shooting a rifle	Peter	
ironing and sewing		
growing up in the country		
going to the beach		
teaching English		
being told what to do		
haircuts		
losing your individuality		
becoming more independent		

3 🔲 [7.2] Listen and complete the first column. Note down as many details in the second column as you can. Compare answers in pairs.

4 Can you remember who said the following? If necessary, listen again, or read the tapescript on p.169 to check.

a) 'I was really looking forward to it.'
b) 'It was quite a shock.'
c) 'I was still quite inexperienced and found it difficult to deal with.'
d) 'It was very daunting.'
e) 'It made me more independent.'
f) 'It made me quite a conscientious person.'
g) 'Looking back, I'm very grateful.'

5 Discuss these questions.

a) Overall, were their experiences positive or not?
b) Do you think military service/boarding schools/au-pairing are a good thing or not?
c) Which experience would you least/most like to have yourself?

▶ Phrase builder

69

Personal vocabulary

Task: who will go on *Shipwrecked*?
Preparation for task

1 **a)** Read about a new TV programme called *Shipwrecked!*

- What will happen in the programme?
- What do you learn about the island where the programme will be filmed?
- What will/won't the participants be provided with on the island?
- How are the six participants being chosen?

b) Have you ever seen any programmes like this?

Useful language

Saying what you want to happen

Personally, I think we should ...

I'm in favour of ...

I think ... is the priority here

I feel very strongly that we should ...

Discussing possible problems

What I want to avoid is ...

One thing that concerns/worries me is ...

... could cause problems

Discussing individual candidates

An important point in his/her favour is ...

... and ... would be an interesting combination

... might not fit in very well with the rest of the group

... would/wouldn't get on very well with ...

I think he/she might have difficulty ...ing

▶ Phrase builder

Shipwrecked!

Shipwrecked! will be a major new TV series featuring six volunteers (plus any children they have) who will go and live on a remote island in the Pacific Ocean for a whole year. They will be accompanied by a cameraman who will have complete freedom to film them.

The aims of the programme are to see how modern people survive in primitive conditions, and how the group manage to get on with each other. The participants will be paid £50,000 each if they complete the year successfully, but nothing if they leave even a day early.

The island chosen is uninhabited and the climate is tropical. It can only be reached by boat and helicopter, and it is an eight-hour journey to the nearest hospital. Participants will be given basic building materials, and emergency food supplies, but they will be expected to gather and hunt for food themselves. The cameraman will have a radio to call for help in emergencies, or if anyone decides to leave.

From several thousand applicants, a shortlist of ten have just attended an assessment weekend, after which the final six will be chosen.

2 ▭ [7.3] You are one of the programme's producers who must decide on the final six participants. Listen to a briefing explaining the criteria that you should use to make your selection, then answer the questions.

a) In what ways can you avoid bad publicity, and ensure that the participants remain on the island?
b) What are the best ways of attracting large TV audiences?

3 If necessary, check the new words below, then briefly read through the notes about the ten candidates on pp.112 – 113. Which candidate:

a) … is humorous and **supportive**, but flirts with all the men?
b) … is very **driven** but lacks a sense of humour?
c) … is a charming **womaniser** who may not realise what he's **letting himself in for**?
d) … has all the right qualities himself, but seems a bit **henpecked**?
e) … is very well prepared physically, but has a secret the group don't know about?
f) … is highly experienced but has a rather **overbearing** attitude?
g) … is well liked herself, but allows her husband to **push her around**?
h) … is extremely attractive to men, but **hasn't got a clue** about how tough life on the island will be?
i) … is very knowledgeable but a natural **loner**?
j) … is reasonably pleasant, but **moans** a lot?

4 <u>Underline</u> the points in favour of each candidate, and write ‼ next to potential problems.

Task

1 Work individually or in pairs. Make your selection of the six best candidates, and think about how to justify your decision to other students. Ask your teacher for any words you need, and write them in your Personal vocabulary box.

▶ Personal vocabulary

2 Work in groups. Discuss and decide on the six best candidates.

▶ Useful language

3 Present your decision to the class, explaining why you chose each candidate. Which did you all agree on? Can you persuade other groups to change their minds?

Reading and vocabulary

Men, women and relationships

1 Read the quotations below about men, women and relationships. Which do you like best? Compare opinions with a partner.

'I married beneath me – all women do.'
(*Mae West, film star, 1940s*)

'A man is incomplete until he is married. Then he is finished.'(*Zsa Zsa Gabor, Hungarian actor*)

'My wife and I were blissfully happy for twenty-five years. Then we met.' (*Rodney Dangerfield, US comedian*)

'All women become like their mothers. That is their tragedy. No man does, that is his.'
(*Oscar Wilde, Irish playwright*)

'Men – we can't live with them, and we can't live without them.' (*Anonymous woman*)

'A wife is a woman who sticks with her husband through all the troubles he wouldn't have had if he hadn't married her.'
(*Antony Mason, author of* A Bluffer's Guide to Women)

2 Look at the words and phrases in the box. Which characteristics do you associate:

- more with women?
- more with men?
- equally with both or do you think it's impossible to generalise?

> being competitive   good social skills   intuition
> being supportive   a tendency to feel guilty
> exchanging confidences   a fear of failure
> a desire for approval   a love of gadgets
> showing off   nagging   being thick-skinned
> gossiping   a fear of commitment

Compare answers with other students. Give examples to support your opinions.

3 **a)** You are going to read extracts from two light-hearted books, *A Bluffer's Guide to Men* and *A Bluffer's Guide to Women*. Read and decide which word should go in each gap: *man/men* or *woman/women*.

b) Compare answers in pairs. Then check on p.114.

The Bluffer's Guide to Men and Women

Approval

(1) ..... Men ..... are suckers for approval. They want to feel that **(2)** ..... women ..... have noticed them and need them. Best of all would be if **(3)** .... admired them. They would also like it if they trusted them, but that would probably be asking too much.

Conversation

The average **(4)** .... uses 10,000 words a day in speech; the average **(5)** .... finds 4,000 perfectly adequate. Around the house, a **(6)** ....'s conversation is especially economical, often reduced to grunts and utterances of one syllable. Telephone calls are for the transmission of essential information, not for gossiping or the exchange of confidences.
For **(7)** .... all information is essential. 'But what were you talking about?' a bemused **(8)** .... may ask a **(9)** .... who has just spent two hours on the phone to someone they saw only that morning.

A Good Cry

Although it is nowadays officially acceptable – even desirable – for **(10)** .... to cry, they will never be a match for **(11)** .... They will never understand how **(12)** .... can, in the right circumstances, claim to enjoy 'a good cry'. Tears make **(13)** .... very uncomfortable, because they feel something is expected of them, but they don't know what.

Nagging

It is important to remember that a **(14)** .... does not nag, but reminds. This point cannot be made too often. **(15)** .... are simply being made aware of the fact that they have not done what they said they were going to do, and therefore need to be prompted regularly, otherwise it won't get done.

Housework

These days (16) .... can and do cook, iron and vacuum, and have even been known to clean the bath. But surveys show that (17) .... still spend four or five times as long on domestic chores as their helpful spouses. The fact is that (18) .... can tolerate a greater degree of grime and disorder before they even notice it. They have the advantage of being thick-skinned – they approach the state of the house rather like the Three Wise Monkeys: 'see no evil, feel no evil, smell no evil'.

Friendship

Friendship is enormously important to (19) .... (20) .... want friends to play with (for example as tennis partners, or as people with whom to watch the Cup Final), whereas (21) .... want friends to talk to. They have friends the way (22) .... have hobbies.

Guilt

(23) .... feel guilty about everything, all the time. They feel guilty about their weight, their appearance, their careers, their mothering skills, the whiteness of their washes. Above all, they feel guilty about not being perfect. They read articles in glossy magazines about 'having it all'. Then they read about the folly of sacrificing quality of life and peace of mind to Superwoman ideals, and feel conscience-stricken about that too.

Commitment

(24) .... find it hard to commit themselves to a relationship. Getting them to do so is like getting hold of the soap in the bath. For (25) .... the very idea of commitment is uncomfortable: 'to commit' – after all, the same verb is used for suicide or being sent to an asylum. They harbour the distinct fear that marriage will change them. (26) .... only hope that it will.

Shopping

The majority of (27) .... dislike shopping. It not only means spending money, but making snap decisions. They like armchair-shopping first, studying advertisements and comparing prices before going out and buying a car, a house or an international corporation. The purchase of a lettuce, cat food or air freshener does not excite them. A mega waste of time, as far as (28) .... are concerned, is window-shopping. This they do not understand at all. The joy of staring at goods which cannot be bought because the shop is closed, is quite beyond their comprehension.

---

4   Discuss these questions with other students.

- Is the text biased against either men or women, or is it equally critical of both?
- Are there any points that you found either particularly true or particularly unfair?
- Are such generalisations about men and women meaningful, or is this just sexual stereotyping?

▶ Phrase builder

Patterns to notice

---
a lack of ...; a tendency to ... etc.

1   Complex characteristics and feelings are often described by compound phrases like this:

a) noun + preposition + noun

fear of failure; fear of rejection; fear of the unknown

lack of self-confidence; lack of ambition

need for approval; need for excitement; a need for reassurance

love of danger; love of adventure

a sense of achievement; a sense of shame; a sense of frustration

b) noun + infinitive

a tendency to panic; a tendency to worry; a tendency to argue

a need to prove yourself; a need to be in control

a desire to please other people

2   The first noun is often qualified by an 'extreme' adjective:

a **total** lack of ambition

an **intense** lack of self-confidence

an **enormous** sense of achievement

---

5   **a)** From the ideas in the box above, think of:

1   at least two things that everyone experiences sometimes. lack of self-confidence
2   at least two things that in your opinion are more characteristic of men than women.
3   at least two things that are more characteristic of women than men.
4   one thing that tends to be more characteristic of young people.
5   one thing that tends to be more characteristic of elderly people.
6   something you yourself feel or have experienced.
7   something you have never felt or experienced.

b) Compare answers in groups.

Writing
A report

1 How much do you think gender roles have changed in your country over the last ten years? In groups, make notes about the ideas below.

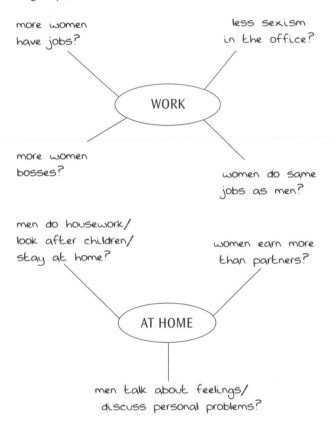

more women have jobs?

less sexism in the office?

WORK

more women bosses?

women do same jobs as men?

men do housework/ look after children/ stay at home?

women earn more than partners?

AT HOME

men talk about feelings/ discuss personal problems?

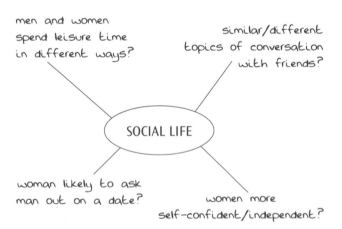

men and women spend leisure time in different ways?

similar/different topics of conversation with friends?

SOCIAL LIFE

woman likely to ask man out on a date?

women more self-confident/independent?

2 a) You are writing a report for a TV company making a programme about changing gender roles in the world. To collect opinions, you will interview students in your class. In pairs, write six questions using the ideas in Exercise 1.

b) Between you, interview at least six other students.

3 Look at the information you have collected and write sentences about your findings, using the language below.

The (vast) majority of		
About .... per cent of		
Many/Not many (of)		said
Very few (of)	those interviewed	thought
A small/significant minority of		felt
It was (generally) felt/ agreed that ...	people	reported
It seems/appears that ...		agreed
Apparently, ...		

4 In the report, it is important to link your ideas together clearly. Decide which phrases are possible in these examples (there may be more than one answer).

a) Some people said that more young adults live alone nowadays, *while/whereas/nevertheless* others disagreed.

b) It was *in addition/also/as well/generally* felt that more men do the cooking and washing-up.

c) Most people said that *even though/even if/although* more women have jobs, the vast majority still earn less than their partners.

d) Apparently, women are much more self-confident and independent nowadays. *On the other hand,/However,/Even so,* they still prefer men to ask them out on a date, rather than vice versa.

e) It seems that more people are working from home these days. *This means that/This is because/This explains why* men are spending more time with their children.

f) A lot of those interviewed said that men talk about their problems more than in the past. *As well as that,/Other than that,/Apart from that,* they felt that the situation had not changed much.

Wordspot

just

1 Read the sentences and look at the diagram. Which meaning (1–5) does *just* have in each sentence? (There may be more than one possibility.)

a) If you ask me, men and women **just** see things differently. `4`
b) Oliver didn't mean to tear your book – he's **just** a baby. ☐
c) You've **just** interrupted me for about the fourth time. ☐
d) – Have you phoned your sister?
   – I'm **just** going to. ☐
e) Could I **just** have a quick word with you? ☐
f) Sorry about the noise – it's **just** our way of having fun! ☐
g) That's **just** the point I was trying to make. ☐
h) Don't take any notice of what Steve **just** said, he doesn't mean it. ☐
i) I saw Carrie in the corridor **just** now. ☐
j) Marco's so rude! I smiled at him and he **just** ignored me completely! ☐

5 Organise your information into these sections:

- an introduction, where you explain the purpose of the report and how you collected the information, e.g.
  The aim of this report is to describe/outline/ discuss ...
  Information was collected via a survey of .... people in ....
- the body of the report, describing your findings. This could be divided into:
  – sections for each area of life, e.g. Work, Home, Social Life, or
  – one section on areas where there have been changes, and one on areas where there has been little or no change.
- a conclusion, e.g.
  In conclusion, it appears/ seems that ...
  Our survey found/showed/ suggests that ...
- Finally, give the report a title, and give each section a clear heading.

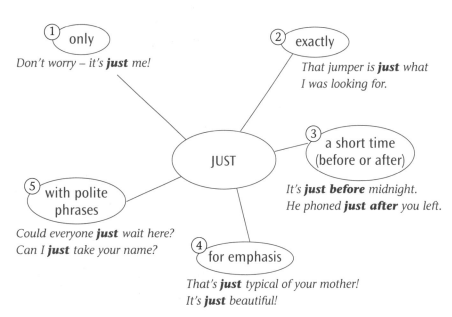

① only
*Don't worry – it's **just** me!*

② exactly
*That jumper is **just** what I was looking for.*

③ a short time (before or after)
*It's **just before** midnight.*
*He phoned **just after** you left.*

JUST

⑤ with polite phrases
*Could everyone **just** wait here?*
*Can I **just** take your name?*

④ for emphasis
*That's **just** typical of your mother!*
*It's **just** beautiful!*

2 Add *just* in the best place in the sentences below (there may be more than one possibility). How does it modify the meaning?

a) I'll take your coat for you.
b) I was so annoyed, I tore up the letter and walked out.
c) I'm looking, thank you.
d) The weather was perfect for my birthday party.
e) These shoes are what I need.
f) I'll be a few minutes and then we can go.
g) Nick arrived after you left.
h) Look! I've found that receipt you were looking for.
i) Lunch is a sandwich. I hope that's OK.
j) Would you mind holding this for me, please?
k) I've got enough money to pay!

6 Exchange reports with another pair. How similar were your findings?

3 🔊 [7.4] Compare your answers to Exercise 2 with the recording. Remember that these are not the only possible answers.

module 8

A question of taste

- ▶ **Reading**: style icons
- ▶ **Listening**: *You're so vain*
- ▶ **Task**: 'rant' about something you hate
- ▶ **Writing**: a tactful formal letter
- ▶ **Vocabulary**: descriptive adjectives
- ▶ **Adverbs**
- ▶ **Adding emphasis**
- ▶ **Wordspot**: *look, sound, feel*
- ▶ **Real life**: comment adverbials

Vocabulary and speaking

What's your style?

1 Look at the pictures. Which instantly appeal to you, and which don't? Write down two words to describe each one.

2 Match the words in the box to the pictures. (There may be more than one possibility.)

> scruffy   sophisticated
> contemporary   traditional
> unconventional   minimalist
> cluttered   dressed up

3 a) 💻 [8.1] Listen to eight people talking about some of these pictures. Which two are mentioned twice? Are their opinions positive or negative?

b) Listen again and write down words to describe the pictures. Check with the tapescript on p.171.

4 **a)** Discuss in pairs. Which of the things in the box below:

- would you never do?
- would you (secretly) like to do?
- have you already done?

Would you....?

- dye your hair bright purple or orange
- have your head shaved
- have your navel, nose or eyebrow pierced
- get a tattoo
- 'invest' half a month's salary on a well-cut classic suit
- buy your clothes from a second-hand shop
- go to dinner in a restaurant wearing trainers
- buy a cute cuddly toy to put on your bed
- fill your home with antique furniture
- wear a shirt with a 'loud' psychedelic pattern
- wear leather trousers
- spend more than $100 on a haircut
- fill your home with abstract art
- cover your walls with photos of your favourite rock star or football team
- paint your bedroom lime green or bright purple
- spend $500 on an ornament that you love
- wear pyjamas with cute cartoon characters on them
- pay $100 a head for a meal in a chic restaurant
- buy yourself a flashy sports car

b) What are the main differences between you and your partners? Tell the class anything interesting you discovered.

5 Write the new words in Exercises 2, 3 and 4 under these headings. Use a dictionary to help you.

for clothes only

for décor only

for many different things

Reading and speaking

1 The four people in the pictures are all often referred to as 'style icons'. What does this mean? From the pictures, describe each person's image.

2 a) In groups, note down anything you think you know about any of them, e.g.

- biographical details and personal life
- their most famous work
- other things they are associated with.

b) Read the four fact files on p.110 and memorise as many key facts as you can. Compare what you remember in your groups. Were you wrong about anything in Exercise 2a?

3 a) Read the quotations on the right made by or about the four people. Using what you learnt from the fact files to help you, mark them as follows:

1 It's instantly clear who it's about.
2 You have to read it a couple of times before you know who it is.
3 You can't work out who it's about.

Which words told you the answers?

b) Compare answers in pairs. To help you with any remaining answers, choose a maximum of three words to check in a dictionary.

c) Are there any quotations that you are still not sure about? Why not? For answers, see p.106.

4 a) In the quotes, these words have a different meaning from their usual meaning. What is it?

1	pretty (a)	5	move (f)
2	class! (b)	6	hot (i)
3	thing (b)	7	cool (i)
4	boy! (b)		

b) Are these words likely to be used in formal contexts, or in a more colloquial style? Do you know any more words like this in English?

5 Discuss these questions with other students, giving reasons for your answers.

- Which of these icons do you find most/least appealing?
- Which other famous people are often considered style icons? Who do you most admire?
- Are there any famous people whose style you particularly dislike?

James Dean

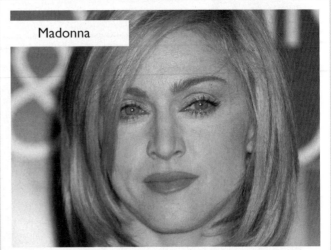

Madonna

Style icons

(a) " For sixty years I've done what I loved most – sing. Fortunately for me, you were out there listening. Together we got through the good times and the bad. Pretty good arrangement (you should pardon the pun). I drink to you. May you live to be a hundred, and may the last voice you hear be mine. "

(b) " *Here is class. She's a wispy, thin little thing, but you're really in the presence of somebody when you see that girl … in that league there's only Garbo, and maybe Bergman: it's a rare quality, but boy, do you know when you've found it!* "

(c) " If she were a painting, she would be an abstract by Picasso, she has so many faces. "

(d) " *…'s voice is as tight as a fist. To sing like that, you gotta have lost a couple of fights. To know tenderness and romance, you have to have had your heart broken.* "

(e) " She conducted her life as discreetly as the way she dressed. "

(f) " *A black humorist might suggest that dying was the best career move he ever made.* "

Audrey Hepburn

Frank Sinatra

(g) ❝ Glamour queens must keep something hidden to retain their audience's attention. If all is revealed, the show is over. For that reason and others, ... chose to keep her personal life personal. ❞

(h) ❝ ... and Elvis were the spokesmen for an entire generation. If Marlon Brando changed the way people acted, then ... changed the way people lived. He was simply a genius. ❞

(i) ❝ Her look is a hot "I'm 100 per cent woman" look, and I think that's great. Rock is full of boys who look like girls and girls who look like boys. I don't understand why people find a girl who does look like a girl offensive – she doesn't have to put on black leather and kick the **** out of a motorcycle gang to be cool. ❞

(j) ❝ If ... sings it, you can be sure it is about the essential dilemma of getting through the night, of relations between men and women – of insecurities, of the sadness that is shared by whole generations. ❞

(k) ❝ I won't be happy until I'm as famous as God. I'm tough, ambitious, and I know exactly what I want.
If that makes me a bitch – okay. ❞

(l) ❝ You only live once, and the way I live, once is enough. ❞

Patterns to notice

6 **a)** Change the verbs in **bold** to add emphasis to the sentences. (There may be more than one possibility.)

1 I'm pleased that we left before the trouble started!
   Am I pleased that we left before the trouble started!
2 I **felt** sorry for Charlie when I saw him yesterday.
3 This flat is a mess. I **think** you have a responsibility to help with the housework.
4 I'm absolutely exhausted! I **need** to get some sleep!
5 I'm sorry, but the way Gina behaves **annoys** me.
6 You'll never believe who was standing beside me in the queue – John's ex-wife! I **was** surprised to see her again!
7 I know you think I don't like your cooking, but I **like** it.
8 I **was** relieved when the day was over!

b) 🔊 [8.2] Listen to some possible answers. Notice the way these auxiliaries are stressed. Copy the voices.

Am I pleased that we left!

The way Gina behaves does annoy me!

▶ Phrase builder

Wordspot

look, sound, feel

1 Choose the best way to complete each sentence.

a) A person who resembles a famous person can be called *a lookalike/ a lookout/an onlooker.*

b) The proverb 'Look before you *jump/leap/strike'*, means you should think about the possible dangers before you do something.

c) To give someone a *dark/dirty/grey* look is to look at them in an unfriendly or disapproving way.

d) If you look *up/up to/upon* someone, you admire and respect them.

e) A sound *bite/clip/grab* is a short phrase taken from a political speech that is broadcast on radio and TV.

f) If you sound *off/on/up* about something, you express strong opinions in an angry way.

g) The sounds produced artificially for film, radio or TV are called sound *affections/effects/efforts.*

h) The recorded music from a film is called the sound*band/play/track.*

i) A feel-*fine/good/well* movie is one that makes you feel happy and optimistic.

j) If you're feeling particularly happy and well, you're feeling o*n top of the mountain/at the top of the tree/on top of the world.*

k) If you have both positive and negative emotions about something, you have *assorted/combined/mixed* feelings about it.

l) 'Feel *free/OK/your way'*, is an expression used to tell people they have permission to do something.

2 📼 [8.3] You are going to hear some sentences. In each case, the word *look*, *sound*, or *feel* has been replaced with a beep. For each sentence write the word that is missing.

a) .... e) .... i) ....
b) .... f) .... j) ....
c) .... g) .... k) ....
d) .... h) .... l) ....

3 a) 📼 [8.4] Answer as many of the questions on the recording as you can. Write the answers in a random order on a piece of paper, **not** in the same order as in the recording.

b) Show your answers to a partner and explain why you wrote what you did.

Why did you write 'good'?

Because I'm very good at giving dirty looks!

▶ Phrase builder

Listening

You're so vain

1 You're going to listen to *You're so vain*, which Carly Simon wrote about an ex-boyfriend. In what different ways can a person be vain?

a) 📼 [8.5] Listen to the song on p.81 and <u>underline</u> three ways in which the man shows that he is vain.

b) Which verse deals with:
- their relationship?
- his lifestyle now?
- his appearance?

2 Listen again and discuss these questions with a partner.

a) Why does she say she was 'still quite naïve' when she had the relationship?

b) What dreams do you think she had, and why were they 'clouds in her coffee'?

c) How do the lines in **bold** add to the image we have of the man?

d) By the end of the song, what's your impression of the man?
- He's shallow, conceited and immoral.
- He's very egotistical but rather glamorous.
- He's an intriguing and rather attractive figure.

e) This song is thought to be about a well-known person. Do you think it is:
- a musician?
- a politician?
- an actor?
- a writer?
  (see p.114 for the answer)

f) Do you know anyone like the person in the song? How does he/she behave?

▶ Phrase builder

You're so vain

You walked into the party like you were walking onto a yacht.

Your hat strategically dipped below one eye,

Your scarf it was apricot.

You had one eye in the mirror **as you watched yourself gavotte,**

And all the girls dreamed that they'd be your partner

They'd be your partner, and ...

You're so vain, you probably think this song is about you

You're so vain, I'll bet you think this song is about you

Don't you? Don't you?

You had me several years ago

When I was still quite naïve.

Well, **you said that we made such a pretty pair**

And that you would never leave.

But you gave away the things you loved

And one of them was me.

I had some dreams, they were clouds in my coffee

Clouds in my coffee, and ... (*chorus*)

Well, I hear **you went up to Saratoga**

And your horse naturally won.

Then **you flew your Lear Jet up to Nova Scotia**

To see the total eclipse of the sun.

Well, you're where you should be all the time

And when **you're not you're with some**

  underworld spy

Or the wife of a close friend

Wife of a close friend, and ... (*chorus*)

Grammar extension
Adverbs

1 <u>Underline</u> the adverbs in these sentences. Which sentences have more than one adverb? Which of these sentences does **not** contain an adverb?

a) I think Carly Simon still secretly admired her ex-lover when she wrote *You're so vain*.

b) She claims that she was 'still quite naïve' when she met the man.

c) I wonder why the song says 'Your horse naturally won'.

d) Madonna is known for her constantly changing image.

e) The first thing most people remember about Audrey Hepburn is her lovely eyes.

f) James Dean had an instantly recognisable image.

g) Throughout his life, Frank Sinatra was romantically linked with glamorous women.

2 In Exercise 1, find:

a) an example of a word that looks like an adverb but is not.

b) two examples of adverbs of 'manner' (they tell you **how** something was done).

c) two examples of time adverbials.

d) an example of an adverb of degree (this tells us **how much**).

e) three examples of adverbs that commonly collocate with either an adjective or a verb.

f) an adverb that could be moved to different positions in the sentence.

▶ Grammar extension bank pp.144 – 147

Personal vocabulary

Task: 'rant' about something you hate

Preparation for task

1 Read about the British TV programme, *Room 101*. Explain the idea of the programme in your own words. Do you have anything comparable on TV in your country?

> **Room 101** is a British TV show in which famous people 'rant' about things, people, habits, etc. that they particularly hate. They try to persuade the presenter to send the object of their dislike to 'Room 101', an imaginary place where all the ugliest and most annoying things in the world go. On average, the presenter accepts about 50 per cent of the suggestions made.

2 [8.6] Listen to four people, Catherine, Essam, Sarah Jane and Pietro, 'ranting' about things they hate. What is each person's pet hate? What reasons do they give?

3 Who said the following? Listen again if necessary, and check.

1 Tapping just drives me crazy.
2 They seem to think they're morally superior to me, and that really gets on my nerves.
3 I find that women are the worst offenders.
4 It's never specific to what you want to speak about, and you never know which one to choose.
5 She immediately put me through to this automated thing.
6 I don't really see what's wrong with eating meat.
7 It just drives me absolutely mad.
8 Nine times out of ten, the bus is late.

4 Which of these four things would you send to *Room 101*? Did anyone say anything that you find offensive, or strongly disagree with?

Useful language

Describing feelings of hate

I really hate the way ...

The main thing I object to is ...

What/One thing/Another thing that I object to is ...

It makes me absolutely furious/sick.

... is/are so annoying/ irritating/disgusting/awful

The thing that really annoys me/drives me mad about ... is ...

I find it/them so/completely/ absolutely ...

It's very frustrating.

One thing that I really can't stand is ...

▶ Phrase builder

Task

1 **a)** Prepare two or three 'rants' about things you can't stand. Use the list below to help you.

- an extremely irritating song/ TV programme/film/book, etc.
- a very annoying singer/actor/ politician/TV personality/ character
- an infuriating personal habit
- an incredibly ugly building/ picture, etc.
- a very annoying machine or aspect of modern technology
- an extremely boring topic of conversation
- a type of food that you particularly loathe
- an animal or insect you find unpleasant
- an aspect of daily life/a daily task you can't stand
- a garment or fashion you hate
- anything else you just can't stand!

b) Spend about ten minutes planning what you will say. Try to include examples of what you mean. Ask your teacher for any vocabulary you need.

▶ Personal vocabulary

2 Practise your 'rant' in pairs. You can use phrases from Exercise 3 in the previous section and the Useful language box.

▶ Useful language

3 Choose one topic to rant about to the class. The other students can ask you a maximum of three questions, before voting on whether or not to send your pet hate to *Room 101*.

Writing
A tactful letter

1 You are starting a new job in a large company. Do you wear:

- the latest fashion?
- a smart suit?
- something unusual, so people will notice you?

2 Veronica works in a large advertising company. She wrote this email, about a junior colleague's appearance, to the Human Resources Manager.

a) According to Veronica, what is wrong with her colleague's appearance?

b) What examples does she give?

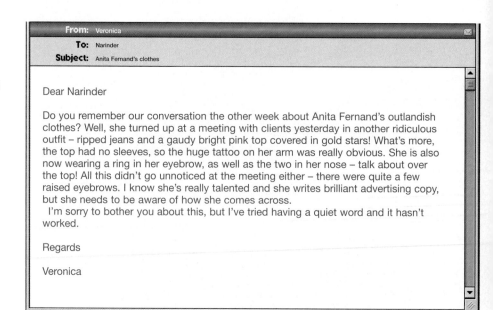

From: Veronica
To: Narinder
Subject: Anita Fernand's clothes

Dear Narinder

Do you remember our conversation the other week about Anita Fernand's outlandish clothes? Well, she turned up at a meeting with clients yesterday in another ridiculous outfit – ripped jeans and a gaudy bright pink top covered in gold stars! What's more, the top had no sleeves, so the huge tattoo on her arm was really obvious. She is also now wearing a ring in her eyebrow, as well as the two in her nose – talk about over the top! All this didn't go unnoticed at the meeting either – there were quite a few raised eyebrows. I know she's really talented and she writes brilliant advertising copy, but she needs to be aware of how she comes across.
  I'm sorry to bother you about this, but I've tried having a quiet word and it hasn't worked.

Regards

Veronica

3 It is company policy to deal with such problems in writing, but Narinder is anxious to be tactful.

a) How might the following make the letter tactful?

- formal language
- understatement
- 'positive' vocabulary
- impersonal constructions (e.g. *It has been pointed out to me that …*)

b) Read Narinder's letter and choose the best alternative.

1st March

RSX Limited

Dear Ms Fernand

I am writing to you because I feel that I must mention **1)** an issue/a problem which **2)** has been brought to my attention/someone has told me about. While the company is extremely pleased with the quality of your work and your innovative approach, **3)** we feel/it is felt that your style of dress is **4)** out of keeping/not entirely in keeping with our image.
I appreciate that the **5)** weird colour/unusual combinations and **6)** flamboyant/outrageous style of your clothes are characteristic of the artistic flair which you bring to your work, but they are **7)** not really suitable/unsuitable for company meetings. I also feel that the amount of body jewellery you wear is **8)** over the top/a little excessive and may **9)** be rather distracting for clients/put clients off, as well as **10)** not setting a very appropriate example/setting a bad example for younger, more impressionable employees.

I would therefore suggest that you wear **11)** less ridiculous/slightly less risqué outfits in future, and ask you to remove the body jewellery and **12)** ensure that the tattoo on your arm is concealed/make sure that you cover up your tattoo.

I trust that you will understand **13)** why I am asking you to do this/my reasons for this request and assure you that the quality of your work is not **14)** the problem/being called into question.

Yours sincerely

Narinder Ray
Human Resources Manager

4 How does Narinder's letter 'tone down' Veronica's message? Find examples of the four ways of being tactful given in Exercise 3a).

5 A college has commissioned two designers to design the front cover of its new brochure. You have been asked to choose the best design.

a) In pairs, look at the two designs on p.111 and choose the best one. Make a list of reasons why you did not choose the other one. Think about:

- how appropriate it is for the cover of a college brochure
- how original it is
- how eye-catching it is
- how colour is used.

b) Write a letter to the designer whose work you rejected, explaining why. The letter should be formal in tone, and tactful. Remember to include some positive points about the design.

Example:
- it's inappropriate >
the approach is perhaps more appropriate for
- it's not original >
we had something a little more unusual in mind

c) Write an email to a friend, telling them about the experience of choosing the design, and what you **really** thought about the design you rejected.

Real life
Comment adverbials

1 Look at the adverbial phrases in **bold** below. Which of them is used:

a) to say that something is good news or lucky?
b) to emphasise that what you're saying is true?
c) to emphasise that something is unfortunate?
d) to say that we hope something will happen?
e) to emphasise that something is strange, surprising or coincidental?

1 **Amazingly enough,** nearly a thousand people came to see the show.
2 **To be perfectly honest,** I've no idea what happened.
3 **I'm glad to say** that no more cases have been reported.
4 **Quite frankly,** I've lost interest in the whole affair.
5 **Thank goodness** there was someone there to help me.
6 **It's a good job** no one saw you.
7 **Much to my surprise,** Teresa has turned down the chance of promotion.
8 **All being well,** she'll be out of hospital by the end of the week.
9 **To tell the truth,** I didn't expect there to be so many applicants.
10 'Andrea comes from a place called Luton. Do you know it?' 'Yes, I do. **Funnily enough,** we nearly moved there once.'
11 He was nearly an hour late, and **to make matters worse,** he was drunk when he arrived.
12 **To her utter astonishment,** he produced a ring and proposed.

2 🔊 [8.7] Listen to the radio interview with Candice de Berg.

a) How is Candice de Berg described? Why do you think she is in London?
b) How would you describe the interviewer's attitude to her?
c) What was the reason for the misunderstanding in the restaurant?
d) How did Candice react to the misunderstanding?
e) How would you describe Candice's attitude to the interviewer?

3 Who said each of the phrases below – the interviewer or Candice? Which of the phrases in Exercise 1 would fit in the spaces?
Listen again and check.

a) .... that our next guest has finally arrived.
b) ...., being seen so much in public can be tough sometimes …
c) but .... there are days when I'd rather just be at home …
d) Well .... you didn't decide to stay at home this evening, then.
e) .... something crazy happened just the other day here in London …
f) and .... , she looked at the napkin and said 'Thank you, but … '
g) and .... they asked me to pay for a new napkin.
h) .... you were able to see the funny side of it.
i) my new movie is called *Single Girl* and, ..., it should hit the screens just before Christmas.

4 With a partner, write the script of an interview with a famous person. Decide if the person will come across well or badly in the interview and why. Use at least five of the phrases from Exercise 1.

▶ Phrase builder

module 9

21st-century lifestyles

Vocabulary and speaking

Work and play in the 21st century

1 Look at the descriptions of inventions predicted for the next few decades.

- Which of these things already exist as far as you know?
- Which most appeal to you?
- Do you think they will catch on or not? Why/Why not?

THE 'INTELLIGENT' HOUSE

This 'smart' fridge will be connected to the Internet as part of a home network that runs your domestic life, interacting with the barcodes on your food, and re-ordering them online as you use them. Virtually all domestic appliances will be linked by computer, so that the fridge can communicate with the cooker and rubbish bin, co-ordinating complex tasks such as cooking a meal. Your electric toothbrush will even be able to let your toaster know that you're ready for breakfast!

GLOBAL GAMES

Children of the future will never be able to complain that there's no one to play with. Equipped with a virtual reality headset, this twelve-year-old is taking part in global games, here a medieval jousting tournament. His opponent, selected for him by the computer, lives on the other side of the world!

HOLOGRAPHIC CONFERENCING

Holographic conferencing and virtual reality meetings will allow people to interact with colleagues and clients via computer, without needing to leave the comfort of their own homes. Through her headset this woman sees a virtual meeting with several people sitting around a table. The people involved live all over Europe.

BEHIND THE WHEEL

Cars of the future will take much of the strain out of driving. The intelligent navigation system in this 2010 model can choose the best route for you by monitoring an online traffic database for hold-ups, while the cruise control keeps a constant distance from the car in front. And if you exceed the speed limit, the speedometer speaks a polite warning to you. Security worries will also be a thing of the past – your car will only allow *bona fide* drivers behind the wheel, recognising them by the irises of their eyes!

2 a) In pairs, make three predictions about the social, economic and personal consequences of such inventions.

b) Compare your ideas with the experts' ideas below. Which of these did you come up with?

But what will it all mean?

I 'Teleworking and **computer conferencing** will mean that a lot more people will either **work freelance from home**, or on flexible **short-term contracts**. The old concept of "jobs for life" will soon be a thing of the past.'

2 '**Highly-skilled** professionals will be under pressure to work longer and longer hours, while much of the **mundane** work will be done by machines, leading to high unemployment amongst **unskilled** workers. By 2050, we are going to have a small number of hardworking rich and a vast majority of idle poor.'

3 'With inventions like cell phones and hand-held computers it is becoming more and more difficult to escape from work – the boundaries between work and leisure are gradually becoming blurred, and in the future it will be harder and harder **to get away from it all**. Already the average American is working 163 hours a year more than thirty years ago – that's the equivalent of an extra month a year.'

4 '**Labour-saving devices** and the resulting **sedentary lifestyle** could well lead to an **epidemic** in **obesity**. It is predicted that the average man will weigh ten kilos more, and the average woman eight kilos more.'

5 'A growth in online shopping and home-working may mean that our city centres become **deserted wastelands**. The physical isolation and loss of **social interaction** resulting from these changes could **put further strain** on family relationships and lead to depression and **mental health problems**.'

6 'There will be a huge growth in the **leisure and fitness industry** as people struggle to combat the effects of **inactivity**, and **social isolation**.'

7 'We will adapt in all sorts of ways that are as yet undreamed of. You should never underestimate the amazing **adaptability** of human beings.'

3 Discuss these questions.

- Which of these predictions most worry you?
- Do you agree with the last expert's optimistic view of human adaptability?
- In what ways might we adapt to the changes in society described?

4 a) Divide the words and phrases in **bold** into the following categories (some words may fit into more than one).

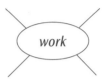

b) Write eight sentences of your own about life today, using some of these phrases. Compare sentences with other students.

▶ Phrase builder

Reading and speaking

1 You are going to read about predictions for the future that didn't come true. Discuss these questions in groups.

- Have you seen or read any old films or books set in the future? What vision of life in the 21st century did they have?
- How did they imagine these things?

> space travel computers clothes food
> daily transport aliens robots

2 Read the article and put these sentences in the correct place.

a) Human nature is the greatest single confounder of all the predictions of decades gone by.
b) Each age has its future fears that turn out to be groundless.
c) Immortality has been a constant theme in futurology.
d) Fifty years ago, the futurologists of the day were confidently forecasting an outlook that was silver, shiny and teeming with intelligent robots.
e) ~~Forecasting what life is going to be like years down the line is a dodgy business.~~ I
f) Neither are there any aliens on the horizon, nor even in the galaxy next door.

3 Discuss these questions in pairs.

a) In what two ways were past predictions about computers wrong?
b) How did people in the 1950s imagine robots?
c) Why does the author believe that all-in-one body suits never caught on?
d) What connection does the author make between cryogenics and freezing strawberries?
e) What's the problem with the mini-planes that were predicted in the past?
f) Why aren't we eating 'nutritionally-perfect pills' instead of traditional food?
g) Does she believe that online shopping will replace traditional shopping?
h) Does she think it will become common for elderly women to have babies? Why/Why not?
i) How widespread does she expect genetic engineering to become?

4 Can you guess the meaning of the following words from the context? Use a monolingual dictionary to check your ideas.

a) lumbering (para. 1)   e) traipse (para. 5)
b) nano-technology (para. 1) f) forego (para. 5)
c) misnomer (para. 3)   g) groundless (para. 6)
d) mucky (para. 4)

5 **a)** Do you agree with the author's final point that 'what we really want', above everything else, is the best for our future generations'?

b) Think of three things that are happening in society today that support this view, and three that contradict it.

▶ Phrase builder

What didn't come to pass
by Vivienne Parry, former presenter of *Tomorrow's World*

1 Forecasting what life is going to be like years down the line is a dodgy business. Even the experts don't always get it right. Take Bill Gates, for example. In 1981, he firmly stated that '640k of memory ought to be enough for anyone.' So it's more than a bit embarrassing for him now that, even on a standard issue home PC, you need 200 times that amount of memory just to run his own company's software. Fortunately for Bill, others predicted that the technological future would involve giant computers that were the size of cities, whereas what we actually have are ever-shrinking models that you can tuck neatly into your pocket, which are hundreds of times more powerful than their lumbering predecessors. Nano-technology is definitely the way forward.

2 ....
They imagined the robots of the future would not only be able to think for themselves, but get on with the housework too. But what have we got? More time-saving devices and what seems like less time. Just how did that happen? And absolutely no sign of a helpful house robot to mix a perfect Martini at the end of a hard day at the cyberface. Face it, we haven't even cracked robotic vacuum cleaners yet.

3 ....

Air tours are not booking moon packages, and space travel is only for the trained or for the fantastically wealthy few. True, all-in-one body suits (the uniform of brave space pioneers) did make a number of fashion appearances – think lycra exercise gear in the eighties – but on the whole, we've realised that body suits are a misnomer, because they don't actually suit bodies, other than those with faultless dimensions. Which brings me to another big fib: perfect bodies in the future. No matter how much nipping, tucking, sucking and filling we do, our bodies continue to traitorously reveal the signs of our increasing years. Sorry!

4 ....

Actually, we do now know how to extend life – by eating less and exercising more. Even so, Californian cryogenics super-salesmen have persuaded some people to part with vast sums of money on a promise that will defrost them when 'the time is right'. But since we haven't yet even perfected freezing strawberries, these poor deluded souls may be nothing more than mucky puddles by 2052.

As for transport, the reason we aren't all buzzing around in our own mini-planes has quite a lot to do with the fact that nobody thought about what would happen when everyone wanted one. Were they going to be stacked high above our streets, stuck in an endless holding pattern while we desperately tried to do our shopping?

5 ....

Nutritionally-perfect pills to replace all our food? Nothing but online shopping, so there's no need to leave your home/computer and traipse round the shops? Both have met with a resounding thumbs down from the public. We simply refuse to give up eating our nutritionally nightmarish fish and chips. And we show absolutely no inclination to forego the pleasure of touching, examining and trying the purchases we make. We love our food and our shopping, thank you very much.

6 ....

In the fifties, concerns focused on monsters and flying saucers. Ours are reproductive. For instance we worry that, come 2052, it will be increasingly normal for grannies to be giving birth, or that male pregnancy will be possible. It's my bet that if you asked 100 women in their sixties, now or in 2052, if they wanted a test-tube baby or double-glazing, 99 per cent would opt for the windows. As for male pregnancy, I have it filed under 'o' as in 'only for the lunatic', along with human cloning and genetic engineering. Yes, it might all be technically possible, and you might well see genetic engineering for very specific and well-defined medical reasons, but it will remain phenomenally risky for the baby. It's an unchangeable part of human nature that what we really want, above everything else, is the best for our future generations.

Grammar extension
Future forms

Read the predictions below and find examples of the following:

- *will* to make a prediction
- *going to* to make a prediction
- two phrases in the Present simple that convey a future meaning
- a 'past' modal used to talk about the future
- a future modal
- a future passive form
- the Future Continuous
- the 'future in the past'
- the 'past in the future'

a) Supermarket experts believe that in a few years we'll be eating far more functional foods, e.g. specially grown food with cancer-fighting properties.

b) Mechanical hearts will soon be used for transplants, removing the pressure to find human donors.

c) The first artificial eyes are set to appear within ten years.

d) Most experts agree that we're going to have to find ways of becoming more active if we are to stay fit and healthy.

e) The labour-saving devices of the future could lead to an epidemic of obesity.

f) A favourite prediction of the eighties was that videophones would take over from ordinary phones, but there is no sign of this happening.

g) It is predicted that by 2020 cash will have virtually disappeared.

h) A radical new form of energy will almost certainly emerge soon.

i) Most scientists don't believe that we will ever be able to travel through time.

▶ Grammar extension bank pp.148 – 151

Listening and speaking
The changing face of tourism

1 Discuss these questions.

- What kind of holidays are popular with visitors to your country?
- Has tourism influenced the town/country where you live?
- What have the positive and negative effects been, and what changes would you like to see?

2 a) You are going to listen to a radio programme about 'eco-tourism'. Can you guess what this is?

b) 🔲 [9.1a] Listen to the first part of the programme.

a) What are most people looking for in a holiday, according to the introduction?
b) Which negative aspects of going on holiday are mentioned?
c) How does Gavin Allan define eco-tourism? Is his definition similar to yours?
d) What does he see as 'the way forward' ?

3 🔲 [9.1b] In the second part of the programme you will hear two holidays described. Complete the grid.

	Holiday 1	Holiday 2
Location		
Reasons to go there		
Typical activities		
Other unusual features		

4 Work in pairs. Look at this list of alternative holidays, including those mentioned in the programme. Would they appeal to you? Why/Why not?

- a yoga retreat in the Sri Lankan jungle
- a four-day water-colour painting course in rural England
- staying with Bushmen in the Kalahari Desert
- a bird-watching holiday in remote Eastern Hungary
- a horse-riding holiday in the olive groves of Northern Portugal
- an archaeology trip searching for dinosaur bones in the Argentine desert
- an Italian cookery course in a farmhouse in rural Tuscany
- a surfing course in a remote beach resort in Mexico
- a survival course in the Rocky Mountains of North America
- camel-trekking in the Sinai.

5 Find out what your partner enjoys doing and what he/she looks for in a holiday. Design a suitable 'activity' holiday for him/her. Include:

• an appealing location
• a rough programme of activities
• the kind of accommodation/level of luxury that your partner prefers.

▶ Phrase builder

Patterns to notice

Describing trends

1 To describe trends, we often use the Present Continuous, particularly with verbs like *become, get (better/worse), develop, increase, improve, deteriorate.*

The tourist industry **is becoming** its own worst enemy.

2 These can be accompanied by adverbs like *rapidly/ quickly/slowly/increasingly,* etc.

A new kind of tourism **is rapidly developing**. Boundaries between work and leisure **are gradually becoming** blurred.

3 We also often use comparative forms and phrases like *more and more* and *increasingly*.

People are living **longer and longer**. **More and more people** are taking to the skies each year. It's getting **increasingly** difficult to escape from work.

6 Use the phrases above to write sentences of your own about trends in:

• the job market in your country
• education
• transport
• holidays and travel
• people's health
• technology
• the media.

Write **five** sentences that you think are true and **three** that you think are false.

Computers are getting more and more sophisticated.
Public exams are becoming increasingly difficult.
The quality of TV programmes is deteriorating rapidly.

7 Read your sentences to other students. Can they spot the false ones?

Personal vocabulary

Task: create a 'time capsule' for future generations

Preparation for task

1 If you could travel in a time machine, which era(s) in the past would you choose to visit? Why?

2 **a)** Which of these things do you find most/least interesting when you are learning about a period in the past?

- important events, wars and politics?
- novels, diaries, newspapers, etc. which give you an insight into the way people thought then?
- everyday objects such as clothes, tools or furniture?

b) Have you visited any museums which have made life in the past particularly vivid?

Useful language

Explaining why you are including things

... will give them an impression/a taste/a snapshot/a good overview of ...

... is a good way of illustrating/demonstrating ...

... would be a good example of ...

Imagining how they will react

... they'll probably find ... very odd/funny because ...

Hopefully, they'll be able to ...

If I was opening the capsule, I'd ...

▶ Phrase builder

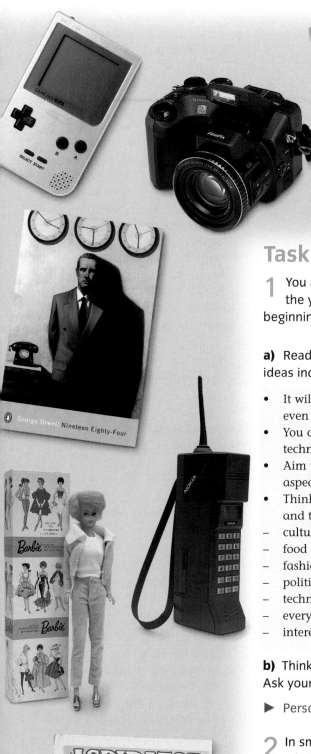

Task

1 You are going to create a 'time capsule', not to be opened before the year 2250, to help future generations understand life at the beginning of the 21st century.

a) Read the guidelines and spend 5–10 minutes making your list of ideas individually.

- It will be the size of a suitcase, and can be sealed so effectively that even fresh food will be perfectly preserved.
- You can put in whatever you like, but should bear in mind that the technology may no longer exist to play our CDs, videos, etc.
- Aim to include about 15 items which best represent the most typical aspects of modern life.
- Think about which of these things you want to represent/include, and the main ideas that you want to get across:
  - culture and entertainment
  - food and drink
  - fashion/design
  - politics and important events
  - technology and media
  - everyday objects that may no longer exist
  - interesting documents, etc.

b) Think about how to explain why you have chosen those things. Ask your teacher for any vocabulary you need.

▶ Personal vocabulary

2 In small groups, discuss and explain your ideas. Together, draw up a list of the 15 best ideas.

▶ Useful language

3 Present your list to the class, taking it in turns to explain why you have chosen those items. One person in your group should write your list up on the board.

Either

Vote for the best individual group's time capsule (you can't vote for your own!)

Or

Vote on the 15 best objects overall. Each student has five votes. Why did you vote as you did?

Wordspot

well

1 Look at the diagram showing the main uses of *well*. <u>Underline</u> any uses that you were not previously aware of.

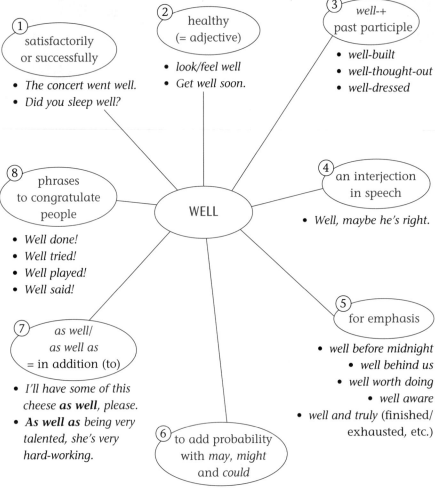

① satisfactorily or successfully
- *The concert went well.*
- *Did you sleep well?*

② healthy (= adjective)
- *look/feel well*
- *Get well soon.*

③ well-+ past participle
- *well-built*
- *well-thought-out*
- *well-dressed*

WELL

④ an interjection in speech
- *Well, maybe he's right.*

⑤ for emphasis
- *well before midnight*
- *well behind us*
- *well worth doing*
- *well aware*
- *well and truly (finished/ exhausted, etc.)*

⑥ to add probability with *may, might* and *could*
- *He **may/might well** be at home today.*
- *Future generations **may/could well** see things very differently.*

⑦ as well/ as well as = in addition (to)
- *I'll have some of this cheese **as well**, please.*
- ***As well as** being very talented, she's very hard-working.*

⑧ phrases to congratulate people
- *Well done!*
- *Well tried!*
- *Well played!*
- *Well said!*

2 As an interjection, *well* can have subtly different meanings. Match the meanings in the box to the uses below.

for emphasis   to pause   to accept a situation   to show surprise
to show anger/annoyance   to show you've finished   to express doubt
to continue a story

a) Well, well! Fancy Andy and Laura getting married!
b) Well, you know what I think, I completely agree!
c) Well, I think she could have phoned and apologised!
d) Well, maybe … what do other people think?
e) Well, let me think.
f) You know what you told me about Erica the other day, well, after I spoke to you, I saw her in the supermarket and you'll never guess what she …
g) Well, if you're sure that's what you really want …
h) Well, I think that's it then.

3 **a)** What do these *well-* + past participle adjectives mean? (The ones marked * may need to be checked in a dictionary.)

well-balanced   well-behaved
well-built*   well-chosen
well-dressed   well-earned*
well-educated   well-written
well-laid-out*   well-prepared
well-fed   well-informed
well-looked-after   well-meaning*
well-known   well-mannered
well-off   well-paid
well-read*   well-thought-out

b) Which of the adjectives above should these things/people be?
- books
- children
- your parents
- shops
- teachers
- a potential husband/wife
- a holiday
- babies
- everyone

Compare answers with other students.

4 Where could you add *well* in these sentences to give emphasis?

a) I think all of you are well aware of the difficulties we have faced recently.
b) By the time we got home, it was after eight o'clock.
c) Personally, I think the end results have been worth all the effort.
d) As you know, you are not allowed to smoke in here.
e) By the time they arrived – two hours late, I was truly fed up.
f) Marta is ahead of the other students in the class.
g) The Chinese were using paper money before people in the West.

▶ Phrase builder

Real life

Collocations with computer terms

1 Work in groups. Discuss and cross out the collocation in each diagram that is not commonly used when talking about computers.

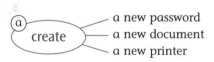
a create — a new password — a new document — a new printer

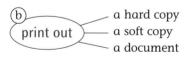
b print out — a hard copy — a soft copy — a document

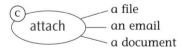
c attach — a file — an email — a document

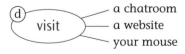
d visit — a chatroom — a website — your mouse

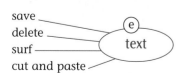
e save / delete / surf / cut and paste — text

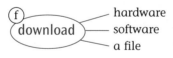
f download — hardware — software — a file

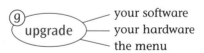
g upgrade — your software — your hardware — the menu

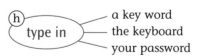
h type in — a key word — the keyboard — your password

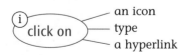
i click on — an icon — type — a hyperlink

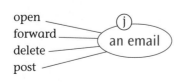
j open / forward / delete / post — an email

2 Work in pairs. **A** imagines he/she is someone who knows nothing about computers (e.g. your grandmother!) and asks **B** to explain five of the terms in Exercise 1. **B** must explain using as little jargon as possible. Use the picture to help you.

3 Describe as precisely as you can the things you always/ usually do, when you:

- start up your computer
- go on the Internet
- check your email
- write a document for work or college on a computer
- shut down your computer.

Are there any other things you often do?

module 10
Truth and lies

Vocabulary and speaking
Is it ever OK to lie?

1 a) Here are some common lies. Who might say these, in what circumstances, and why?

1 'Please don't worry about it, it wasn't all that valuable.'
2 'She/He means nothing to me – it's you that I really love.'
3 'You won't feel a thing, I promise.'
4 'Whatever happens, I hope we can still be friends.'
5 'Don't cry – your rabbit's gone to rabbit heaven. I know he has.'
6 'Sorry, she's in a meeting at the moment. Can she call you back later?'

b) What other things do people often lie about?

2 Read the 12 situations on p.97. In which is the person lying, and in which is the person telling the truth? Are there any cases where it is not clear?

1 A invites his old friend B to dinner, along with some people B really can't stand. So on the afternoon of the dinner, B calls to say he's got a stomach bug and can't come.

2 **Testifying under oath**, a mother tells a court of law that her teenage son was at home with her on the evening that he was actually stealing a car with his friends. As a result, her son **gets away with** the crime, although his friends are sent to prison.

3 A woman asks her best friend if her new dress is too short for her. Her friend thinks it is, but says it looks fine.

4 A man makes a perfect copy of a painting by a famous artist, which is sold to a private collector for a large amount of money.

5 A child has broken his mother's favourite vase, but when she asks, he says the cat did it.

6 A tells B **a rumour** that C and D, both married to other people, are having an illicit affair. B only half-believes the story, but tells several other people anyway.

7 A man goes round calling on old-age pensioners, selling them **bogus** home security systems for hundreds of pounds.

8 A little girl tells her mother that her brother has eaten some sweets that their mother had told them not to eat.

9 A woman has a terrible morning in which everything seems to go wrong. She retells the story throughout the day to various friends, each time adding to the story to make it more amusing. By the end of the day it has changed considerably!

10 A husband asks his wife why she thinks he is putting on weight. She has thought for years that he is inactive and drinks too much beer, and tells him so **bluntly**.

11 A group of young men set up some photos of what are supposed to be aliens. Thousands of people **are taken in**, and they end up selling their pictures to several newspapers.

12 A young woman, who is engaged to be married in a few months' time, starts seeing another young man secretly.

3 Match these phrases to the situations. There may be more than one possible answer.

- [ ] spreading malicious **gossip**
- [ ] **exaggerating**
- [ ] **telling tales**
- [ ] **committing perjury**
- [ ] **conning** people **out of** money
- [ ] **telling a fib**
- [ ] **cheating on** someone
- [ ] **making an excuse**
- [ ] **telling a white lie**
- [ ] **committing forgery**
- [ ] carrying out **a hoax**
- [ ] telling a few **home truths**

4 **a)** Read the situations in Exercise 2 again and mark them 1–4 as follows:

1 = It was right to lie.
2 = It was wrong to lie, but not terribly serious.
3 = It was very wrong.
4 = It was wrong to tell the truth.

Which is the worst piece of dishonesty in your opinion?

b) Compare and explain your answers in groups. Which situations did you disagree about?

c) Which of the things in Exercises 1 and 2 might you say/do? Which would you never say/do?

5 Which words and phrases in **bold** in Exercises 2 and 3 fit into the following categories?

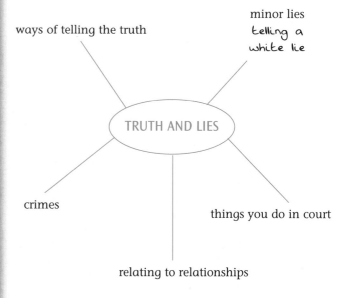

ways of telling the truth

minor lies
telling a white lie

crimes

TRUTH AND LIES

things you do in court

relating to relationships

▶ Phrase builder

Listening
The Unicorn in the Garden

1 Match the two halves of the quotations about lies and truth. Explain what each quotation means. Which do you think are most true?

a) Truth is stranger …
b) It has always been desirable to tell the truth …
c) A truth that's told with bad intent …
d) Any fool can tell the truth …
e) Be sure your lies …
f) Honesty is …
g) A lie can be halfway round the world …

1 beats all the lies you can invent.
2 but it requires a man of some sense to know how to tell a lie well.
3 the best policy.
4 while the truth is still pulling its boots on.
5 but seldom, if ever, necessary to tell the whole truth.
6 than fiction.
7 will always find you out.

2 You are going to listen to a short story by the American humorist James Thurber called *The Unicorn in the Garden*. These are the main characters, objects and places in the story.

a man   his wife   a unicorn   a psychiatrist   a policeman
a strait jacket   a golden horn   the 'booby-hatch'*

a) From the key words, do you expect the story to be:
- tragic?
- amusing?
- magical?
- clever?
- 'dark'?
- childish?

b) Predict briefly what might happen in the story.

> * *Booby* is a type of bird, but also refers to a stupid or crazy person. In this story, *booby-hatch* is taken to mean a mental hospital.

3 [10.1a] Listen to part 1 of the story. In groups, discuss these questions.

a) What did the man see in the garden?
b) What did he tell his wife?
c) How did she respond?
d) How would you describe their relationship?
e) What do you think will happen next?

4 [10.1b] Listen to part 2 of the story, and discuss these questions.

a) Why was the wife so excited?
b) Who did she phone and what did she say?
c) What did she tell them when they arrived?
d) What do you think will happen next?

5 [10.1c] Listen to the final part of the story, and discuss these questions.

a) Were your predictions correct? What happened in the end?
b) Why did the husband live happily ever after?
c) Did the unicorn exist?
d) Which of the adjectives from Exercise 2a would you now use to describe the story?

6 Look at the words in **bold** in the tapescript on p.174. Use the context to guess the meaning, then check in a dictionary.

7 **a)** Look back at the sayings in Exercise 1. Which apply/do not apply to this story?

b) According to the writer, the moral of this story is 'Never count your boobies until they are hatched' – a variation on the proverb 'Never count your chickens until they're hatched.' Can you write a moral of your own?

Patterns to notice

Patterns with *as ... as* + verb

1 Complete the sentence from the story:

The wife got up and dressed .... fast as she ....

2 We can make similar patterns such as *As much as you want, as far as they can.*

(verb) +	as much as as many as as soon as as fast as as long as as often as as far as	+ person	+ want/wanted (like/liked) + can/could + need/needed

---

8 Answer the questions below using an appropriate pattern from the box.

a) 'Buffet: All you can eat for €10.' What does this sign outside a restaurant mean?
   You can eat as much as you want.
b) You're at a very boring party. Your partner asks when you can leave. What do you say?
c) There are no limits on the number of cigarettes you can bring into the UK from EU countries. So how many cigarettes can you buy at the airport?
d) I haven't got enough time to read the whole book by tomorrow. How much should I read?
e) How long should I spend doing my homework?
f) Oh, dear … I can't eat all this. Do I have to eat it all?
g) How often did you go swimming when you were on holiday?
h) It's very urgent that I see you. How soon can you get here?
i) How many people can I invite to my birthday party?
j) Can't you two walk any faster?
k) How long can I keep the computer games you lent me?

Grammar extension 1
Noun phrases

1 Complete the gaps below only when necessary. Sometimes more than one word will be necessary.

a) ....A....... lie can be halfway round ......the..... world while ..the........ truth is still pulling ....its... boots on.
b) I'm sorry I can't come .... evening but I've got .... stomach bug.
c) .... man has been selling .... bogus home security systems to .... old-age pensioners.
d) .... little girl tells .... mother that .... brother has eaten .... sweets that .... mother had told them not to eat.
e) .... group of .... young men take .... hoax photos of .... 'aliens'. .... people are taken in and .... young men sell .... photos to .... newspapers.

2 Find examples of the following in Exercise 1:

1 an indefinite article
2 a definite article
3 a demonstrative
4 a possessive
5 a quantifier

Think of other examples of your own.

▶ Grammar extension bank p.152 and p.154

99

Reading and speaking

1 **a)** Discuss these questions.

- Can you tell when your colleagues/friends/family are lying? How?
- Do you know anyone who is an habitual liar? What kind of things do they say?
- In which jobs is it particularly important that you are trustworthy?
- Are there any jobs in which it is an advantage to be a good liar?
- What characteristics does a good liar need?

b) Make a list of ways in which people often give away the fact that they are lying.

not looking you in the eye

2 Read and see how many of the ways you listed are in the text. What other ways are mentioned?

3 Which statements below are true according to the text? Explain why, in pairs. (There may be more than one correct possibility.)

1   a) Lying makes it harder to spit out the grains of rice.
    b) Lying makes it easier to spit out the grains of rice.
    c) The rice makes your mouth go dry.

2   a) Lie detectors are reliable in the vast majority of cases.
    b) Lie detectors can only work if used voluntarily.
    c) Lie detectors rely on various forms of physical data.

3   a) You don't have to be in the same room as the subject to use the VSA.
    b) The main advantages of the VSA are its cheapness and reliability.
    c) The VSA measures how stressed you are rather than whether or not you're lying.

4   a) People hesitate before lying because they need to prepare their lie.
    b) The less hesitation there is, the less likely it is that you're lying.
    c) The latency period more than doubles when people are lying.

5   a) People blush as the result of a primitive 'fight or flight' instinct.
    b) Special machinery is needed to detect these blushes.
    c) This technology is already in use for security screening at airports.

How do you know when someone is lying?

1 How the ancient Chinese did it

The Chinese used rice. An examination for truthfulness might go something like this: 'Is your name Chiang?' (They know the guy's name is, in fact, Chiang.)
'Yes.'
The interrogators hand Mr Chiang some rice. They have already counted the number of rice grains.
'OK. Put this handful of rice in your mouth. Hold it for three seconds. Spit it out.'
Then they count how many rice grains come out.
'Did you steal the chicken?'
'No.'
'OK. Put this handful of rice in your mouth. Hold it for three seconds. Spit it out.'
Again, they knew how many grains went in, and they count how many come out. If more grains come out after the question about the stolen chicken than came out after the 'easy' question, where the suspect truthfully gave his name, they know he's lying. How? The stress of being caught lying makes the suspect's mouth drier. Fewer grains stick. More come out. Mr Chiang stole the chicken.

2 Modern lie detectors

Modern lie detectors – also known as 'polygraphs' – rely on the same basic principle – that lying causes bodily changes, which can be detected and measured. Having agreed to do the test (if the test is done under duress, the extra stress caused makes the test unreliable), the suspect is connected to three devices measuring blood pressure, breathing rate and electrodermal response (the increased amount of electricity which flows to the skin when we sweat). Increased activity in these areas suggests increased stress … which means the subject might be lying.
Lie detectors have been widely used in the US since the 1950s but they remain controversial and their results are not always accepted by courts.
The results of a test taken by the British nanny Louise Woodward to support her plea of not guilty to killing a child in her care were not admitted as evidence at her trial in Massachusetts. Nowadays, polygraphs are used by the US police, the CIA and the FBI to screen job applicants, but private employers are not allowed to subject job candidates to polygraph examinations, except in a few high-security industries like pharmaceuticals and money manufacturing.

3 Your voice

Cheaper and faster than a polygraph, the voice stress analyser, or VSA is based on the premise that our voice changes when we are under stress – when we're lying for example. The VSA detects the changes, and will work on a telephone, tape recording or from the next room via a wireless mic or bug. The analyser monitors the subject's voice patterns and inflections, and electronically evaluates their relative stress patterns to determine if they are lying or not. Now you can even buy a 'Truth Phone', so when your other half rings to say they're working late at the office, you can immediately know if it's true or not! Research indicates this technology is not very precise at picking up deceitfulness.

4 Hesitation

The period of time between the last word of an investigator's question and the first word of the subject's response is known as 'Response latency'. Research tells us that the average response latency for subjects who are telling the truth is 0.5 seconds … whereas the average latency for liars is 1.5 seconds. This is because the subject is mentally considering whether to tell the truth, part of the truth, or a complete lie. Latencies of two or three seconds should be regarded as highly suspicious … in other words, he who hesitates … is probably lying!!

5 Blushing

According to researchers in the USA, when someone lies you get an instantaneous warming around the eyes … commonly known as 'blushing'. Dr James Levine of the Mayo Clinic in Rochester, Minnesota, speculates that people who lie are afraid of getting caught. 'That fear triggers a primitive response to run away. Blood goes to the eyes so that the liar can more efficiently map out an escape route,' he says. A high-definition, heat-sensing camera can detect such blushes; the new technology has proved more reliable than conventional lie detectors and could offer a new tool for mass security screening at places like airports, office buildings and high-profile events.

4 Think of a word or phrase that could replace the following without changing the meaning.

examination (1)	other half (3)
hand (1)	picking up (3)
bodily (2)	mentally considering (4)
under duress (2)	getting (5)
premise (3)	high-profile (5)

5 Discuss these questions.

- Did you find any of these techniques surprising?
- Which seem to be the most/least reliable?
- In what circumstances do you think such tests should be used? What objections can you think of?
- Have you ever been in a situation where you were telling the truth and nobody believed you?

▶ Phrase builder

Grammar extension 2
Ellipsis and substitution

1 Read the dialogue. Look at the <u>underlined</u> sections. How could they be shortened? You may have to change some of the words.

ANDY:	Have you finished with the paper?
MARIA:	Hang on. I'm just reading an article about lie detectors …
ANDY:	Oh yes, <u>that article about lie detectors</u>. I started reading it this morning but <u>I didn't finish reading</u> it. Is there anything interesting in it?
MARIA:	Apparently **you** can tell someone's lying because **they** can't help blushing.
ANDY:	<u>Do they realise they are blushing</u>?
MARIA:	No, <u>I don't think they realise they are blushing</u>. Tell me, do you ever blush when you talk to me?
ANDY:	No, of course <u>I don't ever blush when I talk to you</u>. That's because I never lie to you.
MARIA:	Is that true?
ANDY:	<u>Of course it is true</u>. <u>I never lie to you, and you never lie to me</u>, right?
MARIA:	So, why are you blushing now, then?

b) 🖭 [10.2] Listen and check.

2 Who do **you** and **they** refer to in the dialogue? Could you substitute these with any other pronouns?

▶ Grammar extension bank p.153 and p.155

Personal vocabulary

Useful language

Making statements

I know this is hard to believe/You may not believe this, but once ...

Believe it or not ...

That's absolutely 100 per cent true.

Checking information

Tell us a bit more about ...

Do you really expect us to believe ...?

Where/What/Why exactly did you ...?

Deciding which statements are true

This one can't possibly be/ must be/might be ...

There's no way (s)he could've ...

▶ Phrase builder

Task: find out if your partner is lying
Preparation for task

1   🔲 [10.3] Amy Wells is 35 years old. You will hear Amy make ten statements about herself. Write the statements below.

1 ....
2 ....
3 ....
4 ....
5 ....
6 ....
7 ....
8 ....
9 ....
10 ....

2   🔲 [10.4] Five of the statements are true and five are false. Listen to Amy play *The Truth Game* with two other players. They have ten minutes to ask questions to find out which statements are false.

3   🔲 [10.5] Which statements do you suspect are false? Listen and check.

Task

1   **a)** Work individually. Write ten sentences about yourself: five should be true and five false. The sentences should be as interesting as possible, but remember that the idea is to trick your partners! Use the grid to give you ideas.

b) Spend 5–10 minutes thinking about how you will answer questions about these things (whether true or false). Ask your teacher about any vocabulary you need.

▶ Personal vocabulary

2   Work in groups of about three. Take turns to read your statements to your partners. They can ask as many questions as they like.

▶ Useful language

3   Decide which of your partner's statements are true and which are lies. Which member of the group persuaded the others to believe the most lies?

Writing
Maintaining attention in a news article

1 Look below at the extracts from a news article about cheating in exams. What technique is used to grab the reader's attention in each case? Which are most suitable for introducing the article/paragraphs? Which make good endings?

(a) If you think cheating is uncommon, read on. You'll be surprised.

(b) Is it the parents' fault?

(c) As one teacher says, 'If I'm marking an exam paper, and the handwriting suddenly changes completely, I just think "Here we go again".'

(d) A girl drops her pen during an exam. As she crouches down to pick it up, she takes a soggy, crumpled piece of paper out of her mouth and frantically reads the notes written on it.

(e) Cheating doesn't work.

(f) Sally had all her history notes written up her arms, hidden under her sweater. The trouble was, when she turned over the exam paper, it was biology.

2 A magazine has asked you to write an article about people who lie in relationships, entitled 'Is technology helping love-rats?' Discuss in small groups how technology like email, the Internet and mobile phones, might make this kind of deception easier. Have you heard of any cases?

" I noticed that she always called me from a mobile phone, and gave various excuses why I couldn't have her home phone number … the mobile was cheaper, the home phone wasn't working, the number was going to be changed … once or twice I heard children's voices in the background, but she told me she was babysitting for a friend, or she was at a children's birthday party. When I asked her to marry me, she accepted right away – not a moment's hesitation – yet she had a husband and two children in Manchester. " **Paul, 35**

" I was sitting watching Crimewatch on the TV one night, and suddenly I couldn't believe what I was seeing: they were showing some CCTV footage from the previous afternoon, of a shopping mall where there had been several thefts – and there, walking hand in hand with another man, was my girlfriend! As far as I knew, she'd been at work that afternoon – she'd even phoned me on her mobile to ask if I wanted to meet later that evening. " **Ali, 28**

" He actually had another wife and home, just 10 kilometres away. The house they lived in was very similar to ours – it was incredible. The rooms were all laid out in the same way, so he wouldn't get confused and walk into the bathroom thinking it was a bedroom. They even had similar colour schemes in the kitchen and living room. He managed to keep the double life going for nearly six years because his job as a salesman meant he was always travelling. Then one day he got caught out: he had two mobile phones – one for each 'life' – and one day I noticed an unfamiliar phone on his desk next to his briefcase: I rang the last number he'd called and a woman's voice answered, saying 'Hi, darling' – well, I asked her who she was, we started talking, and soon the truth was out. " **Marie, 46**

" I suspected that she might be seeing someone else, but when I challenged her about it, of course she denied it emphatically. Then one day I noticed that she'd been sending some emails, and under 'saved emails' I found a whole list of emails to the same address. I only needed to read a couple of the most recent ones to be sure that she was seeing someone else, and was apparently very much in love with him. She obviously didn't realise that the computer was set up to save all her emails automatically. " **Rahul, 29**

" It was like a nightmare, finding out that Fred had married another woman – and she knew nothing about me and our two sons! He met her through a lonely hearts advertisement on the Internet and told her all kinds of lies, including one about his wife dying – just to get her sympathy! She flew all the way to the US to meet him – that's where he'd told her he lived, whereas he actually lived in Scotland. She fell for him completely and they were married two weeks later. This woman seems to think that divorcing me is just a 'legal technicality' that he forgot about. " **Sandra, 48**

3 Read the true stories on the left and <u>underline</u> information relevant to your article.

4 Use the following steps to plan your article of about 250 words.

a) Decide if your answer will be 'Yes' or 'No' to the question 'Is technology helping love-rats?'

b) Make sure that you use enough examples from the true stories to show both sides of the question, but with enough 'weighting' to support your conclusion.

c) Decide whether the style of your article should be informative, amusing or both.

d) Plan your article (4–5 paragraphs), deciding what to put in each paragraph, and how to order the paragraphs.

e) Look back at the techniques for grabbing attention in Exercise 1. Include at least three of these in your article.

f) Decide if you can use any of the useful language below.

- The story/case of X shows us that …
- It is hard to believe that …
- Perhaps the strangest/most shocking case is …
- In another fascinating/sad/ incredible case …
- apparently
- unfortunately
- presumably
- admittedly
- ultimately
- (not) surprisingly

5 Write the first draft of your article. Read it through, checking it against the list in Exercise 4, before writing your final draft.

Real life
Expressing surprise and disbelief

1 [10.6] Listen to a conversation between Mark and his friend Will.

a) Where did Will go last night and who does he claim to have seen?
b) How does Mark respond?

2 Listen and follow the tapescript on p.175. <u>Underline</u> phrases used to indicate:

- surprise
- lack of surprise
- disbelief.

3 [10.7] Listen to some more phrases. Which reactions in Exercise 2 do they show? Repeat, copying the stress and intonation.

a) You're kidding!
b) Do you seriously expect me to believe that?
c) I'm not surprised.
d) I'll believe that when I see it.
e) That's totally ridiculous.
f) No wonder!
g) I'll take your word for it.
h) You're going to do WHAT??
i) You must be joking!
j) You could've fooled me.
k) That's absolutely amazing!
l) Obviously.

4 For each situation below, choose two or three possible responses from the ones above. Choose **three** situations to act out with a partner.

a) A friend tells you she's going to have her hair dyed orange.
b) Your partner is late for your date – as usual, but promises to be on time next time.
c) A friend tells you she's going to have an enormous tattoo of her boyfriend done on her back.
d) A taxi driver tells you that you have to pay double fare as it's after 12.
e) Someone tells you that their dog can sing pop songs.
f) Your colleague tells you she's tired … you know that she's always staying up late.
g) Someone tells you that they've just seen Britney Spears at the local supermarket.

Communication
activities

Module 4: Wordspot p.44

Student A

1 Say this phrase another way: 'I just couldn't understand what he was saying.'

A: I just couldn't get my head round what he was saying.

2 How can we describe a film, story or poem that is very sad and makes us sad?

A: heart-rending

3 What reason could you give for not going out because you've so much work to do?

A: I'm up to my neck in it.

4 Sampras won the tennis final 6–0, 6–0. We can say he won …

A: hands down

5 It's clear that your friend is still very upset about a recent break-up but has no one to talk to about it. What does (s)he need?

A: a shoulder to cry on

6 What might someone have just before they have to address a huge audience?

A: butterflies in their stomach

7 Our cat will only eat one type of cat food. What does she do when we give her another type?

A: She turns her nose up at it.

Module 8: Reading p.78

Answer Key for quotes

a) Frank Sinatra
b) Audrey Hepburn
c) Madonna
d) Frank Sinatra
e) Audrey Hepburn
f) James Dean

g) Audrey Hepburn
h) James Dean
i) Madonna
j) Frank Sinatra
k) Madonna
l) Frank Sinatra

Module 1: Task p.12

a) Practising English outside class

This is vital if you want to make progress, and with dozens of ways you can do it, there must be something that appeals to you! There are songs, newspapers, books, subtitled films, cable TV, internet chat-rooms, and websites (the *Cutting Edge* website at www.longman.com/cuttingedge will give you lots more information about other websites to go to). If you live in an English-speaking country, how about joining an evening class and learning another subject in English, whether it's cookery or wine appreciation? The important thing is that **you** find it interesting.

b) and c) Being active in class and speaking in front of the group

You are much more likely to learn English successfully if you take a proactive approach, and your classroom is the best place to start. People who ask and answer questions are more likely to remember what they've learnt than those who just sit and listen (or look out of the window!). Pairwork and groupwork are the ideal opportunity for shy people to try out what they've got to say, building up their confidence before they speak up in front of the class.

d) Making mistakes

Making mistakes is an important part of learning a language, so fear of getting it wrong should never stop you having a try. However, as an advanced learner you are probably setting yourself high standards now, and this is an area where you really need to take control. Ask your teacher if there is a particular area (like pronunciation, for example) where you need to direct your efforts. Ask your teacher (or even your fellow students) if they will pay special attention to correcting you in this area, and try to go over the mistakes you have made later at home. In writing, of course, accuracy is especially important, so if you're planning on taking any exams soon, this is probably vital. Get into the habit of reading your work through before you hand it in, and go through your mistakes carefully when your teacher gives it back. Ask him/her about anything you don't understand.

e) Making notes

You should! Anything is better than nothing, and make sure it's in a notebook and not on a scrap of paper you'll lose. If you aren't sure about making notes, ask your teacher for some tips, or look at the *Cutting Edge* website.

f) Monolingual Dictionaries

Get one! By this stage you need the up-to-date examples and subtle distinctions of meaning that only a good modern monolingual dictionary can give you. We suggest *Longman Dictionary of Contemporary English*. Again try the *Cutting Edge* website for help using it, or ask your teacher if you could have a lesson on using monolingual dictionaries. Bring it to class, use it at home, make it part of your study habits.

g) Vocabulary

Back to that monolingual dictionary again ...! And also all those things you can do outside the classroom .... (see section a) above). Everything you do in English will help your vocabulary, especially reading. The important thing with reading is to make sure that you are reading something you would enjoy in your own language, so if you don't read much poetry normally, you probably won't get on that well with it in English! If you enjoy reading football reports, how about finding some on the Internet in English? If you enjoy detective stories, why not go down to your local English language bookshop and see if you can find one? Don't feel that you have to write down or even understand every new word you meet – too much time with a dictionary and notebook will kill your enjoyment. You'll pick up a lot without realising it, and you'll probably soon work out the meaning of words that come up again and again.

h) Phrases

Everything that's true about vocabulary is true about phrases too. Use *Cutting Edge Advanced* Phrase builder which gives you lots of extra examples and information about how to use the phrases that you meet in the readings, listenings and vocabulary sections of *Cutting Edge Advanced*. Have a look at it now, for an idea of the kind of information it will give you.

i) and j) Grammar

Some people are more grammar-oriented than others – remember the most important thing is not knowing all the terminology and rules, but how well you can actually use the grammar in your writing and speech. If you are not sure how you rate in this respect, ask your teacher to monitor you for a few lessons and give you his/her assessment. If it's revision you need, have a look at the *Cutting Edge Advanced* Grammar extension bank, starting on p.115. You will see this covers all the major areas of English grammar, with exercises to practise the most tricky points. Your teacher will be able to give you an answer key, so you can start working on it by yourself. Think about buying yourself a good advanced Grammar too.

k) Pronunciation

You probably know by now whether or not you need to improve your pronunciation. If so, here are a few ideas to try. Listen to as much English as you can outside the classroom (satellite TV, the radio or just the tapes from this book!); practise reading aloud from texts in the book (just short sections which you practise over and over again) – it may help to think about a good English speaker that you know (perhaps your teacher or a favourite actor) and imitate the way they speak. Try recording your voice in English – this may help you to see where you could improve. Or ask your teacher to listen and give you some suggestions. There are pronunciation exercises in the *Cutting Edge Advanced* workbook.

l) Writing

If writing is important to you, have a look at the writing activities on the contents pages (pp.2–5). There are also writing activities in the workbook so even if your teacher does not have time to do all the writing activities with the class (other students in the class may have different priorities), you could always do some of them on your own at home. If you have difficulty working out your ideas and writing correctly in English at the same time, try making notes before you start, or even writing a rough draft first. Remember you can improve your writing a lot if you get into the habit of checking your written work yourself before you hand it in.

Module 2: Task p.23

Module 4: Wordspot p.44

Student B

1   My little brother went on a really frightening water ride at Water World Theme park. How did he describe it?

A: **hair-raising**

2   It was a delicious, appetising meal. What's another way to say 'delicious and appetising'?

A: **mouth-watering**

3   My friend is trying to convince me that he's engaged to a film star, but I don't believe him. What do I say?

A: **You're pulling my leg.**

4   He looked so ridiculous dressed in that wig that we had to laugh. What couldn't we do?

A: **We couldn't keep a straight face.**

5   What might a corrupt police officer do when he sees something illegal happening?

A: **turn a blind eye**

6   When I asked him how his wife was, he said she'd left him. What did I do?

A: **You put your foot in it.**

7   A waitress keeps dropping things all over the place! How could you describe her?

A: **all fingers and thumbs**

Module 5: Vocabulary and speaking p.46

A = academic	M = marks
B = break	O = online
C = course	P = professor
E = elementary	R = Reading, Writing, Arithmetic
G = graduation	
J = junior	T = tertiary
L = lectures	U = undergraduate
	V = vocational

Module 1: Speaking p.10

The false piece of information is 'doctor-speak' in **4**.

Module 4: Reading p.39

②

Colour Therapy

Ray Coles teaches a class of ten- and eleven-year-olds.

'I find school very rushed and I only eat when I can find a minute to grab something. I've just moved to the area to take up this job and I really miss having a social circle. When I get stressed at work, I get hyperactive and find it difficult to unwind. I also tend to have difficulty concentrating and suffer from an aching back when I'm tense.'

Prescribed

Colour therapy which is all about light, and involves gazing at various coloured lights to stimulate different parts of the brain.

Ray says: 'I'm open-minded about alternative remedies, so I was ready to give this a go. We began by having a good old natter so that she could get to know me. It was a psychological discussion to talk about what stressed me out, such as school and life at home. She made really constructive suggestions about what I should actually do about my problems, and taught me some quite straightforward relaxation exercises.

'After the discussion she asked me to lie down on the bed and dangled a crystal over my head from head to toe. She said that the energy from some colours was missing from certain parts of my body, but I thought she could have drawn a lot of her assumptions from the discussion rather than picking it up from the crystal vibes. It could have been bluff and guesswork, but she seems extremely genuine in what she believes.

'Next, she switched on the disco lights and left me with them for 20 minutes. When she came back, she dangled the crystal again over certain points of my body and said she could see healing had taken place and certain parts were no longer as tense. I think it's a bit like horoscopes when you read that you'll meet a handsome stranger, you do suddenly begin to notice a lot of strange handsome people around you. An awful lot of the treatment relies on the power of suggestion.

'I was very stressed about my workload and I got things far more in perspective. It was like going to someone for an independent viewpoint, because she gave me a lot of advice on interpersonal relationships. I wouldn't go out of my way to recommend colour therapy, but I would suggest finding someone to go and have a good chinwag with.'

Continuing treatment? No

Module 8: Reading and speaking p.78

James Dean (1931–55)

US actor. Initially a stage actor, he appeared in only a small number of films after making his debut in the 1955 film *East of Eden.*
Dean's instantly recognisable image, featuring blue jeans, a dangling cigarette and a characteristic slouch, made him a cult hero almost overnight, and he has remained a symbol of the rebellious teenager ever since. Always determined to live life to the full, he was addicted to high-speed sports. He was forbidden to engage in any form of sports car racing during the shooting of his last film, *Giant.* The day after filming ended in September 1955, he was heading to Salinas, California, where he was to take part in a race, when he collided with another vehicle on a California highway. Dean died instantly. He was 24 years old.

Madonna (1958–)

US pop star and actor. Perhaps the most successful female artist in popular music, Madonna has always shown the ability to reinvent herself while maintaining full control of her career. The biggest selling female recording star of the '80s, among her biggest fans were a growing number of 'wannabes', teenage girls who copied her independent, don't-care attitude. Constantly changing her image from blonde bombshell to hippie earth mother, from cowboy girl to devoted wife and mother, her success has continued, with albums such as *Like a Prayer* and *Music* bringing popular and critical acclaim. Her film roles have included *Desperately Seeking Susan* (1985) and the title role in *Evita* (1996). She now has two children and lives with her husband, film director Guy Ritchie.

Audrey Hepburn (1929–93)

Actress. Born of Anglo-Dutch parents, she became a Hollywood star in *Roman Holiday* (1951), for which she won an Academy Award. Her other major roles included Holly Golightly in *Breakfast at Tiffany's* and Eliza in *My Fair Lady.* Often playing innocent, childlike characters, her acting was characterised from the beginning by sophistication, modesty, and humour. Audrey's personality – a blend of fragile girl and elegant woman – set her apart from the American

blonde bombshells so popular at the time. From 1988, she gave up her film career and worked for the United Nation's Children's Fund. She died in Switzerland at the age of 63. She was mourned internationally as one of the favourite film actresses of all time, an icon to style, elegance, dignity and charity.

Frank Sinatra (1915–1998)

US singer and film actor. Known variously as 'The Voice', 'The Chairman of the Board' and 'Old Blue Eyes', his career as a singer spanned nearly sixty years. As well as recording more than 1,500 songs, he appeared in nearly sixty movies. As a singer, his cool romantic image brought him worldwide fame. His turbulent love life (he was romantically linked to

many of the most glamorous women of his time and was married three times), extravagant lifestyle and rumours of links to organised crime only seemed to enhance his 'Bad Boy' image – and his appeal to millions of devoted fans. He finally retired from recording at the age of 79, and died in 1998.

Module 8: Writing p.85

Design 1

Design 2

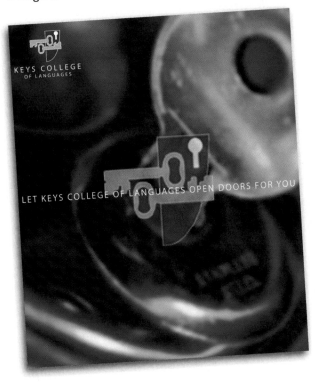

Module 4: Reading p.39

③

Thai Yoga Massage

Dayle Brain teaches ten- and eleven-year-olds.

'I get very stressed and often have a raging headache when I leave school. It feels as though I'm constantly taking painkillers. Like most teachers I crash during the first week of the holidays and get throat infections. I don't know much about these treatments but I wouldn't mind doing something that involves some gentle stretching.'

Prescribed

Thai yoga massage which relieves physical stress and strain and stretches your limbs most effectively. It combines the yoga of India with the acupressure and meridian massage of China. It's like having your yoga done for you.

Dayle says: 'I had only flirted with complementary medicine before. Thai yoga massage is certainly not massage as we know it. It involves much harder pressing and it felt like I was a piece of dough being kneaded. When the practitioner was massaging me (through clothes) I did sometimes think, "please don't do that any more". He didn't actually talk to me apart from when he gave instructions which I found very eerie. If he'd spoken to me more, I would have felt more at ease.

'I felt quite energetic after the first session, but it only lasted the day of the treatment. The next day I felt back to normal. As the sessions went on, the massage got harder and my body felt as though it had been worked on each time, but I never got that feeling of instant energy back again.

'It's difficult to say what benefit the treatment finally had. As the treatments went on, the headaches began to improve and things didn't seem to get on top of me the way they used to. I don't know if this can necessarily be put down to the treatment because stress depends on so many things. Taking time out for myself had a lot to do with it. I feel selfish if I do things for myself. I've spent a whole hour each time letting someone else take over my life and I think that's the key.'

Continuing treatment? No

Module 7: Task pp.70–71

Nick

Background: Investment banker, 34, high earner from wealthy family, single.

Fitness: 7/10

Charming and funny, he got on well with everyone on the surface, but his commitment may start to crumble when the going gets tough – does he really know what he's letting himself in for?

'Impossible to dislike – there's never a dull moment when Nick is around.'
'A bit of a womaniser – he obviously fancied Paula, but he was also flirting with Julia and even with Michelle, who was there with her husband!'

Briony

Background: Nurse, 25, single. Marathon runner.

Fitness: 10/10

Very committed, realistic attitude to the physical challenges. Seemed to understand the value of teamwork in theory, but in practice often worked on tasks individually and did things her own way.

'Briony's a very driven person, almost obsessively determined.'
'She seems a nice person, but very, very serious. A bit lacking in sense of humour.'

Ron

Background: 48-year-old headmaster of a primary school, married to Beverley. They have three children aged 12, 10 and 4, who would accompany them. They spend all their holidays camping, hiking, etc. Has a lot of experience of organising adventure holidays for young people.

Fitness: 7/10

There's no doubting his commitment and his experience would be invaluable to the group. He had a helpful attitude to the others, but one or two seemed to resent his rather overbearing attitude.

'Ron's fine really, but he seemed to push his wife and kids around quite a bit – typical headmaster type!'

Beverley
(Ron's wife)

Background: Domestic science teacher and mother of three, 44, married to Ron.

Fitness: 6/10

Beverley was liked by the group, and seemed to work well in a team. She seems to have realistic expectations of the island and should cope well.

'Bev's a really nice, kind woman, but I wish she would stop running round after her husband all the time.'

Mark

Background: Computer programmer, 31. Mountaineering enthusiast. Single. Stated on his application form that he is gay, but did not want to make this known to the group at this stage.

Fitness: 9/10

Very good in a team – he was popular with the other group members. His mountaineering experience makes him one of the best-prepared candidates.

'Mark's a really nice person, a bit serious, but very likeable. None of the others seemed to realise he was gay, in fact one or two of the women were definitely trying to chat him up!'

Jason

Background: 29-year-old builder, married to Michelle. They have an eight-year-old daughter (Chloe) who would accompany them.

Fitness: 9/10

Obviously highly committed to the project. A quiet man who works well in a team, was very supportive of and liked by the other participants.

'I bet Jason's a bit henpecked.'
'A really good bloke, shame about the wife.'

Michelle

Background: 28. Part-time hairdresser married to Jason, and mother of eight-year-old Chloe.

Fitness: 4/10

Pleasant enough with the other participants, but showed a tendency to moan, which some of the others began to pick up on.

'I didn't really warm to Michelle, to be honest.'

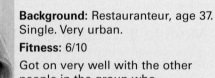
Julia

Background: Restauranteur, age 37. Single. Very urban.

Fitness: 6/10

Got on very well with the other people in the group who appreciated her sense of humour and supportive attitude. Although this is something completely different for her, she does seem to have thought about it, and have realistic expectations

'Julia's great! She had everyone laughing all weekend – a really good sort'.
'Julia obviously fancied Nick a lot, and she also seemed quite interested in Mark, and even tried to flirt with Jason when Michelle wasn't looking.'

Chris

Background: Ex-army marine, 27. Unemployed at present. Divorced with 7-year-old son, who would not accompany him.

Fitness: 10/10

Extremely committed, with invaluable experience to bring to the group. He's a natural loner though, perhaps secretly contemptuous of those in the group who are less tough than he is?

'Very intense, maybe a bit weird?'
'I think Chris is a nice person deep down, but he's very hard to get to know. Trying to keep a conversation going is a real strain.'

Paula

Background: 22, student and part-time model, has never had a full-time job. Single.

Fitness: 6/10

Friendly and cooperative, worked well in a team. Doesn't seem to have a clue about how tough life on the island will be, however.

'I didn't think I was going to like her, but actually, she's a really sweet girl.'
'Paula's incredibly good-looking – it was obvious that practically all the men in the group fancied her. Two or three of the women (Michelle and Julia, for example) seemed a bit jealous.'

113

Module 4: Reading p.39

(4)

Acupuncture

Head teacher Jackie Cox is 53.

'As head of the school, my job involves juggling several roles, and I just don't have time to relieve my stress. I suffer from an inflammatory disease which flares up when I'm under stress, and I'm ill most school holidays.'

Prescribed
Acupuncture, which involves inserting fine sterile needles into various trigger points that run along 12 energy channels throughout the body.

Jackie says: 'I was extremely sceptical beforehand because I don't have much time for this sort of stuff. Still, at my first session the practitioner did a very thorough initial consultation involving my health history and important life events. It was so comprehensive it lasted 90 minutes, and I felt very reassured by her, which filled me with confidence. After that, she got started and, as the sessions have progressed, I've just felt better and better.

'She didn't use big pins to start off with, she just put some very fine ones in my back, and took them out almost immediately, so that helped me with any initial apprehension I might have had. My husband has even noticed a difference in me. He thinks I'm much more laid back about things, and I certainly feel it.

'I've just had a week off and usually I get very stressed during my holidays. I don't really enjoy the break, but it's been a good week. Now I'm back at work, which is a very stressful environment, but I'm just taking it in my stride. It's not a very relaxing treatment in itself – it's very different from having a massage, for example. I got on very well with the practitioner, though. At the beginning of every session, we would go through what had happened in my week. She would ask me how I was feeling and how my stress levels were, before taking my pulses and deciding where she was going to position the needles. I found the process riveting after having been such a sceptic.'

Continuing treatment? Yes

Module 3: Real life p.35

a) Who are the two people involved?
friends   relatives   colleagues   strangers   other

b) Where are they?
at home   at work   travelling
in a public place (e.g. in a café, library)   other

c) What does Speaker A want Speaker B to do?
lend him/her something   help him/her to do something
stop doing sthg   run an errand for her/him   other

d) What is Speaker A's attitude?
extremely polite   fairly polite   casual   other

e) What is Speaker B's attitude?
cooperative/helpful   uncooperative/unhelpful
annoyed/reluctant   other

Module 8: Listening p.80

You're so vain is supposed to be about the actor, Warren Beatty.

Module 2: Reading p.18

Punchlines
1c, 2e, 3a, 4h, 5g, 6f, 7d, 8b

Module 7: Reading and vocabulary p.72

3 women	12 women	21 women
4 woman	13 men	22 men
5 man	14 woman	23 Women
6 man	15 Men	24 Men
7 women	16 man	25 men
8 man	17 women	26 Women
9 woman	18 men	27 men
10 men	19 women	28 men
11 women	20 Men	

Grammar extension bank

Introduction for students and teachers

The needs of an advanced student

At advanced level, different classes – even different individuals in the same class – have different needs. Some learners need to revise certain areas covered at lower levels, some wish to extend their knowledge of more complex areas, and for some, grammar is no longer a priority. For this reason, the grammar in *Cutting Edge Advanced* is designed to be used flexibly according to your needs. A chat with the teacher will help students to work out what their individual needs are.

Two 'strands' of grammar

In each module of the course there are two 'strands' of grammar:

- *Patterns to notice* are small but complex structures typical of spoken or written English, which students may have noticed before, but probably haven't studied explicitly (for example, *Introducing points in an argument* on p.11). These self-contained areas are fully introduced and practised in the module itself, with further practice in the Workbook.

- *Grammar extension* sections feature in each module and focus on a broad area of English grammar which students will almost certainly have studied before (for example, *Continuous verb forms* on p10). The section in the module itself is only intended to give a quick diagnosis of how familiar students are with this area – the main information and practice are provided in the Grammar extension bank at the back of the Students' Book.

What the Grammar extension bank consists of

For each module there is a two-page Language summary, followed by two pages of Grammar practice.

The **Language summary** (in blue) includes both revision of material normally covered at lower levels and more complex details that will help students to use the grammar in a wider range of situations.

The **Grammar practice** (in green) contains 7-9 exercises. Some of these provide global practice of the topic area, but most practise tricky individual points mentioned in the Language summary. The exercises follow the order of the Language summary, and the relevant exercises are signposted with a green arrow after each section of the Language summary.

Different ways to use the Grammar extension bank

Classwork

- **If most students need thorough revision and extension work...**
  The teacher can work through the Language summary in sections, explaining any problems and setting the relevant practice exercises before moving on to the next section. This could be spread out of over several lessons, with further practice between lessons in the workbook.

- **If the class need brief revision work with main focus on new areas...**
  The teacher could set some or all of the Language summary to be read for homework, asking students to come back the next lesson with any problems. Appropriate practice exercises can then be set.

- **If students know most of the material in the Language summary but want to fill in the gaps in their knowledge...**
  The teacher could set some or all of the grammar practice exercises first, then go back to the appropriate sections of the Language summary where difficulties arise, setting further practice exercises from the Workbook as appropriate.

Individual work

If class time is limited and/or most students have other priorities, it may be better for individual students to work on problem areas by themselves as necessary. Individual students can adapt any of the approaches above, asking their teacher about problem areas in spare moments in the lesson.

If you don't want to use the Grammar extension bank at all...!

If time is limited and grammar is not a priority for students, the modules have been designed so that there is still plenty of new input. Even without using the Grammar extension bank, your course will still be challenging and worthwhile!

Continuous verb forms

Ⓐ General

1 We use continuous verb forms to describe actions which we see happening over a period of time.

I hear you're doing a cookery course.

We were watching an interesting series about murders.

I've been trying to phone you. (over a period of time)

When you finish work, we'll be waiting for you outside.

With simple verb forms we are not interested in this sense of duration.

2 We may also see the situation as:

a) temporary.

We're staying with my uncle while our house is being decorated.

b) happening around a point of time.

At 12 o'clock, James was still working on his computer.

Don't phone me at 12.00. I'll be having a meeting.

c) involving change or development.

She was getting more disobedient every day.

There's no doubt the world's climate is changing.

d) incomplete.

We were having a very interesting conversation. (= before you interrupted)

I've been reading Nelson Mandela's autobiography. (= but I haven't finished it)

> The idea of incompletion is especially important with continuous perfect forms. Simple perfect forms emphasise completion (and therefore the result of the action).
>
> *The local council have spent a lot of money on new roads. (= now they are finished)*
>
> *We'd downloaded some files from the Internet. (= this is completed)*
>
> Continuous perfect forms emphasise the action itself.
>
> *The local council have been spending a lot of money on new roads. (= this is how they have been spending their money – perhaps the roads are not complete)*
>
> *We'd been downloading some files from the Internet. (= this was how we spent our time, but perhaps we didn't finish)*

3 The continuous infinitive *(to) be + -ing* also emphasises that an action is in progress at a particular time.

Wherever you go nowadays, everyone seems to be speaking English. (= they are speaking English when you hear them)

Compare this to:

Wherever you go nowadays, everyone seems to speak English. (= they are generally able to speak English)

▶ Exercises 1–3 p.118

Ⓑ Special uses of continuous forms

1 *always* + continuous forms

always + the simple form simply indicates that something happens regularly.

I always start work early.

However, *always* + the continuous form is also common. This stresses the repetitiveness of the action and often indicates that the speaker finds the repeated action surprising, strange or irritating.

Stanley was always dreaming up strange schemes to make money.

Christian's always smiling.

I'm always locking myself out.

We use *constantly, forever, continually,* etc. in the same way.

How can I be expected to work if you're constantly interrupting?

My parents were continually criticising me.

▶ Exercise 4 p.119

2 Past Continuous for polite requests

We can use the Past Continuous to make requests more polite and tentative.

I was wondering if you could recommend a good restaurant.

I was hoping you might help me with this application form.

3 Present Continuous for future arrangements

The Present Continuous is commonly used to describe arrangements for the future.

They're opening that new hypermarket next week.

What are you doing over Christmas?

In this case, either there is a future time phrase in the sentence, or it is clear from the context that we are talking about the future.

See module 6 and module 9 Language summaries

4 Modal verbs

With modal verbs, the continuous infinitive can have a different meaning from the simple infinitive.

*They **might be staying** at the Sheraton Hotel.* (= present possibility)

*They **might stay** at the Sheraton Hotel.* (= future possibility)

*What a terrible noise! They **must be having** a party.* (= logical necessity)

*We **must have** a party soon.* (= personal obligation)

▶ Exercises 5–6 p.119

C Verbs which change meaning in continuous and simple forms

1 State verbs

Verbs which describe states only occur in the simple form.

*Nick **seems** very friendly.*

*I **didn't know** Claire's dad. He died before we met.*

The most common state verbs are:

* *be*

* verbs of possession and unchangeable states (*have, weigh, measure, fit*)

  *Oh dear, this dress **doesn't fit** any more.*

* verbs to do with the senses (*appear, see, look, smell, taste*)

  *The minister **appears** puzzled by the accusations against him.*

* verbs describing thoughts and processes (*think, feel, expect*).

  *I **expect** he'll soon be here.*

2 Verbs to describe states or actions

If the verbs above are used in the continuous form, they become 'actions' of some sort.

a) The verb *to be* occurs in the continuous form when it refers to behaviour which is temporary and/or deliberate (i.e. a kind of 'action').

*Why **is** everybody so unhelpful?* (= they are always like this – a state)

*Why **is** everybody **being** so unhelpful?* (= they are not normally like this)

Note that *is being* cannot be used when there is no volition (deliberate will) involved.

The weather is ~~being~~ very wet at the moment.

b) Other verbs have a different meaning in their continuous and simple forms.

STATES	ACTIONS
*It **looks/appears** to be OK.* (= seems)	*And the referee **is looking** at his watch ...*
	*She's **appearing** in public for the first time.* (= performing)
*I **see** a bright light.* (= with my eyes)	*I'm **seeing** Thomas tonight.* (= meeting)
*I **think** that's all.* (= suppose/guess)	*I'm **thinking** about what you said.* (= considering)
*I **expect** you're tired.* (= imagine)	*I'm **expecting** an important phone call.* (= waiting for)
*I **have** always **admired** Roosevelt.* (= have a good opinion of)	*I **was** just **admiring** your new car.* (= look at with appreciation)
*I **have** a large family* (= possess)	*She's **having** a bath.* (= taking)
*It **weighs** 82kg and **measures** 3 metres.* (= fact)	*The nurse **is weighing** and **measuring** the baby.* (= an activity)
*My suit **doesn't fit** me any more.* (= it's not the correct size)	*A man **is fitting** a new shower unit.* (= installing)

> **Notice!**
>
> A few verbs which describe physical feelings (*feel/hurt/ache*) can be used in either the simple or continuous form to talk about the present moment. There is no difference in meaning.
>
> *Why are you lying down?*   *My back **hurts**/**is hurting**.*
>
> *Are you **feeling**/do you **feel** better today?*

▶ Exercises 7–8 p.119

117

Continuous verb forms

1 <u>Underline</u> all the continuous verb forms in the article below, and decide why a continuous form is used in each case. Look back at the Language summary to help you.

A Tall Story

It's official. We are growing up. According to recent research, the world is getting taller as people lead healthier lives. The average height of Europeans, for example, has been climbing steadily, with an increase of more than 20 cm in 150 years. But manufacturers and retailers appear to be lagging behind – design standards for clothes are over 50 years out of date. Phil Heinrick, founder of the Tall Club in Britain, claims to get 100 letters a day from people who are suffering because of their height: 'they want to know where to get shoes, clothes and furniture for tall people'. Helena Kennedy heard about the Tall Club on the Internet, and was soon attending monthly meetings: 'It's great to be with people who are at least as tall as me – in fact, when I got to my first meeting, someone was measuring all the new members to make sure that they were tall enough to join!' Tall people also hate being teased about their height: 'When I was at school, other kids were always saying things like 'How's the weather up there?' says Helena.

2 Choose the correct perfect form: simple or continuous.

a) 'Did you notice that Anna and Jaime seemed a bit tense?'
   'Yes, I think they'd *argued/been arguing* again.'
b) 'Do you want to come shopping?'
   'I can't – I've *spent/been spending* all my money in the sales.'
c) 'Why can't I go out tonight, Dad?'
   'Because you've *come/been coming* home much too late and you haven't *done/been doing* your homework yet.'
d) 'Why was Jeff so annoyed with you?'
   'Because I'd *left/been leaving* a big pile of photocopying for him to do.'
e) 'What have you *done/been doing* recently?'
   'Oh, mainly working and going to the gym.'

3 Complete the gaps with a verb from the box, in a simple or continuous form.

perform	lose	have	come	reach
promote	take			

No More Lives for Lloyd Webber's Cats

Andrew Lloyd Webber's rule over the West End appears 1).................. to an end after the announcement that he is closing the London production of *Cats*. The musical, which 2)................ £1.4 billion around the world, is the second most profitable in show business history, but its West End production 3)........................ money. Although many of the big shows 4) (still)........................ well, some critics feel that London's blockbuster musicals 5)...................... the end of their natural lives – even *Cats*, which seemed 6)..................... many more than nine. However, Lloyd Webber probably has a few shows in him yet. He 7) (also)...................... others, like the Bollywood musical *Bombay Dreams*, soon to open at the Apollo Victoria.

(adapted from the Daily Telegraph, Jan 16, 2002)

118

4 Change these sentences so that they are true for you, using the same continuous forms. Compare with a partner.

a) I'm trying to save money for a holiday at the moment.

I'm trying to save money for a new computer.

b) I'm always forgetting to switch off my mobile.

c) When I was a child, my friends were constantly teasing me about my hair.

d) I think public services in my country are improving.

e) I'm spending too much time watching TV these days.

f) I'm concentrating very hard on this exercise.

g) People in my country are definitely getting more health conscious.

h) At about this time yesterday, I was having coffee with friends.

5 Match the prompts a–f with answers 1–6 below. Then make sentences from the prompts, using a continuous verb form. Practise the dialogues.

a) I / wonder / like / go / meal
b) You / always / lose / keys!
c) My eyes / seem / get / worse
d) I / hope / you / could / lend / money
e) you / come / for a drink / after / work?
f) we / wonder / you / could / babysit / for us / tonight?

1 Perhaps you need new glasses.
2 Sorry – I'm really short of cash at the moment.
3 I know, I know, but can you help me look for them?
4 Yes, that would be lovely.
5 Sure, no problem.
6 I can't, – it's my mum's birthday, and I promised to go straight home.

6 Which of the infinitives (with or without *to*) in the sentences below are better in the continuous form?

a) She's not at her desk – she might have lunch.
b) Where's Andrei? He's supposed to do his homework.
c) I really must sort out the mess on my desk.
d) You can't still wash your hair after an hour!
e) Do you think Carl's likely to get here before ten?
f) You seem to spend a lot of time on the phone these days.
g) Joe? He's bound to play with his computer game.
h) Right now, I'd like to lie on a quiet beach with a good book.
i) I'd love to come with you to the park, but I'm busy.

7 Finish each pair of sentences a–g with the correct ending from 1–14. What are the two meanings of the verb in each pair?

a) Oh! I wasn't expecting …
   I've got the new plans here, I expect …

b) That jacket looks …
   Sorry, I wasn't looking – …

c) Are you having …
   I don't have …

d) I really don't feel …
   I've got to sit down – I'm feeling …

e) I really admire …
   We were just admiring …

f) Will these books fit …
   They've been fitting …

g) I've been thinking …
   … and I think …

1 a good time?
2 about what you said.
3 really dizzy.
4 that people are taking me seriously.
5 you to get here so soon!
6 the President for his honesty over the crisis.
7 in your bag? Mine's too small.
8 can you show me again?
9 you'd like to see them.
10 you're probably right.
11 air-conditioning at the office – it's chaos!
12 time to do that now – can someone else do it?
13 the wonderful view from this window.
14 great. You should wear it more often.

8 Complete each sentence with a verb from the box in either the present or past, simple or continuous form.

measure   appear   see   look   expect
feel   have   fit

a) Although the others looked nervous, Hobson .... calm and relaxed.

b) I .... through some old photos and I found this one of you and Elena.

c) I thought I heard the doorbell ring. .... anyone?

d) Chris and his new girlfriend .... a lot of each other at the moment.

e) How .... about Lee's plans for the company?

f) Can you keep the noise down? Mum .... a rest upstairs.

g) 'Why .... that space?' 'It's for the new desk I've bought – I hope it ....'

Perfect verb forms

Ⓐ General

1 Perfect verb forms are used **to link two times**. The speaker is looking back from one point to **the time before that**:

a) the past and the present

Present Perfect Simple: *I've lived here for years.*

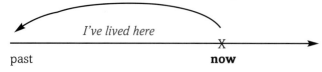

I've lived here

past   **now**

Present Perfect Continuous: *Have you been waiting long?*

b) two points in the past

Past Perfect Simple: *When I got back, they'd all left.*

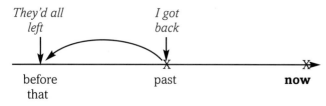

They'd all left   *I got back*

before that   past   **now**

Past Perfect Continuous: *We'd been driving for six hours when we ran out of petrol.*

c) two points in the future

Future Perfect: *By this time tomorrow, I'll have finished all my exams!*

I'll have finished my exams

now   before that   this time tomorrow

Ⓑ Present Perfect Simple and Continuous

1 The Present Perfect Simple links the past and present in a number of different ways:

a) when we are interested in the present result of a past action.

Oh no! The computer's crashed again! (= it's not working now)

There has just been a bad accident on the M6. (= this is news, affecting people now)

b) when an action or state started in the past, but is incomplete or still in progress.

I've been a Manchester United supporter for as long as I can remember.

How long have you known each other?

Or when the period of time in which it takes place is incomplete.

So far this year, there have been a number of exciting new developments.

His girlfriend's phoned about six times today.

> **Notice!**
>
> The Present Perfect **cannot** be used with a time period that is finished.
>
> *Have you been out this morning?*   ✔
>
> *Have you been out last night?*   ✘

c) when an action happened in the past but is still current/relevant in the speaker's mind.

This book has sold over a million copies. (= so it's very successful)

I've been to Italy several times. (= so I know about Italy)

2 A number of time phrases are commonly found with the Present Perfect. These include:

a) present time periods.

today, this week, this year, etc.

b) adverbs whose meaning links the past and present.

for and *since, already, just, recently, ever, never*

c) phrases like *twice, three times, several times,* etc. (see above for examples)

> **Notice!**
>
> We use the Present Perfect in the pattern *the first/second/third time* + clause.
>
> *It's only the second time I've met Harry, but I feel as if we're already friends.*
>
> *Is this the first time you've eaten Korean food?*

3 The Present Perfect Continuous also links the past with the present. The continuous form stresses the duration of the action and so it is commonly found with *how long? for, since, a long time, all day, all week,* etc.

We've been driving for three hours.

I've been rushing around all day.

I'm sorry. Have you been waiting a long time?

When no time expression is used, the continuous form emphasises the recentness of the activity.

I've played squash. (= this could have been at any time up to now)

I've been playing squash. (= and I'm out of breath now)

▶ Exercises 1–2 p.122

C Past Perfect Simple and Continuous

1 The Past Perfect is used to emphasise that one action happened before another action in the past, especially when the sequence is not completely clear from context.

*When I got home, someone **had left** a message on the answer phone.*

*It was obvious from the state of the lock that someone **had tried** to break in.*

Because of this, it is common in reported speech, and after verbs of thought and perception.

*Smith **told** the police he **had never met** the witness before that evening.*

*I **knew** at once that something **had happened**.*

*Miranda **wondered** where her mother **had hidden** the money.*

When the sequence of the actions is obvious, we generally stick to the Past Simple.

*When I **got home**, I **checked** the answer phone for messages.*

2 The Past Perfect is found with some of the same time phrases as the Present Perfect, but they are used in a past context.

*When he met Christina, Jack **had already been** married.*

*It was **the first time I had ever spent** the night by myself in the house.*

*Rosa and Clara **had known** each other **since** their childhood.*

3 We also use the Past Perfect Continuous to describe an action which happened before a particular point in the past. With the continuous form, the speaker sees the action as being repeated or extended.

*We **had** only **been driving** for about fifteen minutes when Jill asked me to stop the car.*

The relationship between the Past Perfect Continuous and the past is the same as the relationship between the Present Perfect Continuous and the present.

*I'**d been trying** to arrange an interview for months. (before she agreed)*

*I'**ve been trying** to arrange an interview for months. (now)*

> **Remember!**
>
> The Past Perfect (Simple and Continuous) is also often used to express the 'unreal' past after words like *if, wish*.
>
> *If you **had been sitting** where I was, you would have had a much better view.*
>
> *I wish I **had** never **met** you!*

▶ Exercises 3–5 p.122

D Other perfect forms

1 We use the **Future Perfect** when we are thinking mainly about one point in the future and want to talk about the time before that. It is 'the past of the future'.

*When her boyfriend gets her letter, she'**ll have left** the country.*

(a point in the future)   (before that)

See Module 9 Language summary

2 We can use a **Perfect -*ing* clause** to mean *when/because* + subject

*__Having__ (= When he had) **completed** his education, he started looking for a new job.*

*__Having__ (= Because I had) **studied** Latin for many years, I found Italian relatively easy.*

The subject of both clauses must be the same.

Because he had passed all his exams, his parents bought him a car.

~~Having passed all his exams his parents bought him a car.~~

▶ Exercise 6 p.123

3 In patterns which are followed by the infinitive form, the Perfect Infinitive *(to) have done* emphasises that we are talking about a past action.

*I'd like **to meet** a famous person. (= present/future)*

*I'd like **to have met** John Lennon. (= past)*

*You should **be** more careful when you're overtaking. (= generally)*

*You should **have been** more careful when you overtook that car. (= past)*

The pattern *would* + perfect infinitive (without *to*) is often used to refer to an 'unreal' past action.

*Without your help, we **would** never **have got** this far.*

▶ Exercises 7–9 p.123

Perfect verb forms

1 Decide if there is any difference in meaning between these pairs of sentences.

a) Have you done your homework?
   Have you been doing your homework?
b) I've lived in this house for over a year.
   I've been living in this house for over a year.
c) Have you been out today?
   Did you go out today?
d) I've been having lots of nightmares.
   I've had lots of nightmares.

2 Cross out the option which is not possible in each of the sentences below.

a) I've seen that movie *three times/a long time/before*.
b) Congratulations! We've *just/never/already* heard the good news!
c) I've been trying to speak to Dr Blake *all day/several times/for hours*. Is he still busy?
d) This isn't good enough Darren – that's the third mistake you've made *for a week/so far this week/since the beginning of the week*!
e) Nicky and Tom have known each other *for ages/since they were little/recently*.
f) Have you been using the computer a lot *lately/in the last few weeks/last week*?

3 Which one of these sentences is correct? Find the mistakes in the others and correct them.

a) I thought I'd remembered everything until I'd got to the church and realised the ring was at home.
b) I'm sorry I'm so late, but I've sat in a traffic jam.
c) I've been looking through your CV and I see that you've been working in three different companies in the last year.
d) I couldn't believe it when Natalia walked in – we'd just talked about her!
e) She said she'd never seen him before in her life, but I know they've met several times.
f) Julia! This is the third time I ask you to be quiet!

4 Put the verbs in brackets into the simple or continuous forms of the Past, Present Perfect or Past Perfect. Then cover the stories and try to remember as much as you can.

a)

When I (1) .... (hear) that Joel
(2) .... (leave) his new job after only a
couple of weeks, I (3) .... (not/be)
particularly surprised. This (4) ....
(happen) several times before. But when he (5) ......
.... (not/answer) any of my phone
messages, I (6) .... (phone) the company
and (7) .... (find out) that he
(8) .... (go) to prison for six months!
Apparently, he (9) .... (steal) money from
the till! I was shocked – I (10) ....
.... (know) Joel for years and he's one of
the most honest people I (11) ....
.... (ever/meet). I'm sure the police
(12) .... (make) a terrible mistake.

b)

Two teenagers who (1) .... (be)
missing since Tuesday (2) .... (arrive)
home safe and well last night. The two sisters, who
(3) .... (leave) home after a family
argument, (4) .... (hide) in woods
a few kilometres from their home. They
(5) .... (not/intend) to stay away for
long, but they (6) .... (get) lost in the
woods and (7) .... (decide) to wait
until somebody came looking for them. Their mother
Helen said she (8) .... (never/give up)
hope of finding them alive.

5 Write or discuss your answers to these questions. Then make new questions to ask, changing some of the words in **bold**.

a) How many **emails** have you **sent** today?
b) How long have you **known** your **best friend**?
c) How many **cups of coffee** had you **had** by **8.00 last night**?
d) How long had you been **learning English** when you first **read a newspaper or a book in English**?
e) Is this the first time you've **studied** the **Past Perfect Continuous**?
f) Is there **anything** you wish you **hadn't said** today?

6 Which four pairs of sentences below can be joined by starting with a perfect participle (*Having* + past participle)? How can the other two be joined?

a) I waited ages for a bus. I decided to walk home.
b) We saw the weather forecast. We decided not to go away for the weekend.
c) I've been here lots of times before. The waiters all know me.
d) The directors have considered all the options. They have decided to close ten regional branches.
e) John's told so many lies in the past. Nobody will believe him this time.
f) Patrick left school with very few qualifications. He found it difficult to get a job.

7 Match a sentence from 1–8 with a response from a–h. Put the verb in brackets in the infinitive, e.g. *(to) go*, or the perfect infinitive, e.g. *(to) have gone*.

1 I'm glad Max didn't come to the film with us.
2 I haven't seen Marti at all lately.
3 Shall we sit in one of these seats here?
4 I've looked everywhere for the cat – he's not here!
5 Hari was really shocked when he opened his present.
6 I'm feeling really exhausted at the moment.
7 Some people were badly injured in the explosion.
8 How did Raul get into the show? It was sold out.

a) I'd prefer .... (sit) nearer the front, if you don't mind.
b) Yeah, but they're lucky .... (survive).
c) I know, she seems .... (disappear).
d) Well, maybe you should .... (take) a few days off work.
e) He pretended .... (be) a sound technician!
f) Don't worry, he can't .... (go) very far.
g) Oh, I'd love .... (see) his face!
h) Me too – he wouldn't .... (enjoy) it.

8 Finish each sentence so that it means the same as the one before it.

a) I'd been to the restaurant once before.
   It ....
b) Sue was very nervous because she'd never flown before.
   Having ....
c) You started trying to give up smoking months ago!
   You've ....
d) It's ages since we enjoyed ourselves so much.
   We ....
e) I bet Sasha's sorry she bought that car.
   I bet Sasha ....
f) I'm glad I didn't live in the 18th century.
   I wouldn't ....

9 Underline all the perfect verb forms in the jokes and explain the use of the perfect form in each case.

a) Patient: Doctor, I'm very nervous. This is the first time I've ever had an operation.
   Doctor: Don't worry, this is the first time I've ever performed an operation.

b) Q: Why did the plastic surgeon collapse?
   A: Because he'd been sitting too near the fire.

c) A: I've come to repair your doorbell.
   B: You should have come earlier, I'm just going out.
   A: But I've been standing on your doorstep all morning ringing your bell.

d) A: Did you meet your son at the airport?
   B: No, I've known him for years!

e) A: I've changed my mind.
   B: Oh good, does the new one work any better?

f) (Can you find the misprint?)
   Foreign ministers today declared that their summit meeting had been a hug success.

123

Modals

Ⓐ General

1 Modals are auxiliary verbs used to give a **judgement** or **interpretation** about an action or state.

The following verbs are often classified as 'full' modal verbs with the features below:

can   could   may   might   must
will   would   shall   should

- they do not have infinitive forms or the 3rd person 's' or tenses

- the negative is formed by adding *not/n't* to the verb

- the question is formed by inverting the modal and the pronoun

- they are followed by the infinitive form without *to*.

2 The following are often referred to as 'semi-modals'. They follow some, but not all, of the above rules. (See F on p.125)

need   dare   have to   ought to

Ⓑ Possibility/probability

1 **Could**, **might** and **may** refer to specific present/future possibilities.

*Steve isn't here, but he **could/might/may** ~~can~~ be in the canteen.*

*They say that it **could/may/might** ~~can~~ snow this year.*

We can make the probability greater by adding *well*.

*This could/might/may **well** be McNally's last appearance at a World Championship.*

2 **Can** is only used to refer to general (or 'theoretical') possibilities.

*In summer, the temperature here **can** reach 35°.*

*Lisa **can** be really moody sometimes.*

3 **Could/may/might have** + **past participle** can all be used to mean that something possibly happened.

*Jay **may/could/might've phoned** while we were out.*

We also use the past form *could have* to say that it was possible for something to happen, but it didn't.

*We **could have taken** a taxi, but we decided to walk home instead.* (= this didn't happen)

4 We can also use **should** to talk about present or future probability. It shows that the speaker is fairly certain about something.

*Have a look in my pockets – the car keys **should** be there.*

*You **shouldn't** have to wait too long, Mr Carr.*

▶ Exercise 1 p.126

Ⓒ Ability and willingness

1 **Can** and **be able to** express ability. The past forms are **could/was able to**.

a) We only use **could** as the past of **can** when we talk about general ability.

*When I was younger, I **could** touch my nose with my feet.*

(= this was something I could do if I wanted to)

b) To talk about a specific event, we use **managed to** or **was able to**.

*Although he was badly injured, he **managed/was able to** crawl his way to safety.* (= This was something he did)

c) **Can** or **could** are often used with verbs of perception.

*I **can** smell something burning.*

*I **could** hear music coming from the upstairs room.*

d) There are a number of other common 'fixed phrases' with **can('t)**.

*can('t) afford   can('t) stand (= hate)
I can imagine   I can't bear it!*

2 **Will** is often used to express that you are willing to do something now, or in the future.

*I'**ll** do the washing-up. You sit down and have a rest.*

- The negative form **won't** expresses unwillingness or refusal to do something.

*Mum, Holly **won't** play with me.*

*I **won't** lower the price, and that's that.*

- To talk about the past, **wouldn't** can mean 'refused to'.

*We tried everything but he **wouldn't** cooperate.*

This can also be used with inanimate objects.

*My car **wouldn't** start.*

▶ Exercises 2–3 p.126

Ⓓ Permission and requests

1 **Can** and **could** are used for both permission and requests.

***Can/Could** I get past, please?*

***Can/Could** you give me a hand to lift this?*

2 **May** and **might** are only used for permission.

***May/Might** I borrow your newspaper for a moment?*

~~**May** you feed the cats for a few days while we're away?~~

3 **Will** and **would** are only used for requests.

***Will/Would** you just wait here for a minute, please?*

~~**Will** I borrow your telephone to call home?~~

4 **May**, **might**, **could** and **would** are more tentative, and therefore more polite than *can* and *will*. However, polite intonation is probably more important than the choice of modal.

▶ Exercises 4–5 p.126

E Obligation/necessity

1 *Must*

a) *Have to* or *have got to* are more common in speech to talk about obligation than *must*, particularly when we talk about obligations which are externally imposed.

*You **have (got) to** be eighteen to vote.*

Must is more often seen in written English, however.

*Applicants **must** be over 18 years of age.* (= from an application form)

The negative of *must* for this kind of obligation is *must not* and the past is *had to*.

*Applicants **must not** be over 35 years of age.*

*When I was young, you **had to** be twenty-one before you could go in nightclubs.*

b) *Must* is often used for advice or recommendation, because it expresses the speaker's sense that this is necessary or important.

*It's an absolutely brilliant film. You **must** go to see it.*

Have to is less common in this context.

c) *Must* also expresses logical necessity (logical deduction).

*That **must be** Isabel's sister, she looks so like her!*

The negative of *must* here is *can't* and the past is *must have*.

*That **can't be** your mother, she looks far too young.*

*Laura **must have gone** home, she's not here.*

2 *Will* is also commonly used for logical necessity.

*Is that the doorbell? It**'ll** be the pizza delivery.*

*It's 8 o'clock, he**'ll** probably have left the office by now.*

3 *Should* is used to talk about the right thing to do. The past is *should have/shouldn't have*.

*These files **shouldn't be** in here – put them in Joel's office.*

*You **should have listened** more carefully to what I said.*

▶ Exercises 6–7 p.127

F Semi-modals

1 *Have to/don't have to* are used to express obligation/lack of obligation.

Note that we use auxiliaries to form questions and negatives.

*What time **do we have to** be there?*

*I**'ve never had to** work as hard as I'm doing at the moment.*

2 *Ought* has the same meaning as *should*. Unlike *should*, it is followed by the infinitive with *to*.

*It's well after midnight. You **ought to be** in bed by now.*

- The past form is *ought to have*.

  *We really **ought to have booked** – there don't seem to be any tables.*

- The negative and question forms are *ought not to* and *ought (I) to*, but *Should* or *Do you think we ought to …?* are preferred.

  *You **ought not to/shouldn't** shout – someone might hear you.*

  ***Do you think we ought to/Should we** ask for the bill?*

3 *Need* can be used as a normal verb, followed by an infinitive (with *to*), a noun or *-ing* form. The past form is *needed*.

*Do you **need to** go to the bathroom?*

*My jacket **needs** clean**ing** – can you take it to the cleaner's?*

- However, the negative has a modal form *needn't*. (Notice that the normal negative form *don't need to* has the same meaning).

  *You **needn't/don't need to** tell me if you don't want to.*

- The past form also has a modal form, *needn't have*. This expresses that something happened which wasn't necessary.

  *You **needn't have** brought milk – I've already got plenty in the fridge.* (= you did it but it was unnecessary)

  This is different from *didn't need to* which simply expresses that it wasn't necessary to do something.

  Because it was Sunday, we didn't need to get up early. (= it was unnecessary, so we probably didn't do it)

- *Needn't/Need I*, etc. are also found in a few fixed phrases, such as:

  You needn't bother. (= often sarcastic, meaning it's not necessary to do something)

  ***Need I** say more?* (= isn't it obvious?)

4 *Dare* is used in the negative and question forms to mean *have the courage to do something*.

*I **daren't** tell him the truth in case he fires me.*

- The past is usually formed with the auxiliary verb *didn't*.

  *I **didn't dare** (to) ask her what had happened.*

- There are certain fixed expressions where the modal form of *dare* is used.

  *I **dare say** (= expect) you'll have a lot of questions.*

  ***How dare you** suggest that I treated you dishonestly!* (= I am very shocked/angry by …)

  ***Don't you dare** make fun of the way I speak!* (= a strong warning not to do something)

▶ Exercises 8–9 p.127

Modals

1 Decide if there is any difference in meaning between these pairs of sentences.

a) They could have missed the train.
They may have missed the train.

b) There may well be severe flooding in the next few days.
There could well be severe flooding in the next few days.

c) It can take up to two hours to reach the top of the tower.
It could take up to two hours to reach the top of the tower.

d We should have another delivery of that paint tomorrow morning.
We could have another delivery of that paint tomorrow morning.

e) He could have sold his story to the newspaper.
He might have sold his story to the newspaper.

2 Rewrite the phrases in bold in this story, using a modal verb.

When her dog Belle (1) **was not willing to eat** her food one evening, Carrie Young became suspicious. 'I called her, but (2) she **was not even able to get up** from her basket. I (3) **was able to see** that something was very wrong.' Vet Andy Marshall found that Belle  had eaten nearly 2 kilos of small stones from the garden path. He (4) **was successful in removing** all the stones in a two-hour operation, and now Belle is recovering after her strange meal. (5) 'It **was possible for Belle to die**,' said Andy. Carrie has taken his words seriously and is replacing all the stones with bigger, less edible ones. (6) 'Belle **will probably be** safe in the garden now,' she smiles.

3 Complete these sentences so that they are true for you.

a) At the moment I can hear ....
b) When I was a child, my parents wouldn't let me ....
c) I can't stand people who ....
d) I have never managed to learn ....
e) I can see .... from my bedroom window.
f) A few years ago I couldn't .... , but now I can/and I still can't.
g) My friends annoy me when they won't ....
h) I sometimes dream about being able to ....

4 Cross out the option which is not possible in six of the sentences below. (In two sentences, all three options are possible).

a) Please *may/could/would* I use your mobile to make a quick call?
b) *Could/May/Can* you get some coffee when you go out?
c) Pass me those scissors, *will you?/may you?/can you?*
d) *Will/May/Can* we have a look round, if that's okay?
e) Perhaps we *might/could/would* discuss this in private, if you don't mind.
f) *Can/Could/Will* you turn that music down, please?
g) *Could/Can/Will* I *have* the day off tomorrow, please?
h) Hold this for me, *can you?/would you?/could you?*

5 Write a request or permission question to match the response given.

a) '... ?'
'OK, as long as you pay me back by the weekend.'

b) '... ?'
'Do you have an appointment, madam?'

c) '... ?'
'Yeah, alright – leave it in the sink and I'll do it later.'

d) '... ?'
'Well ... how long for? She got very upset last time.'

e) '... ?'
'If you've finished all your work, yes.'

f) '... ?'
'Sorry, we only take cash or cheques.'

6 Which of these sentences are likely to be written or spoken? Complete the gaps with a modal verb of obligation. If there is more than one possibility, explain the difference in meaning.

a) Rooms .... (vacate) by noon.

b) He's not in – oh, I know, he .... (take) the children swimming.

c) Passengers .... (leave) luggage unattended.

d) I .... (work) late all week – we've got a big order to finish.

e) You .... (carry) that – the doctor told you to be careful.

f) Marc's in a good mood – he .... (see) the phone bill yet.

g) Hurry up! Dad .... (wait) for us.

h) All mobile phones .... (switch off) in this area.

7 Rewrite these sentences using the verbs *must(n't), will/won't, can't, should(n't), have to.*

a) Is it necessary for you to carry an ID card in your country?

....

b) It is the government's obligation to act quickly to stop street crime.

....

c) I'm sure that's Tamzin's purse – she's just phoned up about it.

....

d) I strongly advise you not to miss the Allstars concert on Sunday night.

....

e) I'm sure you drove like a maniac to get here so quickly!

....

f) It was wrong for you to take the car without asking me.

....

g) How long was it necessary for you to wait for your visa?

....

h) Ring Tim later – it's unlikely that he's had time to unpack yet.

....

8 Complete the gaps with an appropriate form of the semi-modal *ought to, have to, dare* or *need.*

1 I'd love to stay a bit longer, but our babysitter .... leave at 11.

2 You .... do everything he says, do you?

3 I really hate .... wear this stupid uniform!

4 We .... left a bit earlier – we're going to be terribly late.

5 We .... discuss it now if it's inconvenient.

6 I must do something about this room – it .... completely reorganising.

7 Don't .... tell Lisa about the credit card bill – she'll go mad.

8 Sven .... admit that he'd deleted the wrong document.

9 You .... got all dressed up – it's not really a formal dinner.

10 I know it was wrong to steal those sweets, but Lenny .... me to.

9 Match the sentences a–i with answers 1–9.

a) He doesn't live here anymore – he moved away just last month.

b) Come on, keep going. It's not much further.

c) She was in the shop for ages, deciding which mobile phone to get.

d) You sit down – I'll finish clearing up.

e) Did you ask them to refund the money?

f) Phone him and apologise for what you said.

g) I'm sure she didn't mean to upset you.

h) I got you these – to say thanks for everything.

i) Go on, have another slice of cake.

1 I shouldn't really.

2 Yes, but they wouldn't.

3 I can't!

4 He can't have!

5 Oh, you shouldn't have!

6 I dare say.

7 You don't have to.

8 Must I?

9 I can imagine.

Adjectives and adverbs

Ⓐ Word order

1 Adjectives normally come before nouns (*attributive* adjectives) or after verbs like *be, become, look, seem, get,* etc. (*predicative* adjectives)

*We had a **fantastic** holiday.* (attributive)

*Our holiday was **fantastic**.* (predicative)

Most adjectives can be used in both ways.

a) Some adjectives are always attributive, so are only found before nouns.

the **chief** executive	the **only** solution
utter chaos	the **entire/whole** performance
further (= additional) information	**sheer** genius
the **main** difference	the **previous/former** President
a **mere** detail	the **western/southern** border

b) Some adjectives are always predicative, so are only found after verbs.

*I was still **awake** at 2 a.m.*

*She got quite **upset** about her exam results.*

*You two look **alike**.*

c) Sometimes, to express the same meaning, a different adjective is used in the two positions.

*The children **were afraid** of the dark.* (predicative)

*The **frightened children** ran out of the bedroom.* (attributive)

*She **has been ill** for some time.* (predicative)

*There were a lot of **sick people**.* (attributive)

d) Other adjectives change slightly according to whether they are attributive or predicative.

Attributive	Predicative
a **lone** gunman	The gunman was **alone**.
live animals	The animals were **alive**.
a sleeping **baby**	The baby was **asleep**.
a **drunken** argument	The men were **drunk**.
my **elder** sister	My sister is **older** than me.

▶ Exercise 1 p.130

2 Other rules of word order:

a) general before specific

*an **old Hungarian** folk tale*

b) opinion before description

***important domestic** issues*

c) *the first* and *the last* normally come before numbers.

*We are on holiday **the first** week in May.*

▶ Exercise 2 p.130

Ⓑ Compound adjectives

Compound adjectives consist of two or more words which are usually hyphenated.

a) The second part of the compound adjective is often a present or past participle form.

*a **mouth-watering** meal   a **well-known** brand*

b) Some compound adjectives are derived from phrasal or prepositional verbs.

***worn-out** shoes   the most **talked-about** play in London*

c) Compound adjectives are often found with numbers. The noun is in the singular form in these cases.

*a **two-week** holiday   a **hundred-mile** journey*

We can also add another adjective after the noun, with a second hyphen.

*a **25-year-old** man   a **three-mile-long** queue of cars*

d) We add *-like* (= similar to) and *-friendly* (= helpful to) to nouns to form compound adjectives.

*a **child-friendly** environment*

*a **dream-like** state*

e) Many compound adjectives describing appearance are formed with noun + *-ed*.

*a man with **dark hair**   >   a **dark-haired** man*

*a dress with **short sleeves**   >   a **short-sleeved** dress*

▶ Exercise 3 p.130

Ⓒ Prefixes and suffixes

1 We often use prefixes to modify the meaning of an adjective. Some of the most common prefixes are:

anti-	= against	**anti**-war, **anti**-government
bi-	= two	**bi**annual, **bi**lingual
dis-	= the opposite of	**dis**honest, **dis**orderly
in-	= not	**in**complete, **in**competent
inter-	= between	**inter**active, **inter**continental
mal-	= badly	**mal**adjusted, **mal**odorous
mis-	= wrongly/badly	**mis**guided, **mis**informed
mono-	= one	**mono**lingual, **mono**syllabic
multi-	= many	**multi**-purpose, **multi**-cultural
out-	= beyond, outside	**out**dated, **out**lying
over-	= too much	**over**active, **over**worked
post-	= after	**post**-war, **post**-industrial
pre-	= before	**pre**-war, **pre**-industrial
pro-	= in favour of	**pro**-western, **pro**-European
semi-	= half	**semi**-precious, **semi**-professional
sub-	= under, below	**sub**tropical, **sub**conscious
un-	= not	**un**important, **un**grateful
under-	= not enough	**under**cooked, **under**paid

There is no simple way of knowing whether prefixes require a hyphen. Check in a good learner's dictionary.

2 The following suffixes also help form adjectives:

-*able* = (can be)	adjust**able**, believ**able**, break**able**
-*al*	economic**al**, historic**al**, digit**al**
-*ful*	cheer**ful**, truth**ful**, hope**ful**
-*ic*	electr**ic**, symphon**ic**, atmospher**ic**
-*ish* = (quite, not very)	tall**ish**, redd**ish**, warm**ish**
-*ive*	impress**ive**, respons**ive**, invent**ive**
-*less* = (without)	cord**less**, stain**less**, fear**less**
-*ous*	humor**ous**, luxuri**ous**, harmoni**ous**
-*y*	mist**y**, hand**y**, pric**ey**

▶ Exercises 4–6 p.130–131

Ⓓ Gradable and ungradable adjectives

1 Ungradable adjectives have either a very strong meaning, e.g. *fantastic, appalling, unbelievable,* or an absolute meaning, e.g. *unique, right, wrong.*

These 'absolute adjectives' do not normally have a comparative or superlative form.

2 Gradable adjectives can follow words like *very* and *quite* and have comparative and superlative forms, e.g. *very/quite/more/the most interesting, expensive, attractive,* etc.

Ⓔ Adverbs of degree

1 Highest degree

Absolutely indicates the highest degree. Normally it is only used with ungradable adjectives.

*We are **absolutely delighted** to welcome you all here.*

*The weather was **absolutely awful** over the weekend.*

Other adverbs which are used in a similar way: *completely, totally, utterly.*

2 High degree

a) *Very* and *really* are used in British English to indicate high degree. Note that *really* can be used with both gradable and ungradable adjectives, but *very* can only be used with gradable adjectives.

Thank you for a really/~~very~~ wonderful evening.

It was a really/very interesting experience for everyone involved.

In American English, *real* is preferred to *really* in this case.

b) We can add emphasis to *very* by repeating **very** (informal, spoken).

*I'm just **very, very tired** … that's all.*

Or by adding *indeed* (more formal).

*We were both **very tired indeed** by the time we drew up to the hotel.*

c) Note that in British English *not very* + adjective with a positive meaning can be used instead of an adjective with a negative meaning.

*How was the film?   It wasn**'t very good**. (= it was bad)*

d) Similarly we can use *not that* + adjective to say it's not as much as you might expect.

*She would never marry someone she's only just met: she's **not that stupid**.*

▶ Exercise 7 p.131

3 Middle/low degree

Pretty, **rather** and **quite** all indicate middle degree.

a) *Pretty* is common in speech, particularly with positive adjectives.

*We were **pretty happy** with the way we played.*

b) *Rather* is more commonly used with negative adjectives.

*Do you mind if I close the window ? It's **rather cold** in here.*

In British English, *rather* + positive adjective means 'more than was expected'.

*I expected her to be absolutely furious at my suggestion, but in fact she was **rather pleased**.*

c) *Quite* also expresses middle degree with gradable adjectives.

*It was **quite easy** to understand what their gestures meant.*

With ungradable adjectives, *quite* has the meaning of 'completely'.

*I'm afraid it's **quite impossible** (= completely impossible) for you to see Ms Hanson today.*

d) *A bit*, *a little* and *slightly* are all used to indicate low degree. They are normally only used before adjectives with a negative meaning.

*I'm just **a bit worried** you won't find your way … shall I come and get you?*

*On the way home, I began to feel **slightly** ill.*

A bit is less formal than *a little* and *slightly*. However, we often use *a bit, a little, slightly* + comparative adjective with a positive meaning.

How are you feeling today?

*Oh, **a bit/slightly/a little** better, thanks.*

▶ Exercises 8–9 p.131

Adjectives and adverbs

1 Rewrite these sentences correctly so that the adjective in bold is in the correct position or form. (You may need to make other changes to the sentences.)

a) He has a daughter from a marriage which was **previous**.
b) Do you think that difference is **only** between the two computers?
c) What problem seems to be **main**, in your opinion?
d) He tiptoed past the **asleep** guards and ran towards the main door.
e) The roads are full of **afraid** people leaving the city.
f) Too many **ill** people go to work when they should really stay at home and rest.

2 Complete the gaps with the adjectives in brackets, in a logical order (sometimes there is more than one possibility).

a) We recommend 'The Croft', a .... farmhouse in beautiful surroundings, serving a .... breakfast. (*traditional, stone, charming, English*)
b) What was the .... spending of a .... family in the 1950s? (*British, average, typical, weekly*)
c) The combination of .... actors and .... effects make this film a definite contender for an Oscar this year. (*young, state-of-the-art, talented, spectacular*)
d) Click on this site to find out all about the .... concerts and a variety of .... events in your area. (*musical, summer, outdoor, forthcoming*)

3 a) Match the extracts with the text types in the box.

> a TV review   a holiday brochure
> a clothing catalogue   a novel
> an advertisement for accommodation

1 Wear this shirt which fits loosely and has long sleeves with our trousers which have straight legs and boots with high heels. (4)

2 Don't miss the first episode of the psychological thriller in three parts, *Scream Now*, a story which provokes thought featuring a cast who are all stars. (3)

3 This apartment with two bedrooms has a sitting room which is a good size and a balcony which faces south with views that reach a long way. (4)

4 Jenna smiled as her daughter who was 10 years old tipped out the contents of her schoolbag: a birthday card which someone had made at home, an apple which she had eaten half of, a sandwich which was three days old, and a pair of trainers which were covered in mud. (5)

5 Discover the delights of Greece on a tour which lasts five days. Stay in hotels which have three stars and are run by families, and sample food which is cooked at home and local wines. Representatives who speak English are always available to make your stay as easy as possible. (5)

b) Rewrite the extracts using compound adjectives to make them sound more natural. The number of compound adjectives is given in brackets.

4 Match a prefix to an adjective in the box below. Then complete the sentences with the newly-formed adjectives.

> anti-   dis-   in-   mal-   mis-   over-   post-   un-

> .... crowded   .... connected
> .... nuclear   .... grateful
> .... tolerant   .... leading
> .... dated   .... treated

a) I'm fed up with working in an ....overcrowded.... office with no air-conditioning!
b) There was a crowd of .... protesters blocking the entrance to the site.
c) I thought the President made some very .... comments about taxes in the interview.
d) Mr Stevens let me give him a .... cheque for the rent.
e) I thought his new book was terrible – just a collection of .... ideas.
f) Our elderly neighbours have a rather .... attitude towards young people.
g) Callie said some very .... things about the advice I gave her – I was only trying to help!
h) A lot of the organisation's money is spent on rescuing .... animals.

5 Choose a suitable prefix from the box to complete the adjectives. Ask and answer the questions.

> dis   pre-   hi-   multi-   anti-
> sub-   inter-   mono-   over-   under-

a) Do you know anyone who is ....lingual?
b) Why is it a good idea to use a ....lingual English dictionary?
c) Have you ever felt ....dressed for an occasion?
d) Who do you think is the most ....rated film actor at the moment?
e) Would you sign a ....nuptial contract?
f) Do you think smoking in public places is .... social?
g) Have you ever been on an ....continental flight?
h) Would you complain if you were ....satisfied with the food or service in a restaurant?
i) How often do you have ....zero temperatures in your country?
j) What ....purpose gadgets can you think of?

6 Which objects in the box can be:

a) cordless? ....
b) very pricey? ....
c) informative? ....
d) digital? ....
e) washable? ....
f) electric? ....
g) adjustable? ....
h) harmful? ....

> a drill   a radio   a soft toy   a lamp
> a microwave oven   a telephone
> a watchstrap   a toothbrush

7 Cross out any options which are not possible in the sentences below. (Sometimes both options are possible.)

a) I'm *really/very* pleased that you are coming with us and I know the children will be *really/very* delighted.
b) This is a *very/totally* unique piece of jewellery, and I am certain that it's *very/absolutely* valuable.
c) I was *very very/very* relieved indeed when I got to the hospital.
d) Claude thinks Ingrid's *absolutely/very* stunning, but I didn't think she was *that/very* attractive when I met her.
e) It may have been the most entertaining explanation you've ever heard, but it was also *completely/the most* wrong.

8 Tick (✔) the sentences where the adverbs of degree are used correctly. Correct the others, using *pretty, rather, quite, a bit, a little, slightly*.

a) It's going to be pretty hot today – make sure you put on some suntan cream.
b) I know it's a shabby old sofa, but it's actually slightly comfortable to sit on.
c) I'm going to have an early night – I'm rather exhausted after all that decorating.
d) Are you feeling a bit calmer now?
e) I was a bit pleased with the way the children behaved today.
f) I'm rather sure that's the turning, coming up on the left.
g) Mr Quirk is slightly concerned about the number of days you have had off recently.
h) It's quite ridiculous to expect members of staff to accept a pay freeze.

9 Complete the gaps in these film reviews with an adjective or adverb from the box. Sometimes there is more than one possibility.

> absolutely   highly acclaimed   box-office
> delightful   rather   magical   impressive
> eccentric   11-year-old   toenail   world-
> famous   heart-warming

Harry Potter and the Philosopher's Stone

A 1) .... whirlwind of a movie as JK Rowling's 2) .... wizard is brought to life on the big screen with 3) .... breathtaking results. The 4) .... cast includes Robbie Coltrane.

Amélie

A 5) .... smash in France and the winner of several awards, this movie is about a 6) .... lonely, 7) .... woman who spreads 8) .... joy.

Gabriel & Me

From the 9) .... writer of *Billy Elliot* comes this absolutely 10) .... tale of an 11) .... boy who wants to become an angel. Billy Connolly wears silver 12) .... varnish to play the archangel Gabriel.

Passive forms

Ⓐ Passive forms with *be*

1 In passive sentences, the subject of the sentences is **not** the doer of the verb ('the agent') – unlike active sentences.

| Someone | stole my purse.   (Active)
(SUBJECT)

| My purse | was stolen.   (Passive)
(SUBJECT)

2 Normally the agent is not included in a passive sentence because it is unimportant or obvious who the agent is, or because we want to avoid saying who is responsible.

*A man **is being interviewed** in connection with the attack.*

*Several people **were injured** in the explosion.*

*The relevant documents **have been lost**.*

But if the agent is of particular interest, we use **by**:

*Paper money was invented **by the Chinese**.*

3 Note the passive of *-ing* forms.

*Don't you ever worry about **being attacked**?*

*He was upset at **having been omitted** from the final list.*

4 The passive infinitive form (without *to*) is often used after modal verbs.

*There is no limit to what **can be achieved**.*

*I very much doubt whether he **will be allowed** to continue.*

*I really think he **should be given** another opportunity.*

5 Some verbs are not usually used in the passive form. Some of the most important are:

a) intransitive verbs such as *arrive, happen, come, fall, crash*.

He ~~was~~ arrived late.

b) state verbs such as *consist, belong, have, seem, be, depend, exist*.

The Baltic States consist ~~are consisted~~ of Latvia, Lithuania and Estonia.

▶ Exercise 1 p.134

6 Some verbs are most often found in common passive phrases.

*Children **aren't allowed to** smoke in school.*

*Some pupils in the school **are involved** in crime.*

*We**'re supposed to** hand in our projects today.*

*I**'m not used to** late nights any more.*

Ⓑ Using passive forms

1 Normally, the beginning of a sentence tells us what the topic is, and new information is added at the end. When the topic of the sentence is not the agent, the passive is used.

*The Guggenheim Museum in New York **was designed** by Frank Lloyd Wright. It is currently situated in 5th Avenue, but there are plans to move it to Wall Street.*
(the topic is the Guggenheim Museum)

*Frank Lloyd Wright **designed** several well-known buildings, including the Imperial Hotel in Tokyo and the Guggenheim Museum in New York. He died In 1959.*
(the topic is Frank Lloyd Wright)

▶ Exercise 2 p.134

2 We often use the passive when we want a style that is impersonal and objective. For this reason, the passive is common in academic writing and newspaper reports.

*Water **is released** from the reservoir to the turbine.*
(scientific text)

*Italian singer Martina Barrotti **has been cleared** of tax evasion in an Italian court.*
(newspaper article)

The passive is often avoided in less formal contexts (see below).

3 The passive is often used with reporting verbs like *believe* and *think*. These constructions are common in formal writing.

People believe that Bill Gates is the richest man in the US.
(active)

*Bill Gates **is believed to be** the richest man in the US.*
(passive)

It is believed that Bill Gates is the richest man in the US.
(passive)

Other verbs commonly used in this way are: *allege, assume, consider, expect, intend, rumour, know, report, suppose, think, understand.*

*It **is rumoured** that the President is about to resign.*

*The multi-millionaire businessman **was alleged** to have committed fraud.*

*It **is not** yet **known** whether there are any survivors of the attack.*

▶ Exercise 3 p.134

Ⓒ Passive forms without *be*

1 *Be* is often omitted in newspaper headlines.

ENGLAND ~~IS~~ BEATEN AT FOOTBALL

HUNDREDS ~~ARE~~ MADE HOMELESS BY FLOODS

▶ Exercise 4 p.134

2 In relative clauses using passive constructions, the relative pronoun and verb *to be* can be omitted. This is known as a 'reduced relative clause'.

the people (who were) chosen to appear on the show (= the people chosen to appear on the show)

the best play (which has ever been) written (= the best play ever written)

▶ Exercise 5 p.135

3 Passives are often used as adjectives at the beginning of a sentence. This is a fairly formal usage, and is more common in writing.

Locked *away in his prison cell room, he gradually fell into despair.*

Released *in two days' time, 'The South' is probably Manuel Garcia's most ambitious film so far.*

Ⓓ Verbs with two objects

1 Some verbs have two objects, indirect and direct.

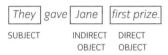

They	gave	Jane	first prize.
SUBJECT		INDIRECT OBJECT	DIRECT OBJECT

In the passive form, the indirect or direct object can become the subject of the sentence.

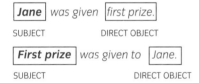

Jane	was given	first prize.
SUBJECT		DIRECT OBJECT

First prize	was given to	Jane.
SUBJECT		DIRECT OBJECT

2 Some other verbs which follow this pattern: *ask, give, hand, lend, offer, pay, promise, show, teach, tell.*

▶ Exercise 6 p.135

Ⓔ Passive forms with *get* and *have*

1 We often use *have* + past participle to talk about services which we arrange and which are paid for, or for things you experience, which may be unpleasant.

*It's really cheap to **have your ears pierced** in this shop.*

*I **had** my bag **stolen** while I was on the Underground.*

2 We can use *get* + past participle for actions which are accidental or unexpected.

*Unfortunately, I fell asleep in the sun and my shoulders **got burned***.

*It's inevitable that some things **get broken** when you move house.*

3 We can also use *get* + past participle when the process is in some way difficult.

*It's taken a long time, but Christopher finally **got** his novel **published***.

4 There are also a large number of idiomatic expressions where *get* + past participle is used to mean 'yourself', e.g.

get dressed (= dress yourself), *get undressed, get changed, get engaged, get lost, get started.*

Passives with *get* are generally more colloquial than passives with *be*.

The couple were married in Rome. (= more formal)

The couple got married in Rome. (= more informal)

▶ Exercises 7–8 p.135

Ⓕ Avoiding the passive

In conversation and other informal contexts, people often avoid the passive, because it sounds more formal. Active verbs with 'impersonal' pronouns like *you, we* and *they* are preferred. Compare the examples:

• ***They arrested*** *him this morning.* (colloquial style; *they* = 'the authorities')
He was arrested *this morning.* (more formal style)

• ***They say*** *he's a multi millionaire.* (usual in conversation – we also use *people* as the subject here)
He is said *to be a multimillionaire.* (formal contexts only)

• ***We use*** *the passive less in conversation.* (less formal)
*The passive **is used** less in conversation.* (more formal)

• ***You should replace*** *the cartridge every three months.* (verbal instructions)
*The cartridge **should be replaced** every three months.* (written instructions)

> **Notice!**
>
> The pronoun *one* also exists in English, but is considered excessively formal by most younger speakers, and is therefore avoided.
>
> ~~One~~ ***You*** *have to be careful here after dark.*

Passive forms

1 Correct the forms in bold.

a) You're late – what **was happened**?

b) That contract isn't worth the paper **it's write** on.

c) She must get tired **of following** everywhere by the paparazzi.

d) My car **was broken down** on the way to the airport and I missed my plane.

e) Do you think Sophie **should be tell** about the accident?

f) I used to **love been taken** to the cinema by my elder brother.

g) I was terrified – we **could be killed**!

h) The cat **was disappeared** one morning and we haven't seen him since.

2 Rewrite these encyclopedia entries so that the topic is at the beginning of each sentence. You will need to change some active forms into the passive, and some passive forms into the active.

a) **Agatha Christie** was an English detective novelist. People know her best for her ingenious plots and for the creation of Hercule Poirot. More than 70 novels were written by her, and they have filmed a number of her books.

b) **Florida** is the southeasternmost state of the USA. People nickname it the Sunshine State. Florida joined the Union in 1845 as the 27th US state. It is popular with tourists and has a thriving cosmopolitan community. Georgia and Alabama border it to the north.

c) **Coco Chanel** was a French fashion designer and trendsetter. Chanel perfumes and 'the little black dress' were created by her, and people have copied her designs all over the world. Her wish for simple, practical clothes inspired her designs and her 'look' was widely influential for many years.

d) **The London Eye** is a huge vertical wheel situated by the River Thames in London. The architects designed it to symbolise the turning of the century. Passengers are taken on a 30-minute flight with views as far as Windsor castle. British Airways sponsored the wheel, but due to technical problems they could not open it on December 31st 1999. They finally opened it to the public on March 1st 2000.

3 Rewrite these sentences using reporting verbs and passive structures.

Example: Everyone knows that the couple are in Mexico.

It is known that the couple are in Mexico.

The couple are known to be in Mexico.

a) There are rumours that Madonna and Gwyneth Paltrow are among the guests at the Versace show.

....

b) We understand that the Princess is expecting her first baby.

....

c) We have reports that an anonymous telephone buyer paid over £2 million for one of Diana's dresses.

....

d) Some people allege that the minister for transport accepted bribes in excess of €15,000.

....

e) Experts think that a recently discovered portrait of Picasso is a fake.

....

f) Organisers expect over 5,000 people to attend the world music festival this weekend.

....

4 The headlines below come from an online news site. Put a suitable past participle into each headline, so that it is passive in meaning. Use one of the verbs in the box.

fine	arrest	find	name	leave	deliver

Example: Prisoner .... by accident
Prisoner released by accident

a) **Criminal .... during visit to accomplice in prison**

b) **Robber's address .... at crime scene**

c) **Man .... $1000 for late library book**

d) **Letter .... 100 years late**

e) **First town .... after Internet company**

f) **Finger .... in bag of popcorn**

5 Match the headlines in Exercise 4 to the sentences below, then join the pairs of sentences using a reduced relative clause.

Example: A prisoner was released accidentally 12 days ago. He has been recaptured.

A prisoner released accidentally 12 days ago has been recaptured.

a) A letter was posted 100 years ago. It has just arrived at its destination.

b) A town was known as Halfway. It has changed its name to 'Half.com'.

c) A man was fined $1,000 for returning a library book a year late. He has described the amount as 'impossible'.

d) A man was wanted for armed robbery. He was arrested when he went to visit his accomplice in prison.

e) A finger was found in a bag of popcorn. Laboratory tests have confirmed that it was human.

f) A piece of paper was left at the scene of a crime. It had the robber's name and address on it.

6 Rewrite these sentences in the passive.

a) Oh, sorry – someone told me that Mr Heaney lived here.

b) We will give candidates ten minutes to read through the exam paper before the exam starts.

c) They sent the wrong phone bill to thousands of people because of a computer error.

d) Did anyone pay you for all the overtime you did?

e) Although they offered me a pay rise, I still decided to leave the company.

f) I wish they had taught me how to cook when I was at school.

g) The company shouldn't have promised those people compensation.

h) What kind of questions did they ask you at the interview?

7 Explain how these sentences are similar or different in meaning.

a) I'm afraid the email was deleted.
   I'm afraid the email got deleted.

b) We had to have the locks changed after the burglary.
   We had to change the locks after the burglary.

c) I've got my finger stuck in the tap!
   My finger's got stuck in the tap!

d) Did you finish your project in time?
   Did you get your project finished in time?

e) The suspect's girlfriend got arrested.
   The suspect got his girlfriend arrested.

f) Our house was broken into last night.
   We had our house broken into last night.

8 Complete the gaps in this article using an appropriate active or passive form of the verb in brackets.

Pop superstar Britney Spears 1) .... (appear) on a live pop show last night and 2) .... (praise) for not making any unreasonable demands. Her fellow American star J-Lo apparently has an entourage of 40 and 3) .... (her dressing rooms/redecorate) before she will set foot in them. Spears 4) .... (surround) by a team of giant minders throughout her two-day visit to Britain. Her visit also includes an interview today on *The Frank Skinner Show*, which 5) .... (screen) later this month. A source on the show said 'The audience 6) .... (give) strict security checks to stop them smuggling cameras in.'

Skinner 7) .... (know) for his direct, near-the-knuckle questioning and 8) .... (not/tell) to tone down his approach for the singer. A spokesman for the programme said 'Britney Spears 9) .... (not/place) any conditions on her forthcoming interview with Frank.'

(Adapted from the Daily Telegraph Jan 19, 2002)

Time and tense

Ⓐ General

The different verb forms of English are often known as tenses. English has twelve verb forms (excluding passives). You have studied the usual ways in which these verb forms are used in modules 1 and 2. See also module 9. However, the relationship between tense and time in English is not always like this.

Present	
Simple	*I live*
Continuous	*I am living*
Perfect	*I have lived*
Perfect Continuous	*I have been living*
Past	
Simple	*I lived*
Continuous	*I was living*
Perfect	*I had lived*
Perfect Continuous	*I had been living*
Future	
Simple	*I will live*
Continuous	*I will be living*
Perfect	*I will have lived*
Perfect Continuous	*I will have been living*

Ⓑ Special uses of the Present Simple

Present Simple for past time

1 The Present Simple is commonly used to talk about past situations:

a) in newspaper headlines.

*Anti-US protest **ends** in violence*

*Minister **quits***

*Strike **brings** city to a standstill*

▶ Exercise 1 p.138

b) when we tell a joke or when we relate the story of a film, book or play.

*A man **goes** to the psychiatrist and **says** 'Doctor, I think I'm a pair of curtains.' The doctor **replies** 'Pull yourself together.'*

*Ingrid Bergman **plays** a rich woman in 19th-century Australia who **marries**, **becomes** an alcoholic and then **falls** in love with her cousin.*

▶ Exercise 2 p.138

2 Present Simple to talk about 'now'

We often learn that the Present Continuous is used for talking about 'now' but sometimes the Present Simple can be used.

a) When we refer to an action which happens **instantaneously** at the moment of speaking, the Present Simple is used. This usually occurs when the words carry a particular importance.

*I **pronounce** you man and wife.*

*I **beg** your pardon?*

*I **name** this ship the Mary Rose.*

b) When describing or commentating on a present action, the Present Simple is used for an instantaneous action.

*Owen **shoots** … and it's a goal!!*

The Present Continuous is used for a longer event.

*And now **I'm slicing** the onions into little pieces, and **putting** them into the saucepan.*

▶ Exercise 3 p.138

3 Present Simple for future time

a) The Present Simple is commonly used to talk about future events which are programmed or timetabled.

*A new production of Mozart's Don Giovanni **opens** at the Royal Opera House next week.*

b) We often use the Present Simple (and Present Perfect) to refer to the future after time conjunctions such as *if, when, before, as soon as, until, once, while, by the time*, etc.

*What'll happen **if** we don't get there in time?*

*I'll phone you **as soon as** we've checked in.*

*You can go home **as soon as** you finish.*

c) We also use the present tenses after relative pronouns such as *who* and *where* and in subordinate clauses introduced by *as, than*, and *whether*.

*The first person **who phones in** with the correct answer will get the prize.*

*I really don't mind **where we stop** as long as I get something to eat soon.*

*You'll probably be on the same flight **as we are**.*

*I'll enjoy the day **whether** the sun **is shining** or whether **it's pouring** with rain.*

d) To describe future events which are officially organised or timetabled, we often use the present form of *be* + infinitive with *to*.

*The Prime Minister **is to visit** India next year.*

*The standard rate of tax **is to be raised** from next April.*

*Is the archbishop **to retire** next year?*

▶ Exercises 4–5 pp.138–139

C Past verb forms in unreal situations

1 Imaginary situations (general)

Past verb forms are used to describe imaginary situations which are contrary to known facts. However, they do not describe the past but either the present or a general situation. They are commonly found:

a) in clauses with *if*.

*If men **had to** undergo pregnancy as women do, there would be far fewer children in the world!*

A variation on this form is the pattern *If + were + infinitive with to*.

*If I **were to tell** you that you've just won $1 million, what would you say?*

> **Notice!**
>
> In the 'unreal' past, *were* is traditionally used with *I* and *he/she*.
>
> *I'd listen to what he has to say if I **were** you.*
>
> Some people still consider this to be more correct, but either version is acceptable in modern British English.
>
> *If it **was** sunny, we could all go to the beach.*

b) after *I wish, I'd rather/sooner, I suppose/imagine* and *it's time*.

Again, these express ideas that are imaginable/desirable, but contrary to the actual facts.

*I **wish** I **had** enough money to buy myself a new scooter.* (= but I don't)

*Suppose you **decided** to sell your bike. How much would you want for it?* (= you haven't yet decided to sell it)

*I'd **rather/sooner** you **didn't smoke.*** (= this is what I would like, rather than what I think will happen)

*You're nearly 28 years old. **It's time you went out** and **looked** for a real job.* (= but you aren't doing this at the moment)

c) when making requests more tentative and distant.

*I just **wanted** to ask you something. Do you have a moment?*

***Was** there anything else, sir?*

*I **was** just **wondering** if you **had** a few moments to discuss something important.*

▶ Exercises 6–7 p.139

2 Imaginary situations in the past

We use the Past Perfect to talk about an unreal situation in the past.

*If it **had been** up to me, I would never have chosen that colour for the living room.*

*I wish I **had** never **met** that hateful man.*

▶ Exercise 8 p.139

D Tense sequence

1 General rules

The verb in a sub-clause is usually in the same tense as the verb in the main clause.

*As soon as I **heard** my mother's voice, (SUB-CLAUSE) I **knew** something **was** wrong. (MAIN CLAUSE)*

If the main clause is in the past, so are the verbs which follow it even if they are still true now.

*From our very first meeting, I **knew** you **were** (are) the right person for me.* (= you are still the right person now, but the fact is only important in relation to the past event)

2 Reported speech

a) The same general rule applies.

*John **tells** me you **work** for a travel agency.*

*Oh, hello! I **saw** James earlier on, and he **told** me you are coming **were coming** to the party tonight.*

*Claire **said** that she will **would** probably be a bit late for the meeting this afternoon.*

After a past tense reporting verb (*said, told,* etc.) the reported words are not in the same tense as the original (direct speech). In the example above, Claire actually said:

*'I**'ll** probably be a bit late for the meeting this afternoon.'*

b) If the fact is still important now, we can use a present tense.

*It was the scientist Sir William Harvey who first proved that blood **circulates** around the body.*

c) With verbs like *say* and *tell* we tend to use the Past Simple to report the exact words and the past Continuous to report the gist of what was said.

*'I'm going to leave my job,' he **said**.*

*John **was saying** how much he hates his job.*

▶ Exercise 9 p.139

Time and tense

1
Rewrite these sentences as newspaper headlines. Remember that articles and possessive adjectives are not usually used in headlines. The number of words in the headline is given in brackets.

Example: The police have launched a crackdown on car thieves. (6)

Police launch crackdown on car thieves

a) A couple have married after a 25-year engagement. (5)

b) The Minister for Education has hinted at changes in the school curriculum. (9)

c) Two brothers drowned after their boat sank in violent storms. (9)

d) A footballer scored a hat-trick but his team was beaten. (7)

e) The veteran actress Googie Withers collapsed on stage at the Theatre Royal. (10)

2
Identify the three text types below. Fill the gaps, using the verbs in the box

ask	go	star	reply	glance	live	tell
shout	change	meet	collect	come		
disappear	fall	have	overtake	start	dream	
know	be (x2)					

Two policemen 1) .... a fast car on the motorway. As they 2) .... at the car, they 3) .... horrified to see the woman at the wheel knitting. 'Pull over!' 4) .... one of the policemen. 'No!' 5) .... the reply. 'Socks!'

Tom Cruise 6) .... as the playboy who 7) .... it all: money, penthouse flat and a beautiful girlfriend. Then he 8) .... and 9) .... in love with a dental assistant and his life 10) .... into freefall.

It's about a girl called Kit McMahon, who 11) .... in a small Irish town where everyone 12) .... everyone and the people 13) .... their lives away. Then Kit's mother 14) .... and her life 15) .... for ever.

3
Who would say the following, and in what situation? Choose the best verb form(s) in each sentence. (Both are possible but one is better.)

a) *I suggest/I'm suggesting* that you think carefully about your version of events, sir.

b) *I name/I'm naming* this ship 'the Argonaut'.

c) And now *we go/we're going* past the largest vineyard on the estate, where the famous Schiava grape is grown.

d) *I swear/I'm swearing* to tell the truth and nothing but the truth.

e) *I put/I'm putting* the mixture into a non-stick tin, which I've warmed in the oven.

f) And *Bryson gets/Bryson's getting* to his feet and ... yes, *he tries/he's trying* to carry on and finish the race.

g) And so *I declare/I'm declaring* this gallery open.

h) As you join us *the minister comes/the minister's coming* to the gates of the house, where dozens of reporters *jostle/are jostling* for position.

4
Match the questions a–h with their answers 1–8.

a) Will you phone us?

b) Where do we change trains?

c) When is Granny going to come and stay?

d) What time does the performance finish?

e) When can I open my presents?

f) Who on earth will notice the mistake?

g) When do your exams start?

h) Will you give me a hand with the painting on Saturday?

1 Some time around 11.

2 Not until you've had breakfast.

3 OK, if I'm not doing anything.

4 In Paris, then Madrid.

5 Yes, the minute I get any news.

6 The week after next.

7 When she's feeling a bit better.

8 Anyone who reads beyond the first paragraph.

5 Match a beginning from a–h with an ending from 1–8, using a word from the box to join them.

> what   whether   until   before   by the time
> who   if   while

a) What shall I do
b) There'll be a reward for anyone
c) I'll book the flight first thing tomorrow
d) Do you think Marcia will agree to do
e) Alec's going to stay in and study tonight
f) It'll all be sorted out
g) You're going to go through all those emails
h) I'll get in touch with the marketing department

1 you find the one from Mr Haig.
2 he wants to or not.
3 you get back.
4 there's nobody there to meet me?
5 you're in the meeting.
6 we suggest?
7 you have second thoughts.
8 gives us information leading to the arrest of this man.

6 Rewrite each sentence so that it is similar in meaning to the one before it. Use the word in bold and an 'unreal' past form.

a) I have to get up at six every morning and I hate it.
wish

....

b) Ingrid is old enough now for her parents to let her make her own decisions.
time

....

c) I don't want you to mention this to anyone.
rather

....

d) I'm not in your position, so I'm not furious.
if

....

e) The plumber prefers you to pay him in cash.
sooner

....

f) They haven't offered me the job yet, so I'm not over the moon*.
were

....

g) Could I possibly speak to you for a moment?
wondered

....

*= absolutely delighted.

7 Complete the questions in a logical way. Ask and answer.

a) If you were to .... a year off, what ....?
b) Imagine you .... back in time, where ....?
c) If you .... English at all, how ....?
d) Suppose everyone .... another language, which ....?
e) If you .... a famous person, who ....?

8 A journalist (J) is interviewing a TV personality, Harvey White (HW), who ran a marathon for charity. Use the prompts to complete the questions and answers.

J: So Harvey, why did you decide to run the marathon?
HW: It was my daughter who persuaded me –
    a) *if/not/be/for her/I/never/get/involved.*
J: And what was the best moment of the race for you?
HW: Oh, getting to the finishing line, definitely …
    b) *I/not/miss/that for anything!*
J: c) *So/you/do/it/again?* You don't have any regrets?
HW: Well only that d) *I wish/I/start/training earlier* – then e) *I/be/better prepared.*
J: f) *There/be/one more thing I/want/ask/you* … is it true that your involvement in the marathon caused problems with your producer?
HW: Look, we'll have to stop the interview here, I'm afraid … g) *It/time/I/get/to the studio* …

9 Cross out any options which do not sound natural in these sentences.

a) It's OK, Sam told me you *don't/didn't* eat meat, so we're having fish.
b) Jack says he *wants/wanted* to move out into the country this year.
c) That was Kate on the phone – she *says/said* she's going to be a bit late.
d) Johnny *said/was saying* 'No' and his boss was so shocked, she didn't say anything!
e) When they told Georgie she *hasn't got/hadn't got* the job, she was really upset.
f) Martina *told/was telling* me that the Waltons' daughter *has been/had been* expelled from school!

Infinitives and *-ing* forms

Ⓐ General

1 Every sentence must have a main verb. In addition, many sentences have infinitives (with or without *to*) and gerunds/present participles (the *-ing* form).

2 These occur in a number of different positions in the sentence, but they are not the main verb (except if they are part of a modal verb – see below).

As the subject:	***Parking*** around here has become more and more difficult.
After the main verb:	I never expected **to win**!
After an adjective:	The result of the election is impossible **to predict**
After a noun:	We didn't have any trouble **finding** our way here.
After a preposition:	Without **seeing** all the evidence, I don't want to comment.
As a clause:	Marina stared out of the window, not even **trying** to concentrate.

3 *-ing* forms can be gerunds or present participles. If the *-ing* form functions as a noun it is a gerund. If it functions as a verb, it is a participle.

Walking is one of the best forms of exercise. (= gerund)

Who's that man **walking** towards us? (= participle)

4 Infinitives and *-ing* forms can be found in both the affirmative and negative forms.

infinitive	*-ing* forms
Try **to hurry**!	**Telling** him was silly.
Try **not to drop** it.	**Not telling** him was silly.
He seems **to be doing** well.	
He seems **to have done** well.	Without **having done** it, I …
He seems **to have been doing** well.	
I want **to be told** the truth.	I prefer **being told** the truth.
I would like **to have been told** earlier.	She's angry about **having been deceived**.

Ⓑ Infinitives and *-ing* forms after adjectives

1 Adjectives are normally followed by the *to* infinitive.

The situation is likely **to get worse** before it gets better.

It's extremely **difficult to understand** why people do this.

2 *Busy* and *worth* are exceptions because they are always followed by the *-ing* form.

Jiang was **busy doing** his homework when I phoned.

We believe that it's a risk **worth taking**.

3 Some adjectives can be followed by the infinitive, or preposition + *-ing* form. The infinitive tends to refer to a particular occasion/situation, the *-ing* form to a more general feeling. Compare:

The old lady was afraid to cross the busy road, so she asked a man to help her. (= unwilling to do something particular, because of fear)

My granny is afraid of being robbed, so she always keeps her money in a money belt. (= a general fear)

4 There can be other differences in meaning too.

• I'm so **anxious** (= worried) **about making** a mistake that I could hardly say a word.

  We are very **anxious** (= keen) **to come** to an agreement as soon as possible.

• It's **good** (= pleasant) **to see you** again.

  I was never **good at** (= clever at) **remembering** names.

• I'm **sorry to interrupt**, but would you mind explaining again?
  (= regret about something we are doing or are about to do)

  Sorry for losing my temper last night. (= to apologise for an earlier action)

▶ Exercise 1 p.142

Ⓒ Nouns with infinitives and *-ing* forms

1 Many nouns are commonly followed by an infinitive form (with *to*).

There are no **plans to replace** the existing Town Hall.

It's **time to take** a long, hard look at our financial situation.

2 Other nouns are followed by *-ing*, or preposition + *-ing*.

There's no **hope of finding** any more survivors now.

We had no **problems finding** accommodation.

▶ Exercise 2 p.142

Ⓓ Verbs with infinitives and *-ing* forms

1 **Infinitives with *to***

a) Many verbs are followed by an infinitive form with *to*.

The police **attempted to break up** the demonstration.

The economic situation **appears to be** improving.

b) Some verbs can have an object before the infinitive.

I want (**you**) to go home.

Verbs like this include: *want, ask, beg, expect, help, need, would like.*

c) Other verbs must have an object.

Politicians **are urging people to vote**.

The police have **warned people to be** careful.

Other verbs: *advise, order, remind, allow, forbid, invite, encourage, permit, teach, force, persuade, tell.*

▶ Exercise 3 p.142

2 Bare infinitives

a) A small number of important verbs take a 'bare' infinitive (an infinitive without *to*). Most important are modals and semi-modals.

See Module 3 Language summary

b) We also use the bare infinitive after *let, make, would rather, had / 'd better*.

*I think we **had better leave** before we cause any more trouble.*

*Please don't **let him upset** you.*

c) The bare infinitive can also be used with verbs of perception (*see, watch, hear, feel*). Notice the difference in meaning between the infinitive and -*ing* form.

*We heard the children **sing** the national anthem.*
(= the whole song)

*We heard the children **singing** the national anthem.*
(= part of the song – in progress)

▶ Exercise 4 p.142

3 Verb + -*ing* form

a) Some verbs are usually followed by an -*ing* form, or a preposition + -*ing* form.

*It's time to **stop worrying** and **start living**!*

*I'd like to **apologise for causing** so much trouble.*

b) A number of verbs have an object + preposition + -*ing* form.

*The police **suspect** Atkins **of dealing** in illegal arms.*

*I don't **blame** you **for being** angry.*

Other verbs: *accuse* (someone) + *of; condemn, criticise, forgive, punish, thank* (someone) + *for; discourage, prevent, stop* (someone) + *from; congratulate* (someone) + *on*.

c) In the passive form, the preposition comes directly after the verb. This is common in newspaper reports.

*Atkins **is suspected of dealing** in illegal arms.*

▶ Exercise 5 p.143

4 Verbs that take both

A small number of verbs can take both.

a) For some verbs the infinitive is used to look forward, the -*ing* form to look backwards.

• *I remembered **to book** the train tickets.*
(= I didn't forget)

*I remember **meeting** him for the first time.*
(= I have a memory of it)

• *We must stop on the way **to get** some petrol.*
(stop for a purpose)

*Dad's stopped **smoking**.*
(= he doesn't do it now)

• *I regret **to tell** you that the performance has been cancelled.*
(= I regret something I am about to tell you)

*I regret **leaving** her.*
(= I regret something in the past)

b) With *like, love* and *hate*, the -*ing* form is normally used in British English, but the infinitive is also common in American English. After *would like*, the infinitive is always used.

*I love **dancing**.* (Br./US)   *I love **to dance**.* (US)

c) The verbs *start* and *begin* can be used with either without any change of meaning.

*I **started/began learning/to learn** English for work.*

▶ Exercise 6 p.143

E Other uses of -*ing* forms

1 -*ing* forms are often the subject of the sentence.

***Blaming** other people isn't going to help.*

▶ Exercise 7 p.143

2 Prepositions are always followed by -*ing* forms.

*Losing your home is **like losing** an old friend.*

3 We often use the pattern *by* + -*ing* to describe the method we use in order to do something.

*You can stop a door from squeaking **by putting** a little oil onto the hinges.*

Remember that *to* is a preposition in the patterns below, and so takes the -*ing* form.

*I'm not used **to living** alone.*

*We look forward **to seeing** you in July.*

F Participle clauses

1 Participle clauses are similar to reduced relative clauses.   See module 5 Language summary

*The woman **who is standing** by the door is my ex-wife.*

*The woman **standing** by the door is my ex-wife.*

2 We use a similar type of clause with verbs of perception like *see, hear, remember*.

*I **saw him**. He was **carrying** a heavy bag out of the shop.*

*I **saw him carrying** a heavy bag out of the shop.*

3 We can also use a participle clause to join two sentences together when they have the same subject.

***Elizabeth** sat quietly in the corner. **She was smiling**.*

> ***Elizabeth** sat quietly in the corner, **smiling**.*

▶ Exercises 8–9 p.143

Infinitives and *-ing* forms

1 Complete the sentences with one of the adjectives from the box, a suitable preposition and the infinitive or *-ing* form of the verb in brackets. (There may be more than one answer.)

> afraid   determined   anxious   possible
> delighted   sorry   advisable   keen

a) Would it be .... (you/take) a later flight?

b) My daughter won't go to bed at night because she's .... (have) nightmares.

c) Kara said she was .... (be) so uncooperative about the holiday.

d) I'm .... (see) so many familiar faces here tonight.

e) I know you're .... (meet) Todd's parents, but I'm sure they'll like you.

f) The doctor said it wasn't .... (Dad/drive) until he's fully recovered.

g) Steven's .... (make) an early start in the morning, so we'd better get to bed soon.

h) Samantha was .... (not/let) us see how upset she was.

2 Rewrite each of the following as one sentence, using the noun in **bold**. If necessary, use a dictionary to help you find the correct construction.

a) You will be able to ask questions at the end.
   opportunity
   You ....

b) We have tried to find the girl. We have failed.
   attempts
   All ....

c) You found your way here. Was it difficult?
   difficulty
   Did .... ?

d) The government has decided to cut taxes. What do you think of that?
   decision
   What .... ?

e) It wasn't necessary to evacuate the building.
   need
   There ....

f) You are retiring next year. Does that worry you?
   thought
   Does .... ?

g) The company is planning to close two factories. How will that affect the workforce?
   plans
   How .... ?

h) Melissa refused to sign the contract. Did that surprise you?
   refusal
   Did .... ?

3 Complete the following so that they are true for you.

a) I have arranged .... this weekend.

b) I aim .... by the end of this year.

c) I often need to be reminded ....

d) My parents always encouraged me ....

e) I would never agree ....

f) It's quite easy to persuade me ....

g) I hate being forced ....

h) I have sometimes been tempted ....

4 Match a beginning from a–j with an ending from 1–10, using a bare infinitive from the box to complete each sentence.

> go   disagree   be   stay   open   slam
> bother   tidy up   tell   discuss

a) Did you see the carnival procession ...

b) Mrs Hughes made me ...

c) Hadn't you better ...

d) I heard Patrick ...

e) Would you rather ...

f) The post should ...

g) You needn't ...

h) Ben's angry because I wouldn't let him ...

i) We could all ...

j) Mr Lee was such a tyrant that nobody dared ...

  1 it and see what it says?
  2 the door as he went out.
  3 past this morning?
  4 arriving any time now.
  5 the office before I left.
  6 with him.
  7 that something was wrong.
  8 this in private?
  9 about the letters now – it's late.
  10 out after midnight.

5 Put one of these prepositions into the correct place in each of the following sentences. If necessary, use a dictionary to help you.

> for   from   with   of   on

a) I must phone Rachel to congratulate her getting engaged.

b) The government has been criticised failing to keep its promises.

c) Twenty people have been charged disturbing the peace.

d) What can I do to discourage my cat scratching all the furniture?

e) I don't blame you handing in your notice after the way they treated you.

f) The four suspects must be prevented leaving the country.

g) I don't think I'll ever forgive Frank forgetting our golden wedding anniversary.

h) I wasn't accusing you cheating, I was just surprised that you knew all the answers.

6 Choose the best verb or verb form to complete the sentences. If necessary, use a dictionary to help you.

1 He just couldn't *like/face/succeed* telling his wife that he'd lost his job.

2 My grandmother *objects/doesn't like/doesn't approve of* girls wearing short skirts.

3 Jack, can you please stop *fiddle/to fiddle/fiddling* with that pen? It's really annoying.

4 Can you imagine never *having to/have to/having* do homework again?

5 I can't *face/stand/help* wondering if Danny was lying about the missing money.

6 I'm afraid I must insist *on you coming/on coming/you coming* with me, sir.

7 Did you remember *phone/to phone/phoning* your mum. She said it was important.

7 Put a suitable -ing form or -ing clause at the beginning of each sentence.

a) .... is a good way of saving money.

b) .... is a good way of relaxing.

c) .... is a good way of losing weight.

d) .... is a good way of meeting new people.

e) .... is a good way of getting to sleep.

f) .... is a good way of remembering things.

8 Rewrite each of the following as one sentence, using a participle clause.

a) I heard the boy next door. He was practising his trombone for hours.

b) The old man went off down the road. He was muttering to himself.

c) We were taking a short cut through the wood. We found an abandoned car.

d) The band kept us entertained all evening. They were playing our favourite songs.

e) Can you hear that strange noise? It's coming from the wardrobe.

f) Susan was thinking about what Gerard had said. Susan drove to the airport.

9 Complete this letter to a newspaper by putting one suitable word in each gap.

Sir,
I was 1) .... to read about the council's 2) .... to build a new entertainment complex on the site of the old church in Manvers Street. I would like councillors to 3) .... how they can 4) .... funding such a project, when they claim that they cannot 5) .... to provide new street lighting in some areas of the city.

Furthermore, the ghastly design for the complex 6) .... even the nearby multi-storey car park look attractive! There has obviously been no 7) .... to design something in keeping with local architecture. The planners also 8) .... to have underestimated the amount of space needed for car parking. Residents already have 9) ....their homes, and with the building of this complex, the situation is 10) .... to become quite impossible.

Last but not least comes the question of noise. It is inevitable that people 11) .... in neighbouring streets will have to put up with groups of people 12) .... the complex late at night. Has the council even considered this problem? I doubt it.

Adverbs

Ⓐ Types of adverb

1 Adverbs are an important way of adding information to a sentence and of modifying the information that is there. There are different types.

Adverbs of place:	*over there, away, at home*
Adverbs of time:	*nowadays, at that time*
Adverbs of manner:	*beautifully, hard*
Adverbs of frequency:	*always, once in a while*
Adverbs of probability:	*almost certainly, possibly*
'Focus' adverbs:	*only, even, especially*
Adverbs of degree:	*very, quite, enormously*

See module 4 Language summary

2 Adverbs can be single words or phrases. Adverbs formed from adjectives often end in *-ly*, but there are many adverbs that do not end in *-ly*.

Ⓑ The position of adverbs

1 **Adverbs of place and time** most often go at the end of the clause or sentence.

*I wasn't aware of any problem **at the time**.*

*I had an odd experience **on the way home**.*

But they are often put at the beginning for greater emphasis.

***On the way home**, I had an odd experience.*

***This season**, United have played very well at home.*

> **Notice!**
>
> a) ***Already*** usually occurs in the 'mid position', but it can be found at the beginning or end of a clause.
>
> *Their daughter is only three, but (already) she can **already** write her own name (already).*
>
> b) ***Still*** usually occurs in the 'mid position'.
>
> *My mother's **still** being prescribed antibiotics.*
>
> At the beginning of a sentence, *still* is often used as a discourse marker to indicate a contrast with what has gone before.
>
> *He's a miserable old guy. **Still**, you've got to admire him.*
>
> c) With questions and negatives ***yet*** usually occurs at the end of the sentence/clause.
>
> *Johnny **hasn't** arrived **yet**. Would you mind waiting for a few moments?*
>
> We can use the pattern *yet* + infinitive with *to* in a more formal context in affirmative sentences.
>
> *We have **yet to see** the full effects of the changes.*

▶ Exercise 1 p.146

2 **Adverbs of manner** are often found next to the word they describe.

***I understand perfectly** what you mean.*

*Many people regard her as being **emotionally unstable**.*

Sometimes changing the position of an adverb can subtly change meaning.

*He was **perfectly aware** that we could see him.*

*He was aware that we could **see him** perfectly.*

> Where there are several adverbs at the end of the sentence/clause, the order is MANNER–PLACE–TIME.
>
> *Dad sat **happily in his armchair**.*
>   MANNER   PLACE
> *Are you going to stay **at home all evening**?*
>   PLACE   TIME
> *United have played **very well at home this season**.*
>   MANNER   PLACE   TIME

3 **Adverbs of frequency and probability** typically go before the main verb and after the first auxiliary or the verb *be*.

*The old man **hardly ever** left his home.*

*Your father was **almost certainly** right.*

*Members of our staff have **frequently** been attacked for no reason.*

• They can also go at the beginning or end of the sentence, but only in sentences which emphasise the frequency/probability.

***Almost certainly**, your father was right.*

***Frequently**, members of our staff have been attacked for no reason.*

~~The old man left his home hardly ever.~~

• Longer adverbial phrases describing frequency normally go at the end of the sentence.

*I visit my grandmother **as often as I can**.*

*I try to go to the gym **once or twice a week**.*

• Adverbs of probability are often used in conversation as single-word answers.

*Will the election result be close?   **Undoubtedly**.*

> If the adverb refers to what will **not** happen, it goes before the negative auxiliary.
>
> *My mother **still doesn't** believe me.*
>
> *They **probably won't** have got your letter yet.*
>
> Generally, we do not put an adverb between a verb and its direct object.
>
> *He took the puppy **gently** out of the basket.*
>
> *~~He took **gently** the puppy out of the basket.~~*

▶ Exercises 2–4 p.146

C Adverbs of manner with and without *-ly*

1 Although many adverbs of manner end in *-ly* (*easily, slowly, clearly*), many do not.

*We went **straight** home when the film finished.*

*Do you have to drive so **fast**?*

2 We do not form adverbs from adjectives which end in *-ly* (e.g. *lively, friendly*). We use *'in a -ly way'*.

*He was looking at us **in a** very **unfriendly way**.*

*She always tries to explain grammar rules **in a lively way**.*

▶ Exercise 5 p.146

3 Some pairs of adverbs have a different meaning with and without *-ly*.

a) *deep / deeply*

Deep is an adverb of manner meaning 'going far down or in'. *Deeply* is often used of emotions, and means 'intensely'.

*The submarine is travelling **deep** below the surface of the water.*

*People in this part of the country feel very **deeply** about this issue.*

b) *free / freely*

These are both adverbs of manner, but *free* means 'without paying' and *freely* means 'without restriction.'

*Railway employees travel **free**. (= without paying)*
*Everyone can talk **freely**. (= without restriction)*

c) *hard / hardly*

Hard is an adverb of manner. *Hardly* occurs in the mid-position and means 'almost not'.

*She works **hard**. (= she works a lot)*
*She **hardly** works. (= she does almost no work)*

d) *late / lately*

Late is an adverb of manner. *Lately* is an adverb of time meaning recently.

*Do you often go out **late**?*
*Have you been going out a lot **lately**? (= recently)*

e) *right / rightly, wrong / wrongly*

Right means 'in the correct way'. *Rightly* is a comment adverb, expressing the speaker's idea that someone was entitled to do or feel something. *Wrong / wrongly* work in the same way.

*I'm sure I'll get it **right (wrong)** next time.*

*Quite **rightly (wrongly)** in my view, they have decided to appeal against the decision.*

▶ Exercise 6 p.147

4 Many **adverb + adjective** and **adverb + verb** combinations are commonly found together and can be seen as set phrases.

*It is one of the most **technologically advanced** societies on earth.*

*It's **highly unlikely** that this project will succeed.*

*The doctors **tried desperately** to save his leg.*

▶ Exercise 7 p.147

5 Verbs such as *feel, look, seem, sound, taste* and *smell* usually take an adjective, not an adverb.

That smells nice! ~~*That smells nicely.*~~

With *look good / well*, both an adverb and an adjective are possible with a change of meaning.

*You're **looking good**. (= attractive)*
*You're **looking well**. (= healthy)*

D Focusing adverbs

Focusing adverbs are used to focus attention on particular words.

1 *Even*
Even is used to emphasise that the following words or information is extreme or surprising.

*I did everything I could to get money. I **even** asked strangers to lend me a few pence.*

2 *Only*
Only has a 'limiting' effect. It usually comes immediately before the word it qualifies.

***Only** you know what really happened that night.*
(= you and nobody else)

*I could **only** answer one of the questions.*
(= I could answer one question and no more than that)

3 *Especially*
Especially emphasises that the information is 'more than the others'.

*I like all kinds of sport, **especially** basketball.*

Note: *particularly* works in the same way.

▶ Exercise 8 p.147

Adverbs

1 Complete the sentences with *still*, *already* or *yet*.

a) I .... haven't had time to look at your proposal, I'm afraid.

b) We've been through this so many times .... – you're too young to go.

c) Government ministers have admitted that they have .... to find a solution to the problem of mobile phone theft.

d) We've .... been along this road once – are you sure you know the way?

e) I don't think that Harry Potter film's on at our local cinema ....

f) Are you .... trying to fix that light switch? Why not just get a new one?

g) I've got to go back to work tomorrow. .... , I've had a great holiday.

h) Is it 8 o'clock .... ? They'll be here any minute and I'm not dressed!

2 Put the words in the correct order in each sentence. (There may be different possibilities.)

a) We've had a wonderful time.
to / <u>We</u> / here / soon / back / hope / very / come
....

b) possibly / a / morning / you / work / give / to / <u>Could</u> / tomorrow / lift / me /? My car's at the garage.
....

c) I haven't seen you for ages. all / sometime / at / for / get / lunch / house / <u>Let's</u> / my / together/.
....

d) the / put / envelope / <u>Elizabeth</u> / quickly / in / then / back / read / carefully / the / it / letter/.
....

e) just / you / hanging / now / see / <u>Did</u> / outside / anyone / around/? My car's been broken into.
....

f) automatically / every / in / the / on / all / 7 o'clock/ rooms / heating / at / <u>The</u> / morning / comes.
....

g) garden / hard / worked / yesterday / the / really / <u>I</u> / in / day / all. / I'm aching all over today!
....

3 Complete the sentences so that they are true for you.

a) I like to .... most mornings.

b) In my country, we hardly ever ....

c) Once in a while, it's nice to ....

d) I would never ever..................... unless ....

e) I .... a couple of times a week.

f) I think people should .... every now and then.

4 Choose an adverb from the box (and nothing else) to answer each question. Ask and answer.

> possibly maybe conceivably hopefully
> (almost) certainly   most likely   no doubt
> definitely (not)   probably (not)

a) Do you think you'll go out tonight? ....

b) Are you going to travel abroad this year? ....

c) Do you think it'll rain tomorrow? ....

d) Are you likely to take an English exam in the next six months? ....

e) Will you have an argument with anyone in the next couple of days? ....

f) Do you think you'll still be studying English in a year's time? ....

g) Would you live in another country if you had the chance to? ....

h) Would your best friend ever lie to you? ....

5 Decide whether the adjectives in **bold** need to be changed into an adverb, and add them in a logical place on the line.

A recipe

a) The simple ingredients in this dish go together and it looks and smells so that you cannot fail to impress your dinner guests. **(perfect/fantastic)**

b) Slice half a kilo of green beans and put them into an sized roasting tin. **(fine/appropriate)**

c) Pour on a little olive oil to coat the beans then chop two cloves of garlic and add that to the tin. **(rough)**

d) Season with salt and ground black pepper, then mix everything together. **(fresh)**

e) Pat the cod steaks with kitchen paper to remove moisture, then put them on top of the beans. **(gentle/excess)**

f) Sprinkle with pine nuts and add a little more olive oil. **(generous)**

g) Cover with kitchen foil and cook for fifteen minutes – you know the cod is cooked when the bone can be removed. **(easy)**

h) Tastes with crusty bread and a crisp dry white wine. **(great)**

6 <u>Underline</u> the correct adverb in each sentence.

a) Look! They've spelt my name *wrong/wrongly* on all these business cards.
b) How *late/lately* did you two stay out last night?
c) We found the whole situation *deep/deeply* embarrassing.
d) If you show your student card to the people on the door, you'll get in *free/freely*.
e) I had *hard/hardly* finished my meal when the waiter came and took my plate away.
f) These holidaymakers are *right/rightly* appalled at the state of the facilities in this hotel.

7 Use a verb from box A and an adverb from box B to complete each of the sentences. You may need to change the form of the verb.

A

> sell   try   feel   understand   go   complain
> club   eat   apologise   react

B

> smoothly   bitterly   well   desperately   strongly
> perfectly   sensibly   badly   together   profusely

a) A lot of people .... about this issue, so be careful what you say at the meeting.
b) The lifeboat crew .... to reach the sinking boat, but the bad weather forced them back.
c) I'm pleased to report that the new range of photocopiers .... very .... over the past six months.
d) It's Trisha's 30th birthday next week – why don't we .... and get her something nice?
e) Ally lost a lot of weight by .... and exercising regularly.
f) The children .... about having to be in bed by 9 o'clock.
g) It's difficult to talk to Joe about his progress – he always .... so .... to criticism.
h) I .... what you mean, madam, and I can assure you that it won't happen again.
i) I thought everything .... very .... this evening, didn't you?
j) My bank manager .... for all the mistakes that had been made.

8 Which of the adverbs in **bold** below are 'focusing adverbs'? Put each adverb into a logical place in each of the quotations.

a) 'Friends are made by many acts – and lost by one.' *(Anon)* **only**

b) 'I don't know anything about music. In my line, you don't have to.' *(Elvis Presley)* **even**

c) 'If a wife laughs at her husband's jokes, is he funny or is she smart?' *(Anon)* **always**

d) 'It takes good manners to put up with bad ones.' *(Anon)* **especially**

e) 'It is easier to forgive an enemy than to forgive a friend.' *(William Blake)* **even**

f) 'Silence is misinterpreted, but misquoted.' *(Anon)* **often, never**

g) 'A brilliant man knows whether the applause for his words is politeness or appreciation.' *(Anon)* **only**

h) 'Nothing is hard if you divide it into small jobs.' *(Henry Ford)* **particularly**

i) 'Answer a letter while you are angry.' *(Chinese proverb)* **never**

j) 'It is the intellectually lost who ever argue.' *(Oscar Wilde)* **only**

Future forms

A General

Many forms are used to talk about the future in English. In many cases, a number of different forms are possible, depending on how we see the event.

1 *will/shall*

The contracted form *'ll* is most common in speech. We use *will/shall* to talk about:

a) predictions based on our feelings and expectations, rather than evidence in the present.

*I believe that, by the end of the 21st century, the world **will be** at peace.*

This use is common in academic writing. Adverbs of probability are often used here.

*A new form of energy **will almost certainly** emerge.*

See module 8 Language summary

b) things we see as 'facts in the future'.

*The meeting **will finish** at 1.00 and then lunch **will be served**.*

c) decisions made at the moment of speaking.

*There's someone at the door ... **I'll ring** you back later, OK?*

d) willingness or refusal to do something.

***I'll sing** at the party if you like, but I **won't wear** a silly costume.*

> **Notice!**
>
> In the question form of the first person *shall* is commonly used to make offers and suggestions.
>
> ***Shall I** carry that for you?*
>
> ***Shall we** move on to the next question?*

2 *going to*

We use *going to* to talk about:

a) our intentions for the future.

*I**'m not going to borrow** any more money from now on.*

b) a prediction based on some present evidence.

*From what I've seen so far, **it's going to be** a difficult game.*

In practice, *will* and *going to* are often interchangeable.

3 'Present' modals

Present modals can have a future meaning.

*The economic picture **may/might/could** look very different in ten years' time.*

See module 3 Language summary

4 Present Continuous

We use the Present Continuous to talk about definite arrangements for the future, where a specific future time is stated or understood.

*What are your plans for **the weekend**? **Are you doing** anything special?*

5 Present Simple

We use the Present Simple:

a) to talk about timetabled future events, or events which are 100 per cent certain.

*The conference **begins** on Tuesday and **ends** on Friday.*

*Tomorrow**'s** Monday.*

b) in subordinate clauses, following words like *if, unless, in case, before, after, when*, etc.

*I'll pass on the message **as soon as** she **gets** back.*

*We will only succeed **if** we all **work** together.*

c) in clauses following *what/who/which* and *whatever/wherever*, etc.

*I don't care what **happens** next year.*

*Don't forget to email me, wherever you **are**.*

It is important to note that in all of these cases the context makes it clear that the future is intended.

See module 5 Language summary

6 Future Continuous

We use the Future Continuous:

a) to talk about an action in progress at a specific time in the future.

*This time next week, I**'ll be doing** my exams.*

*In a hundred years' time, we**'ll probably all be working** when we are 80.*

b) to talk about something which will happen as part of the normal course of events.

*I**'ll be seeing** Anne later this afternoon – I'll pass on your message to her then.*

*I can easily give you a lift, I**'ll be passing** your house.*

c) to ask tentatively/politely about future plans.

***Will** you **be using** the computer later on?*

***Will** you **be needing** anything else?*

7 Future Perfect or 'past in the future'

a) Like other perfect forms the Future Perfect is used to talk about an action which will be completed before a point of time, in this case a point in the future. Compare:

I'll finish my report on Friday night.
(= I will finish it at that time)

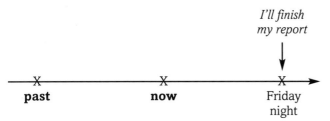

b) The Future Perfect Continuous form can be used to talk about the duration of activities before a point of time in the future, often with *for* or *since*.

I'll have been working in this same building for ten years next month!

Note that the Future Perfect and especially the Future Perfect Continuous are not very common forms.

▶ Exercises 1–4 p.150

B 'Future' phrases

We often use phrases with a future meaning to talk about the future, rather than a future verb form.

1 *about to/on the point of/on the verge of*

We use *about to* to talk about something that is going to happen very soon.

*It's not a good time to to talk. I'm **about to go** into a meeting.*

On the point of + -ing can be used with the same meaning.

*Beckham is **on the point of signing** a new contract with Manchester United.*

On the verge of is used in a similar way.

*Jo is **on the verge of giving** up her university course, because she really hates it.*

2 *is/are to*

We use this form to talk about actions which are officially arranged. This is a common form in news reports.

*The Prime Minister **is to** visit Pakistan early next year.*

3 *(un)likely to*

This is very common for making predictions.

*Mass space travel is **unlikely to** become a reality.*

4 *due to*

We use *due to* in more formal speech or writing to say that something is planned to happen at a particular time.

*The game is **due to** start at 20.00.*

5 *set to*

We use *set to* when something is likely to happen. This form is common in news reports.

*The government is **set to** introduce the reforms early next year.*

6 *bound to*

You use this if you are sure something will happen:

*Carrie's **bound to** be late – she always is.*

▶ Exercises 5–6 pp.150–151

C Future in the past

A number of the forms above have a past form which describes the 'future in the past'.

1 If we talk about plans or intentions in the past, we use the Past Continuous or *was going to*.

*When I was little, I **was going to be** the world's greatest ballerina.*

*We had to go to bed early, as we **were** all **getting up** at 6 the following morning.*

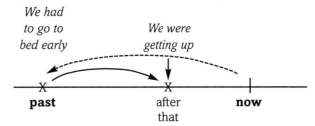

2 We often talk about things which were planned in the past but did not take place.

*We **were going to invite** Henry to the party, (but we couldn't find his phone number).*

*I **was on the point of going** out when the phone rang.*

*I **was about to say** that when you interrupted me.*

*Damn! I **was supposed to phone** my mother last night.*

3 We can use *would* or *was to* to talk about an action which did take place, but was still in the future and not anticipated at the time.

*Bogart met Bacall, who **would** later **become** his fourth wife, in 1944.*

*Who would have believed that this unknown teenager **was to become** one of the world's greatest movie stars.*

▶ Exercises 7–8 p.151

Future forms

1 Which of these sentences do not refer to the future?

a) What time are we leaving for the airport?
b) Most of the country will have scattered showers.
c) My lighter won't work – have you got any matches?
d) Where shall I put these suitcases?
e) That'll be the babysitter – can you let her in?
f) As soon as you get home, can you put the oven on?
g) Who are you going to vote for in the *Pop Stars* contest?
h) On Sundays I'll often have a lie in, unless I'm playing with the local football team.
i) I'll be thinking of you while you're having your interview.

2 Which form of the verb is possible?

a) *'Are we going to get/Shall we get* a takeaway tonight?' 'OK, good idea.'
b) Can you speak to Lily about her homework? She *won't listen/she isn't going to listen* to me.
c) I'm *getting/going to get* fit by the summer.
d) The 14th *is/will be* a Sunday, so the traffic shouldn't be too bad.
e) Oh no, it's broken! Don't worry – *I'll buy/I'm going to buy* you a new one.
f) Did I tell you? We're *moving/move* into our new flat on June 20th.
g) I'm sure you'll have a great time wherever *you'll go/you go.*
h) This traffic's terrible – *we'll be/we're going to be* really late.

3 Put the verb in brackets into the Future Simple, Future Perfect or Future Perfect Continuous.

a) By the time you've found your swimming costume, it .... (be) too late to go to the pool.
b) When Maria retires next week, she .... (work) here for over 30 years.
c) You .... (never/get) a taxi at this time of night.
d) All the best seats .... (go) if you don't ring the theatre soon.
e) Ali will probably be jet-lagged when he arrives – he .... (fly) for about 15 hours.
f) Ring me back at about four – I .... (speak) to Milo about the contract by then.

4 Complete each prediction for the year 2025 with a suitable form of one of the verbs in the box (note that several verbs are in the passive).

> rise   allocate   telework   live
> commit   implant   own

a) More than a third of the population will .... alone.
b) More crime will .... by cyberterrorists than by 'hand-to-hand' criminals.
c) More people will .... virtual pets than real ones.

d) Scanable microchips containing important personal data will .... at birth.
e) 30 per cent of the workforce will ....
f) The Earth's temperature will still ....
g) Lifelong email addresses will .... at birth.

How likely do you think each prediction is? Discuss, adding an adverb of probability where appropriate.

5 Rewrite each sentence so that it is similar in meaning to the one before it, using the word in bold and a phrase with a future meaning.

a) Arrangements have been made for Nuala Campbell to sign a $5 million modelling contract.
   is
   Nuala Campbell ....
b) We've got an appointment to see the solicitor at 11a.m. tomorrow.
   due
   We ....
c) The film's going to start soon – come on!
   about
   The ....
d) It is likely that the phone company Supertel will make record profits this year.
   set
   The ....
e) A new manager probably won't be appointed until after the summer.
   unlikely
   A new manager ....
f) I think Manchester United are certain to win the League cup this year.
   bound
   Manchester United ....

6 Match each headline a–f with the first line of the story 1–6. Fill each of the gaps with *is to*, *is set to* or *is due to* and an appropriate verb.

a) **Beautiful Mind set for clean sweep* at Oscars**

b) **School without electricity to get computers**

c) **Jumbo cream**

d) **Love may disappoint fans**

e) **Soap star cleans up image**

f) **'Wobbly' bridge to reopen**

1 Australian singer Kristy Love, who .... at the Albert Hall on Saturday, may have to cancel the performance because of a throat infection.

2 Ken Bushell, who starred as the psychopathic husband of Mel in *Northside*, ... a comeback in his role as a doctor in a new series.

3 Wendy, a 42-year-old elephant who suffers from eczema, ... with free moisturising cream for the rest of her life by a pharmaceutical company.

4 The story of the brilliant mathematician John Nash, played by Russell Crowe, ... the board* at the Oscars this year.

5 A school in Romania which has no electricity .... top-of-the-range** computers by education officials.

6 The Millennium bridge over the River Thames .... at 10.00 on Friday, after extensive modifications to stop it wobbling.

* in the context of a competition, *a clean sweep* or to *sweep the board* means to win every possible prize.
** *top-of-the-range* means the best you can buy.

7 Choose an ending from 1–10 to complete each of the sentences a–j. Can you explain why each sentence contains the idea of 'the future in the past'?

a) We were going to call in on the way home ...
b) Tariq didn't blame Jan for being annoyed – living in such close proximity to the in-laws ...
c) In 1979 George decided to move to Hollywood, a decision ...
d) I was about to ask for a day off ...
e) When we were 10, we were going to be ...
f) Two weeks later Elvis met Colonel Tom Parker, ...
g) I was on the point of phoning the police ...
h) Joanne hardly got a wink of sleep because ...
i) Although he was optimistic at the time, Sam ...
j) The two children made a promise ...

1 which would change his life forever.
2 would regret his choice of business partner in the years to come.
3 when she turned up safe and sound.
4 which they were to find more and more difficult to keep as the days went by.
5 was always going to be difficult.
6 she was leaving for Australia in the morning.
7 who was to become his manager.
8 rich by the time we were 20!
9 but my boss was in a terrible mood.
10 but it was getting late.

8 Put a name at the beginning of each statement, e.g. your name, the name of a classmate, a friend, a family member, a famous person.

a) .... is about to get married.
b) .... will have moved house this time next year.
c) .... is having friends to stay this weekend.
d) .... will never change.
e) .... is going on holiday soon.
f) .... will have made some important decisions by the end of the year.
g) .... is going to buy some new clothes this weekend.
h) .... will be cooking a meal in a couple of hours' time.
i) .... is on the point of leaving their job.

Noun phrases

Ⓐ Noun phrases

A noun can be preceded by: an article, a demonstrative, a possessive, a quantifier, a noun modifier e.g. *a **university** student*, an adjective or adjectival phrase.

1 Articles

a) The **indefinite article** (*a/an*) is used:

- for something that is new, or has not been mentioned before, in the conversation or text.

  *I had **an** interesting conversation with William yesterday.*

- to classify people or things.

  *Michael Johnson is **a** great athlete.*

- to mean *each/every* in phrases.

  *once **a** day / week / hour   ten kilometres **an** hour*

b) The **definite article** is used:

- to indicate something that is not new, or has been mentioned before in the conversation or text.

  *Do you remember **the** conversation we had the other day?*

- for something/someone that is unique, or unique in that particular context.

  *I usually take **the** children to **the** park on Saturday morning.*

- with superlative adjectives.

  ***the** best fish restaurant in the south-west*

- when we refer to a place familiar to the listener.

  *go to **the** cinema/**the** park/**the** doctor's*

- when further information is given later in the sentence.

  ***the** people I told you about yesterday*

- with rivers, oceans, mountain ranges and a few countries.

  ***The** River Danube, **The** Atlantic, **The** Alps, **The** Czech Republic, **The** United Arab Emirates, **The** United Kingdom*

c) No article (zero) is used:

- with uncountable and plural nouns to talk about things in general.

  People in glass houses shouldn't throw stones.

- to talk about institutions.

  *at **home**, in **bed/hospital**, at **university/school***

- with lakes, mountains and most countries.

  Lake Balaton, Mount Everest, Brazil

▶ Exercise 1 p.154

2 Demonstratives

a) With time expressions, *this* refers to a period close to us in time in the future or past, and *that* refers to a more distant period, in the past or future.

  *Where are you going **this** (= next) weekend?*

  *We can't go **that** weekend, as I'll be in Ireland .*

b) However, in writing, *this* can be used to refer back to an earlier part of the sentence.

  *At the age of 18, Horne joined the army: **this** experience proved to be a turning-point in his life.*

▶ Exercise 2 p.154

3 Possessive adjectives

a) To emphasise the identity of the 'possessor', we use the possessive adjective + *own*.

  *It's disgraceful that she stole money from **her own** family.*

b) When the sex of a person is unknown or unimportant, we can use the plural possessive *their*, even though the verb is singular.

  *Surely everyone is entitled to **their** own opinion.*

4 Quantifiers

a) These quantifiers are used with singular nouns: ***another, each, either/neither, every*** + *day, student*, etc.

b) These quantifiers are usually used before plural or uncountable nouns: ***all (the), any,* both, enough, more, most, no, plenty of, some, a lot of, several, thousands of***

c) *Any* can be used with a singular noun with positive sentences to suggest 'it doesn't matter which'.

  ***Any** guidebook will give you the information you need.*

d) *Much/many* are usually used in negatives/questions.

  *I haven't got **much** time. Were there **many** people?*

e) *A few* or *few* can only be used with plural nouns. A *few* is for a positive idea, while *few* is negative.

  *There are **a few** good restaurants in the market area.*

  ***Very few** tourists ever come to such a remote place.*

  The same difference in meaning applies with *a little/little* before uncountable nouns.

  *We still have **a little** money left from Christmas.*

  *There is **very little** hope of finding any more survivors.*

f) Some quantifiers can be combined.

  a little more/less salt   every few hours

▶ Exercise 3 p.154

5 Noun modifiers

We often use a noun in front of another noun, to define or classify it.

  *The **car** windscreen (NOT the ~~car's windscreen~~)*

  *A **flower/shoe** shop   A **news** programme*

▶ Exercise 4 p.154

Ellipsis and substitution

A Ellipsis

1 'Ellipsis' means leaving out a word or words when they are obvious from the context.

In informal speech, it is common to miss out the beginnings of certain phrases when it is clear *who* or *what* is being referred to. This often happens with:

- imperative *be: (Be) careful! (Be) quiet!!*

- pronouns: *(I) don't think so. (I) don't know.*

- pronouns + *be: (It's) nice to meet you. (I'm) sorry.*

- pronouns + *be* + articles: *(It's a) nice day. (It's a) pity. (It's a) good thing you were here to help.*

- auxiliary verbs + pronouns: *(Have you) got the time? (Are you) coming? (Have you) finished?*

2 Words are often missed out after an auxiliary verb to avoid repetition.

If you're not prepared to lend me the money, then I'm sure Jeffrey is ~~prepared to lend me the money~~.

3 If a verb is followed by an infinitive with *to*, we include the *to* but omit the verb.

There's no need to stay if you don't want **to** *(stay).*

▶ Exercise 1 p.155

B Substitution

Substitution is when a single word is used to replace a word or phrase, often to avoid repetition.

I brought these chocolates home from our holiday. Would you like **one***?*

'Does this bus go to the station?' 'I think **so***.'*

I don't like football, but my wife **does***.*

*'We're going to the Bahamas for our holidays.' '***So** *are we!'*

*'I'm not taking a holiday this year.' '***Neither/Nor** *am I.'*

▶ Exercise 2 p.155

1 Personal pronouns

a) If a pronoun is used in isolation, we always use the object pronoun form.

Who would like to start? ~~I~~ **Me***!*

Similarly, in modern English we use object pronouns as the complement of a phrase.

Who left the door open? ~~It was I.~~ *It was* **me***.*

b) When the sex of a person is not clear or unimportant, we can use:

- either *he/she* or *his/her* depending on the likelihood of the person being male or female.

One of the teacher's main responsibilities is to make sure **her** *students are learning.*

- the plural pronoun *they* or *them*.

'There's **someone** *waiting to see you.' 'What do* **they** *want? Can you ask* **them** *to wait for a moment?'*

c) *You* is often used to mean 'people in general'.

You *never know what* **you***'re going find.*

d) The pronoun *one* is used in more formal contexts with the meaning of 'people in general'.

As **one** *walks through the city,* **one** *is constantly reminded of its turbulent history.*

If the speaker is not stated, *they* is used.

They*'re building a new sports centre opposite the station.*

e) *It* and *there* can be used as the subject of a sentence.

There *are plenty of reasons why*

Who's that? **It***'s Maria (NOT* ~~I am/ She's Maria~~ *)*

It can also be used to refer to 'the situation'.

I've already made **it** *quite clear that I'm not interested.*

▶ Exercise 3 p.155

2 Reciprocal pronouns

a) We use reciprocal pronouns (*each other, one another*) when an action involves two or more people or things doing the same thing to each other.

The important thing is to try to understand **each other***.*

b) Some verbs take a preposition (*with* or *to*).

My two cousins haven't spoken **to each other** *for years.*

c) *One another* is a little more formal and old-fashioned.

Do you promise to love **one another** *for ever?*

3 Reflexive pronouns

a) Reflexive pronouns emphasise that a person is doing the action to him/herself, not to another person or thing.

Here are some extra towels for you to dry **yourself***.*

b) We can also use reflexive pronouns to emphasise who the pronoun refers to.

He didn't write the speech **himself***: one of his PR men did it.*

▶ Exercise 4 p.155

4 *this/that*, etc.

a) When we refer forward to something we are going to say, or something that is going to happen we use *this*.

I hate to tell you **this***, but ...*

b) When we refer back to something we said, or something that has already happened we use *that*.

Sorry about **that***. It won't happen again.*

c) On the telephone in British English, the speaker uses *this* to refer to him/herself; we refer to the other person as *that*.

Hello, **this** *is Alan here. Is* **that** *you, Richard?*

Noun phrases

1 **a)** Cross out **five** unnecessary definite articles in this description of Fisherman's Wharf in San Francisco.

The Fishermen from Genoa and Sicily first arrived in the Fisherman's Wharf area in the late 19th century, and here they founded the San Francisco fishing industry. The district has slowly given way to the tourism since the 1950s, but the brightly painted boats still set out from the harbour on fishing trips early each morning. To the south of Fisherman's Wharf lies North Beach, sometimes known as 'Little Italy'. This lively part of the city has an abundance of the aromatic bakeries and cafés, from where you can watch the crowds. It is home to Italian and Chinese families, with a sprinkling of writers and bohemians*; Jack Kerouac, among others, found the inspiration here.

* bohemians: writers, artists, etc. who like to live differently from the rest of society.

b) Add **ten** definite and **two** indefinite articles in the correct places in this description of Golden Gate Park.

Golden Gate Park is one of largest urban parks in United States. It stretches from Pacific Ocean to centre of San Francisco, forming oasis of greenery and calm in which to escape from bustle of city life. Within park amazing number of activities are possible, both sporting and cultural. Landscaped area around Music Concourse, with its fountains, plane trees and benches, is most popular section. Free Sunday concerts held here are especially popular.

2 Complete the gaps in these sentences with *this*, *that*, *these* or *those*.

a) I don't seem to get much time to myself .... days.
b) I met Billie while she was singing at the Jazz Club. She was relatively unknown at .... time.
c) Oh Jake! .... chocolates were for our dinner guests!
d) Aren't your parents arriving .... Friday? We'd better go to the supermarket tonight.
e) Why don't you wear .... dress you wore to Petra's party? It looked great.
f) When Cristina was introduced to Tom Hall at a concert, she never dreamt that .... man would be her future husband.
g) You're not going to school in .... shoes – they're much too high.
h) I can't really see the Toshiba rep on the 20th – I've got two meetings already .... morning.

3 Underline the best quantifier in each of the sentences below.

a) Would anybody like *little/some/no* more of this soup?
b) For a *few/few/all* hours last Saturday night, our family was united as we watched the final on TV.
c) She ran up and kissed him on *both/every/each* cheek.
d) You should be able to find this kind of pepper mill in *any/all/each* good kitchen shop.
e) Please! Can we have *little/a little/some* less noise in here?
f) There aren't *more/many/plenty of* directors who have been as prolific in their output as Altman.
g) *Any/Very few/Most* children would refuse the offer of an ice-cream.
h) There were cars parked on *either/neither/both* side of the road, so it was impossible for two cars to pass each other.
i) Is there going to be *some/any/enough* room in your house for 70 people?

4 In the extracts below make the style more natural by using noun + noun combinations instead of noun + preposition + noun wherever possible. The number of possible changes is shown in brackets.

A

David Beckham, the captain of England and icon of style who constantly changes his image, has signed a deal to create a range of fashion for boys aged six to fourteen. Beckham's oldest son, Brooklyn, is usually seen dressed in clothes of designers. (4)

B

A man in Missouri stole six electrical transformers from a company of power. He wanted to build a machine of time so that he could transport himself into the future, learn the winning numbers of the lottery, and return to buy the right ticket. The man's boss decided not to press charges. (4)

Ellipsis and substitution

1 Match a sentence from a–h with a response from 1–8, then cross out any words or phrases which can be left out because they are obvious from the context.

a) Can you lock up?
b) Have you got a light?
c) What time does the play finish?
d) Have you phoned Auntie Mel yet?
e) It was lovely to see Stef again, wasn't it?
f) It's very dark out here.
g) Here you are, sir, two glasses of wine.
h) How many times have I told you not to leave the back door open?

1 No, I'm just going to phone Auntie Mel.
2 Yeah, it's a good thing I brought a torch.
3 No, we only ordered one glass of wine.
4 I have no idea, I'm sorry.
5 I'm sorry, I don't smoke.
6 I already have locked up.
7 I didn't leave the back door open, it was Lisa.
8 Yeah, it's a pity she couldn't stay any longer.

2 Cross out any repetitive words or phrases and replace them with words from the box.

(so   do   did   does   one   ones   nor)

a) 'I hope Daniel passes his driving test this time.'
   'I hope Daniel passes his driving test this time, too.'

b) 'I'll probably go shopping this afternoon.'
   'Well, if you go shopping, could you get me some coffee?'
c) Was it this ring you wanted to look at, madam?'
   'No, it was the ring at the front, with the rubies in it.'
d) 'I didn't expect Fran to pick me up from the station, but she picked me up from the station.'
e) 'We went to Paris last weekend.'
   'Really! We went to Paris last weekend! Where were you staying?'
f) 'We didn't understand a word of what he said.'
   'I didn't understand a word. Nobody told me he only speaks Hungarian.'

g) 'Do these trousers look OK?'
   'I think the white linen trousers would look better with that jacket.'
h) 'That man who just went by was the presenter from *The Breakfast Show*.'
   'I thought he was the presenter from *The Breakfast Show* – his face looked familiar.'
i) 'My friend Josef works in the same building as you.'
   'I know he works in the same building as me–I met him in the lift the other day.'

3 Are these statements true of the place where you live? If not, change them.

a) It's quite easy to find your way around.
b) They've pulled down a lot of old buildings recently.
c) You can always find somewhere interesting to go out at night.
d) People find it difficult to get accommodation.
e) You're always bumping into people you know in the street.
f) There has been a big increase in crime in the last year or so.
g) If someone new moves in, the neighbours make an effort to get to know them.
h) There are quite a lot of people living on the streets.

4 Put the following words in order, then think of a context for each sentence.

a) herself / all / blames / this / she / for
   ....
b) at / just / other / stared / they / each
   ....
c) other / speaking / at / we're / moment / not / the / each / to
   ....
d) together / on / pull / come / yourself
   ....
e) any / we / each / more / don't / other / love
   ....
f) really / you / this / make / did / yourself / ?
   ....
g) bit / assert / need / more / yourself / you / a / to
   ....
h) the / ones / I / blue / myself / prefer
   ....

155

Tapescripts

Module 1

Recording 1.1

R = Richard   C = Caroline   J = John
E = Elana

1 R: Sometimes people say there's too much stuff, er, American stuff on the television. I don't agree at all I think it's great we have this choice, erm I wouldn't want to be deprived of all these American shows, American films. Yes, some are good, some are bad, but it would be a shame if we just had, only ever saw British things. No, more American stuff is great. It's great to see French films say, Spanish films, whatever. Choice is what it's all about.

2 C: In terms of an exchange of ideas, I think I think globalisation actually is working and it's quite interesting. If you look at people's, I don't know, CD collections and see the world music that's come to the fore in recent years, I mean that's got to be a positive side of globalisation ... the sort of world world music scene, people travelling, going to different cultures, different religions spreading their words ... I think in that sense yes erm globalisation can sort of help, and you know people to understand each other or to bring about better practices worldwide.

3 J: Well, I think that globalisation has affected my pastime on a Saturday. I am a football supporter and when I was a young boy, practically all the players came from, I suppose, a radius an area around London that must have been about 30 miles, erm and you knew those players from your area. So as the years have gone by, and certainly over the last 10 years, you look down the list of players who are playing for Chelsea football club now and I think there's only one player in the current team that's actually from this country. They come from France, they come from Italy, er they come from Eastern Europe, from Scandinavia, but it's a radical change and it means that in a sense you know my local team has gone global. And I think it has lost something. I think that what has has come in is a sense of big business really rules now.

4 E: Well, the interesting thing I suppose for me, is that the world seems to have dropped into every road that I go down nowadays. Wherever I go you get shops that offer materials and products from Africa and from Afghanistan or from from central and eastern Europe and it seems almost as if you one hardly needs to travel any more because the world has come in on us. Which is lovely to some extent, except being from the African subcontinent, I tend to travel there a lot, I go home quite often and come back with all these lovely materials and products that I think would be unique back in England, only to find that I visit the first market and there the same products are, at the same price, and you lose the sense of uniqueness everywhere, and I find that a little bit of a pity really.

5 R: I took part in the er protests against the er the world trade organisation conference in Geneva. I'm very very in favour of expressing the other opposing point of view to globalisation. I always try to fight globalisation, I try to for example I try to shop from, not from the big high street names but from from small shopkeepers to try and support the er smaller small shopkeepers so that they can survive. Likewise I would never go and buy a coffee in one of those big chains of coffee shops ... I'd always go rather go to a little café somewhere.

Recording 1.2

I = Interviewer   DJ = Dr Jenkins

I: I've come to Kings College, London, to talk to Dr Jennifer Jenkins who's a Senior Lecturer in Applied Linguistics. Now Jennifer, you're quite interested in the teaching and learning of International English, can you explain in general terms what this is?

DJ: It's based on the fact that nowadays the majority of people who speak English around the world are non-native speakers of English – they ... they've learnt it as a second or subsequent language, they use it to speak with each other and therefore, they're not really learning what's always been called English as a foreign language – English to speak to native speakers of English. They're learning it for more international communication, and that has all sorts of implications for the sorts of things that they need to be able to do.

I: So, what would be the main differences between the kind of English that's widely taught around the world today, and perhaps what you describe as a more international form?

DJ: Well, there'd be various differences. There'd be differences in what they need to be able to do when they're pronouncing English, there would be some differences in the grammar, there'd be some differences in, er, use, or not, of idioms.

I: Is there anything that's widely taught when teaching English that would be missed out in International English?

DJ: Yes, I think, for example, that there doesn't seem to be much point in teaching learners to say the T-H, the (θ) and (ð) sounds. Erm, because most of the world's learners of English, speakers of English who are non-native speakers don't pronounce the (θ).

I: And, what is the thinking behind the idea of International English?

DJ: Well, there are two things. One is that the more different groups of people round the world speak English, the more important it becomes to make sure that they have enough in common so that they can understand each other, that they're intelligible to each other and here, pronunciation is very important because their pronunciation is the thing that will vary most, erm among different speakers of English, erm and the second thing would be that now that English is spoken as an international language nobody owns it any more. The native speakers of English don't own it and so don't have the right to expect everybody else around the world, when they speak English, to conform to 'native-speaker' ways of speaking, that everybody has the right to develop their own ways of speaking English.

I: So, what would you say are the advantages for students and teachers of this form of English?

DJ: Well, one one advantage would be that they actually have rather less to do, rather less to learn because instead of trying to learn the entire, erm, way of speaking of a native speaker, which is incredibly complicated and most learners never do achieve this in any case, so

they've got less to do, but they're also allowed to, erm, keep something of themselves in their English. They're speaking English as say a Japanese speaker of English or, erm, an Arabic speaker of English, a Spanish speaker of English, erm and therefore, they are allowed to be themselves in English.

I: Right, and how do you see English being learnt and spoken in, say, 30 years' time? How do you feel it will have changed?

DJ: Well, the English that's being spoken internationally, I think, for example, will have no longer, erm, say British-based or American-based idiomatic language because this is not useful for international communication so that will have gone. I think that, erm, quite probably, the nouns that we call, erm, uncountable nouns like 'information' and so on, will have become countable nouns for international use. I expect, in Britain, we'll carry on talking about, erm, information as a 'piece of information', but quite possibly the rest of the world will be saying 'three informations' without treating it as an uncountable noun. I think, quite likely, the third-person-singular 's' in the Present Simple tense will have gone for international use. Erm, I think, in pronunciation, I think the 'th' ([think]) sound will have gone and possibly the 'th' ([the]) sound as well. Most learners will say, instead of 'th' ([think]), will say a 's' or a 't', as most of them do anyway at the moment, erm, but it will just be legitimate then.

I: There must, on the other hand, be students who will want to speak English the way that they perceive it to be spoken in Britain or America. So, what would you say to that?

DJ: Well, I'd say, first of all, I'd want to explain the facts to them, the fact that they are the majority that the non-native speakers of English are the majority. And having explained that and also the fact that they're much more able to express themselves, who they really are, their identity, in English, if they keep something of their background, of their 'mother tongue', I would then say that we can't patronise learners, that if learners still want to learn to speak as closely as possible to a native speaker, say a British or American English, it's their choice, and the important thing is to give learners choices so that they can make up their own mind what it is they want to do.

157

I: Well, Dr Jenkins, thank you for talking to me about that. It'll be interesting to see how far things change.

Recording 1.3

1   American English

Around 10,000 people gathered in Washington this week to protest against the globalisation policies of the International Monetary Fund and the World Bank, which were holding their annual general meeting in the nation's capital. Riot police used tear gas to disperse the marchers and several hundred were arrested over three days of protests. Following the recent protests in Seattle, which attracted an estimated 60,000 people, extra police were on duty to ensure that all scheduled meetings were permitted to go ahead, although four European finance ministers were unable to attend one meeting after being cut off by street protestors.

2   Indian English

More than 70 million Hindus have begun to gather on the banks of the River Ganges in the northern state of Uttar Pradesh for the religious festival of Maha Kumbh Mela. The festival is held every twelve years, in order to commemorate the mythological falling to earth of four drops of a liquid believed to confer immortality. The event began this week with a parade of sadhus – Hindu holy men living lives of strict simplicity – accompanied by parades of elephants and richly-decorated chariots. A thirty-square-mile tent city has been built to house pilgrims who have travelled from all over the world for the event, described by many as the 'largest religious gathering on earth'. Bathing in the River Ganges on one of the six selected days is said to wipe away the sins of seven lifetimes.

3   Australian English

An unexpected downpour of rain last weekend helped to douse the bushfires which have been raging in New South Wales for the past fortnight. Around 45 mm of rain fell in the space of only eight hours, putting out many of the fires which have devastated 740,000 acres of bushland in the Blue Mountain area, and have threatened the suburbs of Sydney, causing the evacuation of over 5,000 people. No lives have been lost, but the fires have killed thousands of sheep, and driven poisonous insects and snakes into the nearby city. Animal welfare workers fear that the local wildlife populations will take many years to recover.

Module 2

Recording 2.1

It was Mr Passey who saw I could also act. He gave me the chance to prove it in our school production of Benjamin Britten's *Let's Make an Opera*. Mr Passey was the director, but even before we opened, he told my parents he was beginning to have last-minute doubts. 'Lately,' he said, 'the boy … he hasn't put much effort into his performance … I don't know what he's going to be like.' It was only after I stepped on stage that first night that both he and I found out what I was about as an actor. I heard the laughter for the first time; I could see and feel that living organism that is an audience, and my love affair with it began at that instant.

We did a week at school with a cast made up of pupils and teachers. It was such a success that two months later the headmaster agreed that we would do a performance on a proper stage in South London, at the Town Hall, Brixton. The public was invited, and it was a proud night for the school. There was coverage in the South London press.

The second half of *Let's Make an Opera* is a rather dark and Dickensian tale telling the story of one of the children who were forced by sweeps in Victorian England to climb up to clean the narrow chimney passages. I was Sam, the young sweep boy and the opera's hero, who is rescued from his terrible fate, brought into a loving home and turned into a gentleman. In the first scene of the opera little Sammy is pushed out on to the stage while everyone sings 'Up the chimney, up you go …'. In response, Sammy pleads 'Please don't send me up again …' and the company keeps singing, pushing their brushes, 'Up the chimney, up you go …!' At the end of the first verse the two villainous sweeps (played with relish by Mr Livingston, the headmaster, and Mr Anderson, our French master) come along and rip off poor little Sammy's shirt. At the end of the second verse they rip off his raggedy pants and he is left standing in his tattered shorts, a miserable tyke with soot all over his pathetic frame. Then they push the poor boy up the chimney.

On opening night, the hall was filled to capacity with parents, teachers and pupils; Mum and Den were in the audience, and Nan as well. The night was in aid of the Church of England Children's Society, and everybody was there, representatives of the Church, local dignitaries and, top of the list, the Mayor of Lambeth.

Behind the curtains, I was manic with stage fright. I can scarcely remember getting ready for the performance. At last the moment came, the curtains opened and the opera began. 'Up the chimney, up you go!' They ripped my shirt off. 'Up the chimney, up you go!' But this time I grabbed my trousers and absolutely refused to let go. Little Sammy stood firm, grasping his drawers with an iron grip. Mr Livingston was convinced I was overacting and decided to take matters into his own hands. 'Ah-ha,' he ad-libbed, lunging across the stage at me, 'Little Sam doesn't want to go up the chimney!' He cuffed me on the head and pulled off my tattered trousers. There was nothing on underneath, not a stitch. I was so nervous beforehand, I had simply forgotten to put on my shorts.

So I stood there, stark naked, in full view of the audience, and the Mayor, completely surrounded by chaos. There was anarchy in the stalls, as pupils started cheering, the girls whistled and pennies were thrown on the stage.

Mr Livingston was livid, of course, and using his bare hands he pulled the curtains across on the performance. The noise from the audience died down, and for the next few minutes the only audible sounds in Brixton Town Hall signified that the mother of all beatings was being administered to my backside.

Recording 2.2a

Her name was Mrs Thompson. As she stood in front of her fifth grade class on the very first day of school, she told the children a lie. Like most teachers, she looked at her students and said that she loved them all the same. But that was impossible, because there in the front row, slumped in his seat, was a little boy named Teddy Stoddard. Mrs Thompson had watched Teddy the year before and noticed that he didn't play well with the other children, that his clothes were messy and that he constantly needed a bath. And Teddy could be unpleasant.

At the school where Mrs Thompson taught, she was required to review each child's past records and she put Teddy's off until last. However, when she reviewed his file, she was in for a surprise. Teddy's first grade teacher wrote, 'Teddy is a bright child with a ready laugh. He does his work neatly and has good manners.' His second grade teacher wrote, 'Teddy is an excellent student, well liked by his classmates, but he is troubled because his mother has a terminal illness and life at home must be a struggle.'

His third grade teacher wrote, 'His mother's death had been hard on him. He tries to do his best, but his father doesn't show much interest and his home life will soon affect him if some steps aren't taken.' Teddy's fourth grade teacher wrote, 'Teddy is withdrawn and doesn't show much interest in school. He doesn't have many friends and he sometimes sleeps in class.'

By now, Mrs Thompson realised the problem and she was ashamed of herself. She felt even worse when her students brought her Christmas presents, wrapped in beautiful ribbons and bright paper, except for Teddy's. Some of the children started to laugh when she found a bracelet with some of the stones missing, and a bottle that was one-quarter-full of perfume. But she stifled the children's laughter when she exclaimed how pretty the bracelet was, putting it on, and dabbing some of the perfume on her wrist. Teddy Stoddard stayed after school that day just long enough to say, 'Mrs Thompson, today you smelled just like my mother used to.'

After the children left she cried for at least an hour. From that day on, she no longer felt as if she was just teaching reading, writing and arithmetic. Instead, she began to teach children. Mrs Thompson paid particular attention to Teddy. As she worked with him, his mind seemed to come alive. By the end of the year, Teddy had become one of the smartest children in the class.

A year later, she found a note under her door from Teddy, telling her that she was still the best teacher he ever had in his whole life. But the story doesn't end there. Twenty years went by before she got another note from Teddy. This time he explained that after he got his degree, he decided to go a little further. The letter explained that she was still the best and favourite teacher he ever had. But now his name was a little longer – the letter was signed Theodore F. Stoddard, M.D. Doctor of Medicine.

Recording 2.2b

For many years, Matenko the great comedian, had performed in all the great theatres in the country, and was the particular favourite of the King and Queen, who he never failed to entertain with his brilliant wit and clever tricks. But now Matenko was growing old, people no longer laughed at his jokes and everyone had seen all his tricks a hundred times. Finally, it was decided that he must retire. The King invited Matenko to his palace and told him, 'The Queen and I are very sorry, Matenko, that it is time for you to retire. Take this purse of money with you when you go and live in your native village.' Matenko was heartbroken.

He and his wife sadly carried their belongings to the little cottage which the king had given them. Soon, they had almost no money left. 'How can I earn a living?' wondered Matenko. 'Telling jokes is the only trade I know.' At last the two old people were starving. 'There is nothing else to do but lie down and die,' said Matenko in despair one day. Then suddenly he had an idea. 'Wait, there is just one chance that we may not have to starve. Wanda, trust me and do just as I tell you.' Then Matenko explained his plan to her.

That evening Wanda put on her best clothes, and chopped a raw onion so that tears ran down her wrinkled cheeks. Then she went to the royal palace to see the Queen. 'Your Majesty,' she sobbed. 'My poor Matenko is dead.' The Queen felt very sorry for the old woman, and gave her a purse full of money to pay for a funeral and to buy food for herself. 'We have 50 gold pieces! Hoorah!' cried Matenko, and he danced around the little cottage as he counted the coins in the Queen's purse.

The next day, Matenko chopped another raw onion and went to the palace to see the King. 'Your Majesty,' he sobbed, 'my poor wife is dead.' The King felt very sorry for his old favourite and gave him a purse before sending him home. 'Hoorah!' cried Matenko when he reached home. 'Now we have 100 gold pieces ... a small fortune!!' Then he kissed his wife and told her the rest of his plan.

On the sideboard in their little cottage he set two big, lighted funeral candles, and beside them he laid the two purses with all the gold pieces still in them. Then he told Wanda to lie down on the bed. 'Cross your arms over your chest, and don't move. You must pretend to be dead,' he told her. Then he lay down beside her, crossing his arms over his chest. And so they lay and waited.

Meanwhile, as soon as Matenko had left the palace with his purse of coins, the King hurried to his wife's chamber to tell her that the old jester's wife had died. 'But, my dear, you must be mistaken,' said the Queen. 'It is the jester, not the jester's wife who is dead.' Then they began to quarrel about which one of them was right. In the end, they agreed to go to the jester's cottage to find out.

When they knocked and walked into the little cottage they found the candles lit, the purses on the sideboard and Matenko and Wanda, who were obviously dead. 'But which of them died first?' asked the Queen. 'It must have been Matenko.' 'No, it must have been Wanda,' said the King. They began to quarrel again, when Matenko jumped up from the bed and said, 'Your Majesty, my wife died first, but I was dead before her.' When they had recovered from their astonishment, the King and Queen were too happy to see the old couple still alive to be really angry. When Matenko explained why they had pretended to be dead, the King and Queen promised to send them money whenever they needed it.

Module 3

Recording 3.1

I = Interviewer   R = Rosemary

I: Rosemary, what are the most common situations where people have problems in communicating?

R: Well, probably one of the main situations where people have problems communicating is where they're unsure of who they're talking to. So for instance going to a party and it's a room full of strangers, people you've never ever met before, that generally for most people will prove to be a little bit of a difficult situation. Erm I suppose the second area is where people are unsure of what they're talking about, so the content worries them for whatever reason. And the third area is where we're in a situation of speaking to an audience who we perceive are very different to us, so they are different in terms of their age, their experience or their status.

I: So that's quite general so why don't we, can we think of a specific example, maybe that party again?

R: Oh, let's suppose you're erm introduced to someone, again a total stranger you've never met them before and you don't know them, erm you are introduced to them and you from the introduction you gather that they are actually quite an important person, they've got high status, they're very experienced, they're much older than you, and all of a sudden you think 'my goodness, why would they possibly want to listen to me?' and we feel totally lacking in confidence.

I: Erm in that situation, what are, what are the most common mistakes they're going to make?

R: Probably one of the most common mistakes, will be they would want to speak too much, they'd say too much. Er all this information would come out of their mouths er but what they really should be doing in that situation is asking some questions to get the other person talking to them, not too many questions because if we ask too many questions it sounds like an interrogation, but getting the balance right between giving some information but also asking for information as well through questioning. Probably one of the other things they would do tied into that, would they wouldn't, they wouldn't pause enough. They wouldn't erm stop, to allow the other person to reflect on what they've said and to give them time to think about what they're going to say next, and to reflect on what's being said to them. So that would be something we need to be careful of and to always remember that when we do pause when we communicate, it will seem a lot, seem quite a length of time to us but it won't to the person we're speaking to.

I: And what about eye contact?

R: Well, if we don't look at someone they immediately think that they can't trust us or we're not telling the truth, so eye contact is very important. We've got to make sure we get it right … if we give too much they could perceive that we er we rather like them a little too much, or maybe we're being a little aggressive towards them. So we've got to get the eye contact about right, about three seconds in general is about right before we move away from the face then come back to the eyes.

I: A situation I often find I have trouble with is when I need to complain about something. What sort of mistakes might I be making?

R: Well I think it's very common to feel uncomfortable about making a complaint. Probably one of the most common things that people do in that situation is they're tempted to say far too much, so they become very unclear about the nature of the complaint … they're not precise enough. And they may well be tempted to speak far too quickly as well because actually we want to get to the end of the complaint because we don't particularly like complaining in the first place. We may also fall into the trap of not listening enough to what the other person has said because actually we may be becoming emotional too and therefore we listen less actively to what the person's saying to us and they in turn may not listen very well to us either so the whole erm complaint may become totally out of hand and we may end up completely falling out with one another. So, that's probably why complaints can be very difficult to er to handle.

I: So those are the problems you might encounter when you're complaining. How do you make a successful complaint?

R: Well, the first thing to do is to think and plan how you're going to voice your concerns. So don't go straight into it – you've really got to think and consider what's going what needs to be said. Make sure the sentences are short. Take out any language which could be seen as being emotional and irritating to the other party. And then wait and be prepared to get a response from the other person whom you've made the complaint to – and really listen, actively, to what they are saying and summarise or test your understanding of what they've said to make sure you totally understand their point of view.

I: And when you summarise something, how, how do you do that effectively?

R: Well, if you think of summarising as being simply restating, in a more compact form, what the other person has said to you, so that you've included all the key things and make sure that you've understood exactly what they're saying to you. So restating in a compact form what's been said to us.

I: How do you summarise why good communication is so important?

R: Because in whatever situation we're in we always have to deal with people and we have to communicate with people. And if we're going to get the best out of people and build relationships successfully, whether it be at work or in a social situation, we need to have good communication skills and we mustn't think that good communication skills are something that we all naturally have ... it's something that we all need to work on to make sure that we build good relationships.

Recording 3.2

a)

A: Karen ... hi ... are you in the middle of something?

B: Sort, of ...

A: Well, shall I come back later?

B: No, no it's all right ... what can I do for you?

A: Sorry to disturb you ... I'm having a lot of trouble with my computer. Every time I try to print something, I just get an error message.

B: Have you tried just turning it off and starting again?

A: Yes, well it just seems to keep on happening ... I thought if you had a minute you might come and look at it for me ... you did say if there was anything ...

B: And you've tried re-starting it ...

A: Yeah, I've done that ... same thing, it just keeps freezing when I try to print ...

B: OK well, I've just got to finish this, if you'll just bear with me for a minute ...

A: Right.

B: OK, just let me send this off and I'll be right with you.

A: Thanks ... sorry to be a nuisance.

B: No, that's all right.

b)

A: Neil?

B: Hmm?

A: Do you fancy a walk?

B: What, you want to go for a walk? Now?

A: No, I thought you might ... y'know ... a bit of exercise ... do you good.

B: No, not particularly. I'm OK here, thanks.

A: Right.

B: What made you say that?

A: Nothing ... no reason. Neil?

B: Yeah?

A: Can I ask a really really big favour?

B: Depends what it is.

A: You know the dry cleaner's down the road?

B: Mm.

A: You know it shuts at 8.00, doesn't it?

B: Ah! You want me to pick up your dry-cleaning.

A: It's just a couple of things, oh go on ... I'd be really grateful.

B: So that's why you asked if I wanted a walk.

A: Well, partly yes, although I did think you looked like you wanted something to do.

B: I see ... and is there something preventing you from going?

A: It's just that I wanted to see the end of this programme on the telly ... I'm really into it now.

B: Oh, are you?

A: Oh, go on. I'll make you a cup of tea when you get back.

B: Oh, all right then.

A: Here's the ticket – there's two coats, a skirt ...

c)

A: Hi, how're you doing?

B: Fine, thank you.

A: May I disturb you for one moment? We have a small problem here and I wonder if you might be able to help me.

B: What's the problem exactly?

A: As you'll have seen, the flight is very full this morning, so there are no spare seats anywhere.

B: Yeah?

A: We have a family with three small children. Unfortunately they're sitting separately, and obviously they would prefer to sit together.

B: Yes ... and you want me to move.

A: Would that be at all possible?

B: Well, I'm very comfortable here actually ... I did ask for an aisle seat.

A: Well, we can move you to an aisle seat if you prefer. We would very much appreciate it if you could help us here.

B: Well, I don't see why I should ... I mean I did ask for an aisle seat. Why don't you ask someone else?

d)

A: … and as I said, there's absolutely no way we can … Excuse me a moment … James, yeah … yeah I can hear you, yes just about. Right … well I'm just having dinner … right … listen … I'd better ring you back, is that OK? Right … sorry about that. I'll just give him a ring ba …

B: Excuse me, sir.

A: Yes?

B: I must ask you not to use your mobile phone in the restaurant. Perhaps you could make your call outside, if you don't mind.

A: Oh … I didn't realise …

B: It is the policy of the restaurant. Some diners complain that it's disturbing for them.

A: Fair enough. If you say so.

B: Thank you sir. Enjoy the rest of the meal.

Module 4

Recording 4.1

a) Water while-you-wait
You can never drink enough water, so keep a bottle of filtered water in your car and drink it while you wait at red lights. This is an especially useful health tip for people who spend a lot of time on the road.

b) Musical relief
Music can bring calm and peacefulness to anxious moments. And the beauty is, it can travel with you. If you find music soothing, bring a walkman with you on public transport, while waiting in queues, or when you're out walking or jogging.

c) Empty your brain
Just like a dustbin, the brain can overflow with unwanted 'rubbish'. Make an effort to empty your brain of all thoughts for five minutes three times a day. Visualise travelling through a white tunnel in which you leave behind all your unwanted thoughts and feelings.

d) Your mind
Your mind is like the surface of a lake. It is calm and smooth until anxious thoughts start ruffling the surface. Drain the lake. Empty your mind. When there is no water, there is no surface. When there is no mind, there can be no anxiety. The empty head is the beginning of wisdom.

e) Unblocking your emotional flow
Do you find your emotional flow blocked by unwanted feelings? Unblock your flow by asking a friend to be your feelings facilitator. If your friend refuses, release your emotions by screaming loudly for ten minutes. Afterwards, write a loving letter to your friend, explaining why you feel let down.

f) Skip-to-it
Increasing your level of fitness can often seem difficult and impractical, but it doesn't have to be. Skipping is one of the quickest ways of getting up your heart rate, and the best thing is, you don't need lots of time, space or expensive clothes and equipment.

g) Stressed out?
Go outside, lie down on your back, spread your arms and legs in an X-shape and stare up at the sky. Stay in that position until you can feel your connection to the infinite. If you hear the rumble of traffic, you may be lying in the middle of a road. Ask the infinite if you can call back later.

h) Getting rid of the clutter in your life
Make space for yourself by getting rid of the clutter in your life. Throw away your unwanted clothes. Burn your old files. Clear out the rubbish in your attic. Dispose of your grandmother.

i) Stress in the workplace
When you are experiencing stress in the workplace, there is nothing more soothing than a herbal tea. Make the tea in a large mug, add a generous spoonful of organic honey, and pour the contents over the desktop PC of the person who's been annoying you.

j) Instant air-conditioning
If you don't have air-conditioning in your car, don't despair. Place an icepack or block of ice in an ice chest on the back seat of your car. Leave the lid off. The ice will gradually cool the air, which will make those long, balmy drives bearable.

k) Colour your thoughts
Whenever you feel stressed, take a few minutes to think of a relaxing colour such as pale blue, white, mauve or green. Bathe yourself in this colour in your mind and then tackle your stress. See how much calmer you feel.

l) New beginnings
Break through to a whole new life in less than a day. Here's how. Buy ten self-help books. Take them home. Put them in a pile on the floor. Sit on them. Watch television.

Recording 4.3

… so these are our finalists. Before the judges make their decision, let's have another look at the stories that first brought these outstanding men and women to our attention.

A British couple have made history by becoming the first husband-and-wife team to walk to both the North and the South Poles. After a 56-day trek across the frozen Antarctic Ocean, Mike Thornwill, 38, and his wife Fiona, 33, have become the first couple to reach the South Pole. They ended their journey by renewing their wedding vows outside the Amundsen-Scott Ice Station. During the trip they endured temperatures as low as –50°C. The previous year, they spent 61 days walking to the North Pole. Mr Thornwill spoke to the BBC by satellite phone: 'It's absolutely awesome … I am not so emotional at the moment, I feel quite cool about the whole thing. But I am incredibly proud of my wife.' The expedition was organised to raise money for cancer research and children's charities.

Child psychologist Camila Batmanghelidjh, whose family came to Britain from Iran in the 1970s, had had a dream ever since her own difficult childhood – to open a drop-in centre where under-privileged children from troubled homes could take refuge when they were not at school. She finally found the premises in South London that she had been looking for to make her dream a reality, but was soon warned that the centre would be overrun by local teenage gangs, many of whom carried knives, and even guns. Rather than trying to keep these wild teenagers out, Camila made a highly courageous decision: that she should open her doors to them too. But experience convinced her that they would never respond to the authority of middle-class social workers, so again she made a very unusual decision, to recruit as careworkers young men who were themselves ex-gangsters and drug dealers, to whom these youngsters would be better able to relate. 'Of course it was very difficult at first – there was a lot of conflict between ourselves and these young men who were working in the centre. In some ways they were much stricter than us – when youngsters broke the rules, they wanted to take them outside and beat them up! But eventually, I think, we learnt to coexist.'

Three retired women on a day trip to France attacked and disarmed a man who attempted to steal their car at gunpoint. The women were sitting in their car when the thief pointed a loaded gun through the window and tried to grab the car keys. To the robber's surprise, Joan Windsor, 70, grabbed the gun and started hitting him with it, while the driver, Jean Douglas, punched him on the arm. The gunman managed to push the two women out of the car and drive off, but he hadn't counted on Anne Aylward, 69, who was still in the back seat and attacked him until he lost control of the car and crashed into a concrete flower tub. Mrs Aylward was taken to hospital and treated for cuts and bruises, and later released. Mrs Windsor, who was still holding the gun when the emergency services arrived, said later, 'This won't stop us enjoying ourselves. My sister calls us the 'Have a Go-Golden Girls'.

When 44-year-old police constable Glynn Griffith heard over his radio that a mother and three children were trapped on a sandbank surrounded by the incoming tide, he didn't hesitate for a second. Although the coastguard were on their way in a lifeboat, Constable Griffith knew that by the time they arrived, the tide would almost be in and feared that it would be too late for the mother and her family. So in spite of the perils of quicksand as well as the tide, which constantly undermined his footing, the brave father of three waded out for over a mile to guide them off the sandbank in a race against time. This was what his boss, Superintendent Tony Burden had to say about him: 'In taking the prompt action that he did, without a thought for the danger to himself, Constable Griffith almost certainly averted a tragedy. We are all very proud of him.'

Module 5

Recording 5.1

1 Well I think for me at school I did history and French and Maths, and I wish I'd done woodwork because I'm incompetent in my house … I can't put up a shelf, I can't paint a wall, so it costs me a lot of money to have decorators in, or my uncle who is a painter/decorator himself, so I really wish I'd done woodwork.

2 Well, one subject that I wish I'd learnt at school is typing, because you know it's very important in everyday life and I still only type with two fingers and if I'd had the time it would have been a really nice thing to have done and I think it would have helped me in my life.

3 The one practical skill that I really wish that I'd been taught in school is note-taking because I find it extremely difficult to follow what people say to me in meetings and take notes at the same time, and because my memory's very short, I often forget those things, so that's definitely one skill that I wish I'd been taught at school.

4 I wish I'd learnt economics at school so that I could understand what I was reading in the business section of the newspapers.

5 Cooking! Like I went to an all boys school and I wish I'd been taught a little bit more about the fundamentals of cooking 'cos I really enjoy it now but I just ... I missed some of the little points I think, to start off with.

6 Well, I wish I'd concentrated more on learning languages really. I really didn't put my mind to those things really and now they'd be very useful.

7 ... (it'd) probably be about life, like day-to-day life, like bills and you know, how to organise yourself and how you run a home and things like that, just ... I think that would have been great.

8 I think it's really important that people learn to do first aid, I would have loved to have done a first-aid course because I think it's really important to know what to do in an emergency. You may never need it, but if you have the skill, it's always there.

9 Not really actually, I went to an American High School where we were taught home economics, accounting, typing, car mechanics, taught to drive ... it's really hard to think of anything. It was a very well rounded ... lots of choices available.

Recording 5.2

I = Interviewer   W = William Atkinson

I: In what practical ways do you try to prepare your pupils for life in the adult world after they've left school ... for being a member of the community, as it were?

W: There are a number of ways in which we try to teach citizenship within our school. First of all through our assemblies – we have daily assemblies in the school, and through those we get across issues to do with the organisation of management and the living together, because citizenship is all about, fundamentally, it's about people living together, it's about people organising their group in a way that allows people to flourish and no one individual to have an undue influence on what is actually going on.

I: And how do you actually teach pupils to 'organise their group'? What practical experience do they get, in this respect?

W: We have representatives from each class on a school council. The school council is able to make observations about the management, the organisation of the school. They're able to suggest things that need to improve in the school, that need to change. Essentially we try to give them a say within the organisation of the school ... One of the other skills that we teach is to do with er being able to work with other people – teamwork yah, so the ability to be a member of a group, to listen within that group and also to develop a degree of empathy and tolerance of other viewpoints and perspectives within that group ... and the need to channel one's energies into the common good rather than simply pursuing the one's own interests.

I: So do you have actual lessons called 'teamwork'?

W: It's not a timetabled subject as such, but what it is, it's an approach that we try to weave in to the normal teaching that we do in the school. Having said that, if we're now talking about an area like drama, in drama there are overt attempts to work as a team, to develop these team skills that I've just touched on, so in that part of the curriculum you'd find it. If you were also to go to physical education, again in physical education you will find the teachers trying to develop good interpersonal skills within groups, and to develop the team as an entity that's greater than the individual in order to actually win a game in an inter-team sport, for example.

I: Why do you consider teamwork to be such a vital skill?

W: We're very interested in equipping young people to play their role in adult life and part of that is in a workplace, and it is rare that anyone in a workplace work by themselves – they're always a member of a smaller or larger team and that requires some skills to be an effective and productive member of that team so the kind of skills that we're teaching in schools have application not only inside the standard structured education system, but they have direct application inside in a work environment outside and indeed in the social context outside. And increasingly, living in a highly competitive, technological age, I think it's going to call for more and more people working together, sharing … so I think the need for the kind of skills that we've been talking about will actually grow in the future.

I: And as well as these practical skills, do you try to deal with wider social issues at all?

W: I think it's important to to deal in schools with those big issues that society's facing at this particular time. Drugs and alcohol will be a case, early pregnancy would be something, the intolerance that exists in certain sections of our society to do with homophobia, racism, sexism, these are issues which we in school try to deal with, within our overall er active citizenship programme within the school. To that end, we do bring in from outside er organisations and individuals who have expertise in this area to actually share with our youngsters … and having outside facilitators who are not teachers often is a very effective way of grabbing the attention of the young people er because they're seeing somebody who may have been involved in drugs, for example, may have been involved in crime, and been able to articulate why they were involved, what they got out of it, and why they stopped, yah. So engaging with the wider community in school is something that's increasingly important.

Recording 5.3

The most common circumstances in which you might have to resuscitate someone is either because they've had a heart attack, or because they've drowned, or had an electric shock or maybe because something has fallen on them. So the first thing to remember is to approach the patient with caution … be aware of possible dangers to yourself, like electric cables, or falling objects, etc. Self-preservation comes first, for obvious reasons.

Before you start trying to resuscitate them, you need to check that they're not just asleep, so shake them by the shoulders and say their name or whatever, and see if you can wake them up.

If they do need resuscitation, it's either because they've stopped breathing, or because their heart has stopped beating, but you should always deal with the breathing first. Oxygen is the number one thing that the body needs – four to six minutes without oxygen can cause irreparable damage to the brain … so that's always the first thing to think about.

The reason the person isn't breathing may simply be that the airway is blocked … they've swallowed their tongue, as you might say … and so very often all that's needed is to open up the airway. This is actually very simple – you just place two fingers beneath the chin, and use them to lift the head back, and that will be enough to straighten up the airway. You may well actually hear a deep intake of breath when this happens. But if you aren't sure whether or not they are breathing, then put your ear close to their mouth, and you will probably be able to feel their breath tickling your ear, and then you know it's okay.

If the patient still isn't breathing, you need to start mouth-to-mouth resuscitation at this point. To do this, you pinch their nostrils together hard, with one hand, and hold their chin with the other hand so that their head is tilted back. Then you need to cover their mouth with your mouth … this is really important. You need to completely seal their mouth so that no air can escape – that's why you're pinching their nose. Then you press down hard, and breathe into their mouth, watching out of the corner of your eye to see if their chest is expanding … you should just see it rise slightly.

Then you take your mouth away to allow the air to be exhaled, then repeat again four to six times. Repeat the breaths at about the same interval that you breathe at yourself. If they're breathing for themselves by now then that's fine … you can turn the person onto their side and put them into the unconscious position. If not, deliver two more breaths, and see if that does it.

If they aren't breathing by this stage, the problem may well be that their heart has stopped … and at that stage you would need to check the pulse and if necessary give a cardiac massage. But remember the number one priority in this kind of emergency is always to get the patient breathing. Any questions so far?

Module 6

Recording 6.1

£10:

The answer is obviously B. The world's first coins were produced – or minted – in ancient Lydia, in what is now Turkey – about 2,600 years ago. The coins were made of electrum, a mixture of gold and silver. The other items didn't appear till the twentieth century.

£25:

A company goes 'bust' when it cannot continue because it has no more money, but a person who has no money is often described in colloquial language as 'broke', or even 'flat broke'. The answer's A.

£50:

All of these words refer to sums of money people receive at different times. A professional person gets a 'fee' when they do a piece of work; people get a 'pension' when they retire; you get a 'subsidy' when you need money for an unprofitable business … but you don't normally get any of these from your parents. The answer's C, 'pocket money'.

£100:

'Valueless' and 'worthless' both mean that something has no value, so it's worth nothing. 'Pricey' is an informal word for expensive, but the item can be bought; so the correct answer's B, 'priceless'.

£250:

To say a company is 'in the red' means that the company owes money – but it doesn't necessarily go out of business. If it 'breaks even', it doesn't make a profit … in which case it would be 'in the black' … the only phrase that means it goes out of business is D, it 'goes bankrupt'.

£500:

All of these words describe sums of money you give to different people at different times, but only two of them relate to crime or dishonesty! A 'tip' is the money you pay a waiter or a hairdresser for doing a good job; a 'deposit' is part of the full price of something – you pay it when you agree to buy something then pay the full amount later, so again there's nothing illegal about that. A 'ransom' is the money you pay a kidnapper, so that certainly does relate to crime. But if you want to persuade a person in authority to do something dishonest, you pay them 'a bribe', so the answer's B.

£1,000:

You can probably guess that 'tight-fisted' means someone who hates spending money, and perhaps 'miserly' too. 'Stingy' has the same meaning, so the odd one out is A, 'flashy', which actually means that you like spending lots of money on things that show everyone how rich you are!

Recording 6.2a

The story of Stella Liebeck is often quoted as a symbol of what has come to be known as 'Compensation Culture' in the USA today. Listen to the facts … and make up your own mind.

One morning in February 1992, Stella Liebeck, a 79-year-old woman from Santa Fe, New Mexico, drove 60 miles with her son, Jim, and her grandson, Chris, to Albuquerque airport in order for Jim to catch an early flight. After she dropped Jim off, she and her grandson stopped at a burger restaurant for breakfast. Her grandson, who was driving the car, parked so that Stella could add cream and sugar to her coffee. She put the cup between her knees and tried to pull the lid off. As she tugged at the lid, the cup tipped over and scalding coffee poured onto her lap. She screamed and a horrified Chris rushed to help her.

Stella received burns over 16 percent of her body, and was hospitalised for eight days. Her daughter stayed home for three weeks to look after Stella following her release from hospital. Treatment for her burns, including skin grafts, lasted for more than two years. Eventually, Mrs Liebeck wrote to the burger company asking if they would consider selling their coffee at a lower temperature and to refund her medical expenses – about $2,000 – plus the lost wages of her daughter who stayed home to care for her. The company offered her just $800.

Only then did Stella consult a lawyer, who advised her to sue the company. The jury awarded her

$160,000 in actual damages and an extra $2.7 million dollars in punitive damages against the fast-food restaurant in question. The sum was eventually reduced to $640,000, but not before there was a huge outcry in the US media, and Stella Liebeck had unwillingly become a national celebrity.

Recording 6.2b

D = David   B = Beth

D: OK, so what's your, what's your take on this Stella Liebeck thing?

B: Well, I think she was entitled to some compensation …

D: What do you mean … some compensation … what do you mean by some compensation?

B: Well, let's be blunt about this, she burned herself, she had to undergo medical treatment, her family member had to take time off of work …

D: What I find really interesting is when you just said that she burned herself, now not once did she admit that it was her fault, you've just said she burned herself, and that's exactly what I think, she burned herself so … she shouldn't get any compensation from them.

B: Yeah, but David, the coffee was absolutely ridiculously hot, it's one thing for a company to serve hot coffee but it was 180 to 190°.

D: Companies would not serve coffee that hot if the public didn't demand in the first place that they got really hot coffee … you … do it the other way round, you'd probably get people suing them for having cold coffee …

B: Yes I know …

D: … and their tooth fell out or, I mean … you know ridiculous …

B: But the coffee that you have at home isn't that hot, and people say 'Oh coffee's great' …

D: Yeah, bu …

B: … and that's the temperature they want it, it's 135 to 140, I mean that's a significant difference.

D: You have to ask yourself …

B: … in temperature …

D: You do have to ask yourself why they have it that kind of temperature, I mean presumably they have it that kind of temperature because people want it that kind of temperature …

B: Well, OK. I think people want it hot but I – you do have to realise as well that there've been approximately 700 cases of people being burned by scalded – scalding coffee, so …

D: Right …

B: I mean obviously restaurants and, and take-out food places have got to take this on board …

D: There …

B: … they just can't sell it that hot …

D: There may well have been 700 cases of people being burned by scalding coffee, but … but … they didn't all sue, did they? I mean, she's the only one … only one who's sued.

B: No, she's …

D: As far as I know anyway …

B: … she's the most famous one because she got most money out of it.

D: I'm sorry, I'm sorry, no way should she have give … have been given that money … no way.

B: Look, the fast-food chain makes 1.3 million dollars a day selling coffee … they could afford this.

D: It is ridiculous, it is ridiculous to claim that, just because a company makes a lot of money and they can afford to pay people compensation they good … they, they should … it's … the thing is, nowadays what happens is that we, we have to blame someone, and the person to blame is never yourself, never yourself, it's always somebody else's fault, always.

Recording 6.5

A was awarded £20,000 (or $30,000) damages following the review of his play. He said later 'I stand really strong on the side of fair comment and opinion about the theatre. If you're going to use something like that, get your facts right.'

B was awarded a total of $3 billion dollars by the Californian court – the largest sum ever awarded in a case of this kind. Members of the jury explained that it had been their intention to 'hurt' the tobacco industry.

C received just £1,500 ($2,250) – about a month's salary – as compensation for losing his job.

D was initially awarded $450 million – the amount by which the value of her late husband's companies had increased during their marriage. However, this was later reduced to $88 million when her husband's son appealed against the decision.

Module 7

Recording 7.1

1 The trouble with my sister is that if I do something she isn't happy about, she won't just say what's wrong. She sulks for ages and ages before she tells you what's the matter. And it's the same if we have an argument about something. She can't just put it behind her and move on – I hate it.

2 I share a room at college with my friend Laura, and she's really good fun. She's always laughing and everything. The only problem is that she never stops talking. When she comes in, she'll tell you everything that's happened to her, everything everyone's said to her, in minute detail. Sometimes you wish she'd just shut up, just for a few minutes to give you time to think.

3 One big difference between me and my wife is mornings. I jump out of bed really bright and breezy, you know, singing along to the radio, and she just loathes the morning. She crawls out of bed with her eyes half closed and just growls at everyone until she's had at least two cups of coffee. You hardly dare speak to her, it's terrible!

4 One major problem between my ex-husband and me was tidiness. He was incredibly tidy – I would say fanatically tidy, and he used to go mad at me if I left things lying around. He was always picking things up and folding them, and tutting and sighing to himself. It was awful.

5 The worst thing about Tony, my ex-flatmate, was his moods. One day he'd be really friendly and full of jokes, and then suddenly the next day, for no reason you could see, he'd be really down, and you could hardly get a word out of him. You never knew where you stood with him.

6 The thing that most annoys me about my son is the way he turns on the TV the moment he walks into the room, or puts on a CD or whatever. And he never turns anything off when he's finished. Then he'll go into another room and put something else on. It's infuriating.

7 I'm living with a landlady at the moment, but I'm going to move out. I just can't stand it any more. She never stops moaning … every time I see her it's something different. She's always waiting for me when I come home, with her latest problem. It's driving me mad!

Recording 7.2

C = Catherine   P = Peter   L = Liz

C: Peter, did you use to be in the army?

P: Yes, in my time, you had to do national service when you were eighteen years, and it was compulsory, so you had no choice …

C: So how did you find it?

P: Well, I remember at the time I was really looking forward to it … it was an opportunity to go abroad and … er … live in other countries and, it was quite a shock when I got in.

L: What, what were you looking forward to? I can't imagine anything worse than being in the army!

P: Well, it was … I don't know, it was exciting … it was that boy thing, and shooting a rifle, and going abroad … Yes, I remember I was really looking forward to it. The first thing they put in my hand was an iron and they showed us how to iron a shirt, which wasn't what I wanted to join the army for, because I'd never ironed a shirt in my life … and then the next thing they did was they … they showed us how to sew a button on a shirt, and how to darn a hole in a sock. I think it was about six weeks before I was even allowed to get my hands on a rifle at all.

C: Yeah, what about you, Liz, when did you leave home?

L: Oh, I … well I went to boarding school when I was eleven … erm … I'd had a wonderfully free life growing up in the country in Australia, and suddenly at the age of eleven my parents decided that they wanted me to go to a school in the city. What about you?

C: Erm, well I started doing some au-pairing when I was 18, erm I'd done French 'A' level so my French was relatively good … but erm still … y'know speaking, conversation and living in the French language for a month was very daunting.

L: And was it different to how you imagined it was going to be?

C: Erm, I can't remember now what I'd imagined but I mean we had some fantastic times – the weather was gorgeous every single day … and we'd go down to the beach every day … erm … the kids were a good age so they could go off and play … erm … but it wasn't all kind of playing on the beach (sailing) … the parents really wanted them to learn English whilst I was there so one of my roles was to teach them English … erm … which for an eight-year-old and a ten-year-old on their summer holiday was not what they wanted to do at all … so we had quite a lot of battles, trying to get them to sit down at that dining-room table and do their work

L: But what was it like, what was it like actually just living in a … you know a place that you hadn't been to before, with a family that you weren't … that you didn't know … and living under somebody else's rules?

C: It … difficult … being an au pair you're told what to do … you're there, you're getting paid, you're living in their house, and you have to abide by their rules. I don't like being told what to do and to be told to go and put on the milk, to sweep the floors, put the washing out – I find quite hard work, but after a couple of weeks you get to know the routine so you start doing those kind of things yourself without having to be told … erm … but I did have moments when I just kind of stormed up to my room and shut the door, 'cos at eighteen, I was still quite young, I was still quite inexperienced and I found it quite difficult to deal with that.

L: Well, I suppose that's something that you had to do as well, didn't you, live under under the rules of the army, that must've been …

P: That's right, yes, the discipline was very, very hard but … erm … there's one, another story that I remember about being in the army, because … er … suddenly we found ourselves in a long hut with about thirty beds … er … with a short space between each bed and from all walks of life, we came from everywhere and the man opposite me, he was a huge man and he was one of these people that you avoided eye contact with, because … er … if you so much as glanced at him, he looked as if he was ready to … er … to attack you, and he had this thick, Elvis Presley-style hairstyle, and … er … on the second day we were marched to the barber shop to have our hair cut and they just cut the whole lot off, and I remember him standing outside, afterwards, and he was, he looked like an overgrown schoolboy, and he was crying, there was … tears running down his cheek, and he was quiet for about two days, and then after that you couldn't have met a nicer person. He did everything, he joined in everything and he was, he was really completely different.

C: So it was just his hair gave him an ego.

L: Perhaps that's … was his way of coping in an alien environment.

P: Could be! Yeah!

C: How did you feel about having your head shaved, then, I mean did you …

P: Well, they didn't actually shave it, they just they gave us what was known in those days as 'a short back and sides' …

C: But did you feel like you lost your individuality?

P: Yeah, because that was the whole idea, to make, to make you work as … as one unit … so that if they if they shouted 'Jump', then thirty men jumped at the same time, because … er … that was the whole objective, to … erm … to discipline people and to make you an effective force.

L: How did that affect you? How do you feel about it now, looking back?

P: Erm … well … at the time, it was … it was a bit scary … but looking back now, I think it was, it was a good time.

L: Erm, how boarding school affected me … well I said earlier it made me a more independent person, and at the time, at the time I hated it … I hated the rules, I hated the regulations, but it did, it did as I said, give me independence, but it also made me a quite conscientious person, because I got used to studying, and I think as a result of that, I developed into a very different person, at the end of the day, than I would have done had I stayed in Australia, you know, living my free life in the countryside. So I suppose looking back, looking back I'm very grateful that my parents made that decision to send me away, but certainly I didn't feel that when I was eleven.

Recording 7.3

Hello everyone, and erm thanks for coming along today … sorry … as you know, we are going to be making our final selection of the six candidates very soon, so I just want to remind you of the main things you need to bear in mind. Obviously I don't need to tell you that our number one priority is audience ratings. This is a big project for us, and it's going to be shown at prime time against stiff competition on the other channels, so we need something that's going to capture people's imagination, and pull in big audiences. Now as we already know, the candidates have been assessed on their fitness, ability to work in a team, knowledge of survival techniques, etc. etc.

and all that is very important. The last thing we want is participants dropping out halfway through their time on the island and going to the newspapers before the show is broadcast with lots of negative publicity – we mustn't be seen to be irresponsible in other words.

It's very important that we make sure that the people we select are likely to stay on the island for the full year. However, a perfectly balanced and perfectly trained group is not necessarily going to be what creates the maximum interest … what captures viewers' imagination, as I mentioned earlier. So, what else do we need to do to give the show that extra something, and pull in the viewers? Well, previous attempts at this kind of show have told us that it's very important to have different types of people that different viewers can identify with – erm, different ages, different types of backgrounds, different interests, single, married couples, etc. etc. etc. so that's something extremely important to bear in mind. OK?

Another pretty obvious thing is that viewers have got to find the participants attractive and interesting in some way. I don't just mean physically attractive, though obviously that helps – well, after all they'll be appearing on our TV screens in shorts and swimsuits for the next year, but also attractive, sympathetic, interesting as people, as personalities … the sort of people they'd be interested to get to know themselves. Related to that, and equally important is the potential for what we could call 'interesting interaction' between the participants. OK we want them to get on well and operate as a team, but we all like a bit of drama too – the hint of romance, maybe, a touch of conflict and one or two personality clashes, jealousies, etc. Of course we need to be very careful here, but I think you all know what I mean … something to get the viewers talking about the show the next day at work, and watching next week to find out what happens next, so that's another very important consideration. Anyway all that remains now is for …

Module 8

Recording 8.1

1 This is the kind of house that I would love to live in, because it's airy and spacious and it's tidy, but I could never live in a house like this, because I have two cats and two dogs and everything gets too messy.

2 Oh, she's beautiful, all pretty and elegant and sweet and young, just … I feel warm and good.

3 I personally don't like it. I think it's a bit … it's very over the top and very, very, very bright, but in the same breath I like to see people and admire anybody who could wear that, because it just shows individuality and creativity and confidence which is, I think appealing.

4 This I really like. I like this because of the clean lines. I like the fact that it reflects things, the reflective surface really mirrored mirrored in the water underneath it – I think is fantastic. I love the way it's sort of ship-like, almost – erm, it stands out so well against the background. I think it's beautiful, I think it's beautifully designed.

5 I think she looks really elegant in this picture. It's it's a very sort of classic elegance, a very sort of classy lady erm, and very … the clothes are are … you can tell they're very expensive, they're very well cut, and she's made up to look as if she isn't made up … it's very sort of naturalistic. The earrings are a bit large, they're a bit gaudy really, but apart from that, I think she looks, yes quite exquisite.

6 I think it's quite obscene when children are abused almost, treated as adults, their sort of childhood is actually robbed from them … they're dressed up like dolls, they're not real children.

7 I like his grungy-looking jumper, I think it looks really good on him, I think they're really good colours although he looks really scruffy, I think he looks really cool as well.

8 … erm, well, well about grunge … I guess it used to be really popular about five years ago, and erm I don't really like it, I think it's all a bit dirty, and it's really just an excuse for not washing properly.

Tapescripts

Recording 8.6

C = Catherine   E = Essam   SJ = Sarah Jane
P = Pietro

C: What I really hate is automated telephone answers – when you try to phone up a company and you get a recorded voice and you have to choose different options and they tell you press one if you have a problem with your invoice or press two if you have a problem with something else and it's never specific to what you want to speak about and you never know which one to choose, and it takes you like three minutes to get through to speak to an actual person, and you it's costing you money all this time and it's very frustrating. I was phoning up the hospital the other day and I wanted to speak to somebody specifically, and I spoke to a person and they said is it about appointments and I went 'well kind of …' and she immediately put me through to this automated thing without even saying 'I'm just putting you through' just like blanked off, and that was something which didn't answer my question at all. I had to put the phone down and phone up again to actually speak to a human – so I hate them.

E: Bad manners, and I'm afraid from my experiences I find that women are the worst offenders, particularly in the morning. I have a bus stop outside of my house, I arrive outside at the bus stop and I wait in line, and lo and behold, it's most of the men who'll wait patiently in line and join the back of the queue. However women have this very sly habit of side-stepping men particularly when they're not looking, walking to the front of the queue and jumping on the bus ahead of you and nine times out of ten the bus is late, the bus is full and who gets on ahead of you, it's the woman in front, and the doors close and you have to wait for the next one.

SJ: Something that drives me absolutely mad is repetitive noises, like someone tapping a pencil, or using a fork against a plate to tap, a beeping noise from an alarm system going off or something like that. I can take one or two or three beats and then I go crazy, and everyone asks me well how can you listen music, but then it's all mixed up and then it's all right for some reason but just the tapping drives me crazy and I can sit in a room full of a hundred people all talking and eating and someone can be tapping their fork and I can find them, and someone said to me once I should listen to try and find bombs because I was so good at this … it just drives me absolutely mad … even strangers in a lift I would turn to and ask them to stop tapping because it makes me so crazy.

P: Well the one thing I really hate is vegetarians. Erm, I mean I don't eat a lot of meat myself, but I have quite a lot of vegetarian friends and they seem to think that erm they're morally superior to me and that really gets on my nerves actually. Erm, I guess I don't eat a lot of meat and I have a great deal of respect for animals, but I think at the end of the day we're all animals and animals eat other animals, so I don't really see what's wrong with eating meat.

Recording 8.7

J = Johnny Taylor   C = Candice De Berg

J: Welcome back, this is Johnny Taylor here on Drive Time and I'm very glad to say that our next guest has finally arrived … and we're very lucky to have her in the studio with us to talk about her new film. All the way from the USA, Candice De Berg.

C: Hi there.

J: Candice welcome …

C: It's my pleasure …

J: Candice, obviously you are known as a major style icon … your face is in all the top fashion magazines, you're seen at all the most fashionable parties … tell me, what's it like to be so much in the public eye over in the States?

C: Well, to be perfectly honest, being seen so much in public can be tough sometimes … I mean I am lucky to be invited to so many things … but to tell the truth there are days when I'd rather just be at home, watching a video, talking to my cats, y'know … just doing normal stuff.

J: Well it's a good job you didn't decide to stay at home this evening, then. Tell me, do you ever get tired of being recognised everywhere you go … does it become a bore ever?

C: Well, funnily enough something crazy happened just the other day here in London that made me think about that. I was having dinner with a very dear friend and the waitress came over and she said 'Can you sign here, please?' and I'm thinking 'Oh no, another autograph' so I asked her 'who's it for?' and she looked a little confused, she said something and I just heard the name 'Bill'.

J: I see.

C: So I wrote on the napkin 'To Bill, with deepest affection, Candice De Berg' and much to my surprise, she looked at the napkin and said 'Thank you, but I meant can you sign for the bill please … can you sign the credit card slip?' She didn't want an autograph at all.

J: Oh dear.

C: … and to make matters worse … they asked me to pay for a new napkin.

J: Oh dear, how embarrassing … thank goodness you were able to see the funny side of it.

C: Excuse me?

J: Fortunately you were able to appreciate the humour of the situation.

C: Oh, yeah yeah sure, sure. After we'd left the restaurant, my friend and I had a real good laugh about it.

J: Right. So your new film. When will we be seeing that?

C: Erm, well my new movie is called Single Girl and, all being well, it should hit the screens just before Christmas, and I play …

Module 9

Recording 9.1a

P = Presenter   G = Gavin Allan

P: With the holiday season once again upon us, millions of people all over the world are busy thinking about their annual holidays … a chance to put our feet up, relax and do nothing for a week or two. Sitting in a traffic jam on the way to the coast, queuing up at a packed airport terminal or fighting your way through the crowds to find a free spot on an overcrowded beach may not be the best thing to put you in that relaxed holiday mood, but for millions of us, it's worth it for those blessed few days where we can forget about work and truly get away from it all.

But with more and more people taking to the skies every year, all too often the tourist's search for tranquillity … or a touch of genuine local colour is ruined by thousands of other tourists all doing the same thing. It's as if the tourist industry is becoming its own worst enemy. It is in response to this problem that a new kind of tourism is rapidly developing –

eco-tourism, as it's often known, and in today's programme we ask whether this is the future of the tourist industry. Gavin Allan is the director of a tour company which specialises in eco-tours. Gavin, what do we mean eco-tourism?

G: Eco-tourism is really about sustainable tourism. The holiday and leisure industry too often is about exploiting our resources, erm going for the quick money if you like, and we've all seen the damage it can do to the local environment. We can all think of places where the local economy has gained in the short term through tourism, but in the end, the very things that attracted the tourists may be lost. Eco-tourism is really about preserving these assets for future generations. We've got to think in the longer term … the way forward must be to respect and maintain local environments. So, if you like the tourist has to adapt to the local lifestyle rather than vice-versa. I think this has got to be the way forward in the future.

Recording 9.1b

P = Presenter   M = Matthew   J = Joanne
I = Isabelle

P: So, ecotourism also involves taking tourists away from established holiday destinations to places which are much less frequented – the Kalahari desert, for example, isn't on the usual list of 'Been There, Done That, Got the T-Shirt' places. Virtually inaccessible to foreigners until a few years ago, the desert occupies an area of nearly a million square kilometres in central southern Africa. Here in what is truly one of the most inhospitable places on earth, the only people who can survive are the Kalahari Bushmen … until now that is. A British travel company is offering an eleven-night all-inclusive tour of the Kalahari and five-star hotels, afternoons lazing by the swimming pool and sophisticated cuisine are definitely not on the menu. Matthew and Joanne Wyatt have just returned from their holiday in the Kalahari. Matthew, what made you visit such an out-of-the-way sort of place?

M: It is an extraordinary place, and an extraordinary way of life … what we're doing really is getting in touch with the way our ancestors lived thousands and thousands of years ago. The lifestyle that the bush people have is pretty much unchanged over the centuries. They're hunter-gatherers – the men go hunting and the women gather food from wherever they can find it, and they share everything … so we had to fit in with that.

J: The thing is, you're not just a guest here. If you're a visitor, you can't just put your feet up and let everyone else do the work. You're expected to muck in and do your bit … and so you have to join in with that way of life … so being a woman I was part of the gathering party.

P: And what kind of things did you come back with?

J: Well, usually some sort of leaves that tasted rather like spinach which they used to make a salad … nuts … but there are also these beetles, there are these enormous yellow and black desert beetles which they actually bake … in the hot sand.

P: Good Lord. And you actually eat them?

J: Yes … funnily enough … they tasted rather like crab … a little bit crunchy outside … delicious … especially when you're hungry.

P: As for the men … what did they get up to?

M: As a man I was part of the hunting party, which I'm afraid to say wasn't all that successful. We spent a lot of time nearly catching things … usually our catch would consist of a hare or a bullfrog or two …

P: And what does that taste like?

M: It tastes like nothing on earth actually … like nothing else on earth.

P: … and that's just one of the eco-tourism options now on offer. Among the other eco-holidays, you can have a taste of the gaucho lifestyle, staying and working on a cattle ranch on the borders of Chile and Argentina, join archeologists in the North African desert, or live the life of a religious hermit on an uninhabited island off the west coast of Ireland.

But if roughing it isn't quite to your taste, perhaps you'd like to use your holiday to learn a local craft or skill? And these days it seems you can learn almost anything, from Italian cookery in Tuscany, to riding Lusitano horses in Northern Portugal. We caught up with journalist Isabelle Fahey, who had just spent two weeks on a yoga retreat in Ulpotha, in the Sri Lankan jungle. Isabelle, describe the experience to us.

I: It's paradise, there's no other word for it. You are surrounded by glorious scenery, you can swim in mountain lakes, take showers in waterfalls and take midnight strolls through the paddy fields! The yoga takes place in bamboo-roofed pavilions and there is a local medicine man on hand to give ancient Ayurvedic treatments … you learn so much, and it's like being in heaven!

P: Even though there's no electricity or hot water?

I: No, there are no traditional western luxuries, but I can guarantee that you will come back feeling thoroughly spoiled!

P: Thank you Isabelle, it's obviously been a wonderful experience! So, whatever your tastes, it seems there's an eco-holiday to suit you, and perhaps this is how we'll all be spending our holidays in a few years, instead of lying on the beach in the Mediterranean, who knows!

Module 10

Recording 10.1

The Unicorn in the Garden

Part 1

Once upon a sunny morning, a man sitting in his breakfast **nook** looked up from his scrambled eggs to see a white unicorn with a gold horn quietly **cropping** the roses in the garden. The man went up to the bedroom where his wife was still asleep and woke her. 'There's a unicorn in the garden,' he said, 'eating roses.'

She opened one unfriendly eye and looked at him. 'The unicorn is a mythical beast,' she said and turned her back on him. The man walked slowly downstairs and out into the garden. The unicorn was still there; he was now **browsing** among the tulips.

'Here, unicorn,' said the man, and he pulled up a **lily** and gave it to him. The unicorn ate it gravely. With a high heart, because there was a unicorn in his garden, the man went upstairs and roused his wife again.

'The unicorn,' he said, 'ate a lily.' His wife sat up in bed and looked at him coldly.

'You are a booby,' she said, 'and I am going to have you put in the booby-hatch.'

Part 2

The man, who had never liked the words 'booby' and 'booby-hatch', and liked them even less on a shining morning when there was a unicorn in the garden, thought for a moment. 'We'll see about that,' he said. He walked over to the door. 'He has a golden horn in the middle of his forehead,' he told her. Then he went back to the garden to watch the unicorn; but the unicorn had gone away. The man sat down among the roses and went to sleep.

As soon as the husband had gone out of the house, the wife got up and dressed as fast as she could. She was very excited and there was a **gloat** in her eye. She telephoned the police and she telephoned a psychiatrist; she told them to hurry to her house and bring a strait-jacket. When the police and the psychiatrist arrived, they sat down in chairs and looked at her, with great interest.

'My husband,' she said, 'saw a unicorn this morning.' The police looked at the psychiatrist and the psychiatrist looked at the police.

'He told me it ate a lily,' she said.

The psychiatrist looked at the police and the police looked at the psychiatrist.

'He told me it had a golden horn in the middle of its forehead,' she said.

Part 3

At a solemn signal from the psychiatrist, the police leaped from their chairs and seized the wife. They had a hard time **subduing** her, for she put up a terrific struggle, but they finally subdued her. Just as they got her into the strait jacket, the husband came back into the house.

'Did you tell your wife you saw a unicorn?' asked the police.

'Of course not,' said the husband. 'The unicorn is a mythical beast.'

'That's all I wanted to know,' said the psychiatrist. 'Take her away. I'm sorry, sir, but your wife is as crazy as a jay bird.' So they took her away, **cursing** and screaming, and shut her up in an institution. The husband lived happily ever after.

Recording 10.6

M = Mark   W = Will

M: Will … Will!! Could you pass one of those?

W: Er, what sorry?

M: Could you pass me one of those forms from over there?

W: Oh yeah … there you go … Oh dear … sorry, I just can't get going at all this morning … d'know what's the matter with me.

M: What … were you up late again last night? Out clubbing again?

W: Well, not that late, we went to that new place … what's it called … I got home about 6, I suppose.

M: You didn't get home till 6??

W: Well I got a couple of hours' sleep … I was up at 8 to go for a run in the park … still feel tired though.

M: Well, I'm not surprised.

W: Ran for three miles … didn't seem to do me a lot of good, I must say.

M: No wonder you're tired after all that exercise.

W: Anyway, you'll never guess who was there.

M: Where … in the park?

W: No, in the club, dummy.

M: Well, I don't know, do I?

W: You know Jasmine Ellis?

M: What? Jasmine Ellis, the supermodel?

W: That's her … she was there … with some friends of hers.

M: You're kidding!

W: No, seriously … and you're not going to believe this – she asked me to dance … just like that … 'May I have this dance with you, sir?' Really!

M: No! No, you're right … I don't believe you

Pearson Education Limited
Edinburgh Gate, Harlow
Essex CM20 2JE, England
and Associated Companies throughout the world

www.longman/cuttingedge

© Pearson Education Limited 2003

First published 2003
Fourth impression 2005
Set in 9/12.5pt ITC Stone Informal
and 10/13pt Congress Sans

Printed in China. GCC/04

ISBN 0582 469430

Author acknowledgements

We would like to thank the following people for their help and contribution: Dr Jennifer Jenkins, Rosemary Bailey, William Atkinson, David Albery, Beth Neher, Karen Adams, Brian Baldock, Catherine Timothy, Peter Ball, Peta McRedmond, Sarah Jane Fischer, Richard Northcott, John Newton, Caroline Mapus-Smith, Pietro Alonghi, Elana Katz. We would also like to thank Debra Emmett for her editorial input and everyone at Pearson Education for their support and encouragement, in particular Jenny Colley (Senior Publisher), Naomi Tasker (Senior Editor), Sarah Hounsell (Senior Designer), Andy Thorpe (Mac Artist) and Alma Gray (Producer).

The publishers and authors are very grateful to the following people and institutions for piloting and/or reporting on the manuscript:

Michael Nutt, Eastbourne School of English, Guy Monk, New College, Nottingham, Claire Wallace, Bell School of Languages, London, Stella O'Shea, John Sutter, Hammersmith and West London College, London, Kate Fuscoe, Samantha Tennant, Hampstead School of English, London, Nanna Challis, Frances King School of English, London, Wendy Armstrong, The British Council, Milan, Katherine Johnson, CLIC International House, Seville, Mike Carter, CLIC International House, Seville, Robert Armitage, International House, Barcelona, Birgit Ferran Eichmann, Escola Oficial d'Idiomes de L'Hospitalet, Barcelona, Mark Baker, Hampstead School of English, London, Kenny Graham, Bell School, Cambridge, Frances Eaves-Walton, Kenna Bourke, Fiona Dunlop, Wimbledon School of English, London, Frances Eales, International House, London.

We are grateful to the following for permission to reproduce copyright material:

The Barbara Hodgensen Agency Inc and Rosemary Thurber for an extract from "The secret life of Walter Mitty" from My World and Welcome to it by James Thurber © 1942 James Thurber. Copyright renewed 1971 by James Thurber; Dennis Publishing for extracts from "Late to bed, late to rise can make you…wise" published in The Week 2nd October 1999 issue 224, "The worries that ruin childhood" published in The Week 26th February 2000 issue 244, "Good parents don't push" published in The Week 22nd April 2000 issue 252, "We all have genius within us" published in The Week 24th March 2001 issue 299 and "TV is good for toddlers" published in The Week 20th October 2001 issue 329; Hal Leonard Corporation for the lyrics "Tears of a Clown". Words and music by Stevie Wonder, William 'Smokey' Robinson and Henry Cosby © 1967 (Renewed 1995) Jobete Music Co Inc and Black Bull Music c/o EMI April Music Inc; Illawarra Mercury for an extract from "Broke backpacker wins $250,000" published in Illawarra Mercury 29th April 1999; Irish Independent for the extract "A toss of a coin costs contestant dear" by Isabel Hurley published in Irish Independent 4th March 2002; Lonely Planet Publications for an extract adapted from the Lonely Planet's Guide to Beijing; Random House Group Ltd for an extract from Parcel Arrived Safely – Tied with String by Michael Crawford published by Century; Redwood Publishing Ltd for an extract from "What didn't come to pass" by Vivienne Parry published in Marks and Spencer's Golden Jubilee Special Magazine 2002.

In some instances we have been unable to trace the owners of copyright material and we would appreciate any information that would enable us to do so.

Illustrated by: Adrian Barclay (Beehive Illustration agency) p.13, pp.48–49, p.103; Melanie Barnes pp.26–27, p.41, pp.66–67, pp.88–89; Paul Burgess (Private View) pp.56-57, pp.82–83; Alex Green p.98; Neil Gower p.35; Graham Humphreys (The Art Market) pp.22–23, p.108; Alison Lang (The Black and White Line) p.95; Domanic Li (The Organisation) p.86; Annabel Milne p.53; David Newton (Début art Limited) p.36; Peter Richardson pp.60–61; Jerry Tapscott p.10, p.28, pp.72–73, p.84, p.100, p.118, p.119, p.122, p.123 x 2, p.126, p.127 x 2, p.130, p.135, p.138, p.143, p.147, p.150, p.155; Fred Van Deelen (The Organisation) pp.62–63, p.146.

Photo acknowledgements

We are grateful to the following for permission to reproduce copyright photographs:

Advertising Archive for 6 bottom left; The Argus, Brighton for 43 top; Atlantic Syndication/*Evening Standard* for 42 bottom; Bubbles for 18 right, 112 top right; Celador International (www.celador.co.uk) for 59; Cephas for 90 centre; Collections for 68 centre, 77 (e), 112 bottom right, 130; Corbis UK for 9 bottom left, 18 left, 19, 32, 33 top, 45 top, 70-71, 74, 76 (b) and (d), 78 top and bottom, 79 top, 80, 90 bottom, 110 top left, top right and bottom left, 113 top left, centre right and bottom; Suki Dhanda (suki.dhanda@virgin.net) for 38 all; Dorling Kindersley Picture Library for 93 top left; Education Photos/John Walmsley for 46 bottom left and bottom right, 51 right, 69 bottom, 104 both, 112 centre right, 113 top right, centre left; EMI Records/Cover by MC Productions and The Apple staged by Peter Blake and Jane Haworth photographed by Michael Cooper; wax figures by Madame Tussauds for 92 centre right; Eye Ubiquitous for 8 top, 15 bottom right, 51 centre, 69 centre, 112 bottom left; Getty/Image Bank for 6-7 bottom, /Stone for 33 bottom, 42 top, 91 top, 96 bottom right, /Taxi for 16 (c), 30, 71 top and bottom; Ronald Grant Archive for 118; Sonia Halliday Photographs for 91 centre; Robert Harding Picture Library for 69 top, 81, 96 top right, 101; Image State for 16 (a), 17 (e), 37, 54, 46 centre and bottom centre, 75, 76 (a), /Pictor for 68 bottom, 112 top left; Impact Photos for 8 centre, 9 top and bottom right, 16 (b), 17 (d), 20 top right, 45 bottom, 46 top right, 76 (c); Chris Moat (cmm@benenden.kent.sch.uk) for 90 top; Jeff Moore (jeff@jmal.co.uk) for 6 top left, 20 top left, 68 top, 92 bottom right; Moviestore for 93 top right, 131; North West Evening Mail, Barrow-in-Furness for 43 bottom; On Track International (www.ontrackinternational.com) for 31; Robert Opie Collection for 92 bottom centre, 93 centre left below, centre right and bottom; PA News Photos for 17 (f), 96 bottom right; Panos Pictures for 7 bottom right; Pearson Education for 11 (Trevor Clifford), 93 top centre right; Penguin Books Ltd – Penguin Classics 2000. Cover painting, *Abstract Painting* 1992 by Stephen Conroy, reproduced courtesy of Marlborough Fine Art, London for 93 centre left above; Pictures Colour Library for 46 top left, 51 left, 91 bottom, 96 bottom, 142, 151; Popperfoto for 8 bottom, 15 top and bottom left, 147; Powerstock for 45 top left; Redferns for 24, 25 top, 79 bottom, 110 bottom right; Rex Features for 58 both, 77 (f); RMN for 96 top left; Science and Society Picture Library for 92 top left, top centre, top right, centre left, bottom left, 93 top centre left; Sony Music Entertainment Inc for 25 bottom right; South American Pictures for 6 top right; Topham Picturepoint for 20 bottom, 77 (g), 134. 135. 138, 147 top and centre, 151 top, 154 both.

The cover photograph has been kindly supplied by Getty Images/Image Bank.

While every effort has been made to contact copyright holders, the publishers apologise for any omissions, which they will be pleased to rectify at the earliest opportunity. .

Picture Researcher: Liz Moore